PUBLIC VENTURE CAPITAL

PUBLIC VENTURE CAPITAL

Government Funding Sources for Technology Entrepreneurs

2000 Edition

Henry Etzkowitz

Magnus Gulbrandsen

Janet Levitt

Harcourt
Professional Publishing

San Diego   New York   Chicago   London

99 00 01 02 03 EBA 5 4 3 2 1

CONTENTS

PREFACE

Public Venture Capital is an invaluable resource you will use again and again when seeking an inside track to government dollars. Relatively few entrepreneurs are aware that government funds from programs with acronyms like SBIR, ATP, Dual Use, ManTech, DARPA, and Act II can provide both initial and later-stage venture capital for their companies. Moreover, public venture capital programs do not require equity in exchange. Funding is available to technology start-ups and innovative firms through a variety of government programs.

The purpose of this book is to familiarize you with the concept of public venture capital and to illustrate how you can use the above-mentioned programs to fund technology endeavors. *Public Venture Capital* brings together information and resources on programs that make funds available to technology entrepreneurs and innovative firms on a competitive basis. Whether your interest is in a specific project or technology idea or you are looking for more general information regarding public venture capital, this book will be specifically helpful to you.

Public Venture Capital provides insight and helpful hints—based on interviews with successful applicants and current program officers—on how to win government funding awards. More important, it provides the tools needed to gain access to relevant programs and people. These tools include:

- In-depth information about current programs;
- A Quick Reference section with names, email addresses, and phone and fax numbers of program managers; and
- Special indexes that provide quick ways to approach programs, people, and topics.

This book is organized to allow you to go from broad topic areas to your specific areas of interest. For example, if you have a specific project in mind you can go to the Science and Technology Preference Index and spot where your project fits in. From this starting point you will be guided elsewhere in the book to find leads for making appropriate contacts, to find more information about current programs in your field, and to learn how and why these programs were founded.

Public Venture Capital will be of practical interest to:

- Technology entrepreneurs and innovative firms (large and small)
- Advisors (lawyers, accountants, and consultants) of these firms
- Teachers and students in entrepreneurship courses
- Public and corporate libraries
- Policy-makers concerned with issues of science- and technology-based economic growth at the federal and state levels

- Universities, national laboratories, and firms trying to encourage employee entrepreneurship

In contrast to private venture capital, government is not trying to earn a profit. Its objectives are to generate jobs, to assist the growth of the economy, and to increase tax revenues in the long term. Thus, government programs may offer funding to a broader range of technologies than do private venture capital firms.

We wish to acknowledge Lucia Venancio (Science Policy Institute, SUNY, and the Federal University of Rio de Janeiro) for help in preparing the Name Index; and the technology entrepreneurs and program managers who graciously allowed us to interview them and gave generously of their time.

We look forward to putting together future editions of *Public Venture Capital*. We welcome comments regarding how we can serve you better. Please contact:

Public Venture Capital Editor
Harcourt Professional Publishing
525 B Street, Suite 1900
San Diego, California 92101

Henry Etzkowitz
Magnus Gulbrandsen
Janet Levitt

ABOUT THE AUTHORS

Henry Etzkowitz is Associate Professor of Sociology at the State University of New York at Purchase, where he serves as Director of the Science Policy Institute. He is Contributing Editor of *Technology Access Report*, a newsletter for the technology transfer community. Dr. Etzkowitz regularly publishes in such journals as *Research Policy, Science and Public Policy, Journal of Technology Transfer, Minerva,* and *Science.* He is also a member of the Board of Advisory Editors of *Minerva: A Review of Science, Learning and Policy.* Dr. Etzkowitz's forthcoming books are *The Second Academic Revolution: MIT and the Rise of Entrepreneurial Science* (London: Gordon and Breach) and *Athena Unbound: The Advancement of Women in Science and Technology* with C. Kemelgor and B. Uzzi (Cambridge: Cambridge University Press). He has been awarded numerous research grants from the National Science Foundation and other foundations. He is U.S. organizer of the bi-yearly International Conference on University–Industry–Government Relations: "The Triple Helix" (Amsterdam, 1996; New York, 1998; Rio de Janeiro, 2000). He received a B.A. in history from the University of Chicago and a Ph.D. in Sociology from New School University in New York City.

Magnus Gulbrandsen is Researcher at the Norwegian Institute for Studies in Research and Higher Education (NIFU) and Ph.D. student at the Department of Industrial Economics and Technology Management, Norwegian University of Science and Technology. He is also Contributing Editor of the Nordic quarterly journal *Forskningspolitikk* (Research Policy). He has published papers (both internationally and in his native Norway) about issues such as university–industry relations, entrepreneurship, and the organization and management of research and development. His Ph.D. thesis, about the relationship between research quality and organizational factors, will be published in 2000.

Janet Levitt has been a consultant to entrepreneurs, inventors, and small growth companies for many years, helping them organize, plan, and obtain financing. Prior to that, she analyzed business proposals for a leading venture capital firm and was a security analyst and a portfolio manager for two large New York City banks. Currently, she is the manager of a New York–based charitable foundation. She holds an A.B. in chemistry from Barnard College, an M.A.T. in chemistry from Harvard University, and an M.B.A. in finance from Columbia University. Ms. Levitt is currently a member of The New York Academy of Sciences, The New York Society of Security Analysts, The Harvard Club of New York City, The Barnard Business and Professional Women, Inc., and The Financial Women's Association of New York, Inc. She was elected to Iota Sigma, an honorary chemical society, while at Barnard College, and Beta Gamma Sigma while at Columbia Graduate School of Business.

ABOUT THE COMPUTER DISC

The CD-ROM provided with *Public Venture Capital* contains many helpful tools, including venture capital sources, bank funding sources, solicitations for proposals with detailed descriptions of the programs and requirements, criteria for application and judgement of proposals, and points of contact for agencies and offices.

Subject to the conditions in the license agreement and the limited warranty, which is displayed on screen when the disc is installed and is reproduced at the end of the book, you may duplicate the files on this disc, modify them as necessary, and create your own customized versions. Installing the disc contents and/or using the disc in any way indicates that you accept the terms of the license agreement.

The data disc is intended to be used in conjunction with your word processing software. There are versions of each document in WordPerfect® 6.0 and Microsoft Word® 6.0, both for Windows™. If you do not own either of these programs, your word processing package may be able to convert the documents into a usable format. Check your owner's manual for information on the conversion of documents.

Installing the Templates

To install the files on the disc using Windows 95 or above, select the Control Panel from the Start menu. Then choose Add/Remove Programs and select Install. If you are using Windows 3.1, choose File, Run from the Windows Program Manager and type D:/INSTALL in the command line or type D:/INSTALL at the DOS prompt. You will be asked a series of questions. Read each question carefully and answer as indicated.

First, the installation program will ask you to specify which drive you want to install to. You will then be instructed to specify the complete path where you would like the files installed. The installation program will suggest a directory for you, but you can name the directory anything you like. If the directory does not exist, the program will create it for you.

You can choose to install the entire system (both Word and WordPerfect files) or just the files for one application. The program will automatically install the files in Word and/or WordPerfect subdirectories.

Opening the Files

Open your word processing program. If you are using Microsoft Word or WordPerfect 6.0, choose Open from the File menu. Select the subdirectory that contains the loaded files to list the names of the files. Highlight the name of the file you want to open and click OK or press ENTER. You can also open a document in the Windows Explorer (in Windows 95 or above) or from the File Manager (in Windows 3.1) by highlighting the name of the file you want to use and double-clicking your left mouse button.

Refer to the Disc Contents section of the book to find the filename of the document you want to use. The Disc Contents is also available on your disc in a file called "Contents." You can open this file and view it on your screen or print a hard copy to use for reference.

Word Processing Tips

Microsoft Word and WordPerfect are equipped with search capabilities to help you locate specific words or phrases within a document. The Find option listed under the Edit menu performs a search in both Microsoft Word and in WordPerfect 6.0.

Important: When you are finished using a file you will be asked to save it. If you have modified the file, you may want to save the modified file under a different name rather than the name of the original file. (Your word processing program will prompt you for a file name.) This will enable you to reuse the original file without your modifications. If you want to replace the original file with your modified file, save but do not change the name of the file.

Print Troubleshooting

If you are having difficulty printing your document, the following suggestions may correct the problem:

Microsoft Word

- Select Print from the Microsoft Word File menu. Then choose the Printer function.
- Ensure that the correct printer is selected.
- From this window, choose Options.
- In the media box, make sure that the paper size is correct and that the proper paper tray is selected.
- Check your network connections if applicable.
- If you still have trouble printing successfully, it may be because your printer does not recognize the font Times New Roman. At this point, you should change the font of the document to your default font by selecting the document (CTRL + A) and then choosing Font from the Format menu and highlighting the name of the font you normally use. Changing the font of the document may require additional adjustments to the document format, such as margins, tab stops, and table cell height and width. Select Page Layout from the View menu to view the appearance of the pages before you try to print again.

WordPerfect

- Select Print from the WordPerfect 6.0 File menu. Then choose Select.
- Make sure the correct printer is selected.
- From this menu, press Setup.
- Ensure the correct paper size and paper source are selected.
- You may be having difficulty because your printer does not recognize the selected font. You can correct this problem by changing the base font of the document to your default font. From the Edit menu choose Select All (or preL+A). The entire text of the document should be highlighted. Then choose Font from the Layout menu and highlight the font you normally use. Changing the font of the document may require additional adjustments to the document format, such as margins, tab stops, and table cell height and width. Select Two Page from the View menu to view the appearance of the pages before you try to print again.

DISC CONTENTS

Document Title	File Type	File Name
Program Solicitation FAQs	html	DOE08.htm
Program Solicitation Main Menu	html	DOE09.htm

Department of Transportation (DOT)

SBIR Program General Information	html	DOT01.htm
SBIR Program Solicitation	doc	DOT02.doc

Department of Education (ED)

About the SBIR	html	ED-01.htm
Request for Proposal	doc	ED-02.doc
SBIR Contacts	html	ED-03.htm
SBIR Program Schedule	html	ED-04.htm

Environmental Protection Agency (EPA)

Research Program	html	EPA01.htm
SBIR Program Report—Pg. 1	html	EPA02.htm
SBIR Program Report—Pg. 2	html	EPA03.htm
SBIR Program Report—Pg. 3	html	EPA04.htm
SBIR Program Report—Pg. 4	html	EPA05.htm
SBIR Program Report—Pg. 5	html	EPA06.htm
SBIR Solicitation	html	EPA07.htm

National Aeronautics and Space Administration (NASA)

1999 SBIR Program Solicitation	pdf	NASA1.pdf
1999 STTR Program Solicitation	pdf	NASA2.pdf
About Solicitations	html	NASA3.htm
Program Overview	html	NASA4.htm
Program Schedule	html	NASA5.htm
Sources of Assistance	html	NASA6.htm

National Science Foundation (NSF)

Instruction Guide—Chapter 1	html	NSF01.htm
Instruction Guide—Chapter 2	html	NSF02.htm
Instruction Guide—Chapter 3	html	NSF03.htm
Instruction Guide—Chapter 4	html	NSF04.htm
Instruction Guide—Chapter 5	html	NSF05.htm
Instruction Guide—Chapter 6	html	NSF06.htm

Document Title	File Type	File Name
Instruction Guide—Chapter 7	html	NSF07.htm
Instruction Guide—Chapter 8	html	NSF08.htm
Instruction Guide—Chapter 9	html	NSF09.htm
Instruction Guide—Chapter 10	html	NSF10.htm
Proposal Checklists	html	NSF11.htm
Proposal FAQs	html	NSF12.htm
Proposal Forms	html	NSF13.htm
United States Department of Agriculture (USDA)		
Assurance Statement	doc	AGR01.doc
Considerations	html	AGR02.htm
Definitions	html	AGR03.htm
Evaluation Criteria	html	AGR04.htm
National Environmental Policy Act Exclusions Form	doc	AGR05.doc
Program Description	html	AGR06.htm
Project Solicitation	html	AGR07.htm
Project Budget	doc	AGR08.doc
Project Summary	doc	AGR09.doc
Proposal Cover Sheet	doc	AGR10.doc
Proposal Preparation	html	AGR11.htm
Sample Proposal A	html	AGR12.htm
Sample Proposal B	html	AGR13.htm
Scientific Information Sources	html	AGR14.htm
Submission Forms	html	AGR15.htm
Submission of Proposals	html	AGR16.htm
Topic Areas	html	AGR17.htm

PART I
PUBLIC VENTURE CAPITAL

Public venture capital is a hidden U.S. asset. High-tech entrepreneurs often are not aware of grants and matching funds available to them through government funding sources. Many firms do not apply for monies from federal government programs such as SBIR (Small Business Innovation Research) and ATP (Advanced Technology Program), mistakenly thinking they are ineligible. How can one explain the paradox of technology entrepreneurs—who need funds to help start or expand their business—often not being aware of public venture capital?

Virtually all technology entrepreneurs are aware of private venture capital. Many time the early venture capital firms created new entrepreneurs simply by suggesting the possibility of forming a firm to scientists and engineers who had invented new technologies. Often these inventors saw themselves as entrepreneurs only after they were introduced to the possibility by a venture capitalist.

Early venture capital firms, in addition to providing a source of funds, prided themselves on providing business acumen in assisting the founding of new firms. In 1946, the founders of the first venture capital firm, American Research and Development Corporation (ARD), stated that the purpose of their firm was to provide a vehicle for spreading risk among a variety of ventures and to provide technical entrepreneurs with capital and business advice.

The invention of the venture capital firm was the culmination of a depression-era search for a strategy of economic renewal. In succeeding years, as the amount of funding committed to the industry grew, private venture capital moved upmarket to the so-called mezzanine stage of financing, just prior to an initial public offering (IPO). With notable exceptions, even today most entrepreneurs find it extremely difficult to get venture funds to support the early stages of firm formation and product development.

The purpose of this book is to increase high-tech firm founders' awareness of the public funds available to support the "start-up" process. Government funding sources have to some extent filled the monetary gap created by the shift of private venture capital to other uses. In addition to family, friends, and "angels," a complex quilt of federal, state, and local programs has arisen to support technology start-ups.

Originally, some of these programs were intended to give small business increased access to government research and development (R&D) contracts. Over time, the programs have become sources of "public venture capital" to help technology entrepreneurs start their companies. In addition to providing funds, government R&D programs targeted at small firms often have managers who can play an advisory role for entrepreneurs who have received grants and contracts to develop new technology.

Nevertheless, relatively few technology entrepreneurs know of the existence of public venture capital, much less how to compete for it. Private-sector success is highly publicized, but the government's role in creating the conditions for economic growth and job creation through technological advance is less well known. This lack of awareness of the role that public entrepreneurship plays in the economy leaves programs such as the Advanced Technology Program (ATP) and Small Business Innovation Research (SBIR) open to misunderstanding and vulnerable to attack. Since its inception, SBIR has given out more than 40,000 awards; the ATP has given out more than 500 since its inception.

Together, public and private venture capitalists in the United States have helped to create the strongest growth engine for new technology and business development in the world. *Public Venture Capital: Government Funding Sources for Technology Entrepreneurs* provides information and policy analysis about the federal programs that have developed over the past 30 years. Although certain gaps persist, these programs play a significant role in encouraging the transition of technology from research findings to useful products and services.

National economies each have their special assets. For instance, Italy's strengths include the introduction of handsome design and production through networks of small firms. Germany's talent is applying new technology to the upgrading of traditional industries. Japan's strengths reside in reducing production costs through application of logistical techniques and in empowering workers to improve the products they manufacture. The United States' specialty lies in creating new industries and new firms through technological innovation and entrepreneurship supported by a complex web of public and private initiatives.

Technological innovation is the wellspring of the U.S. economy. It is an important source of new jobs in less-developed areas as well as in the high-tech regions of our country. Although the U.S. economy is increasingly based on technology, relatively few people are aware of the role that federal policies and programs play in encouraging technology entrepreneurs to develop new products and services. This volume analyzes the role of the federal government in promoting technology-based economic development and recognizes the public servants who initiate and run these programs.

CHAPTER 1 • PUBLIC FUNDING OPPORTUNITIES FOR PRIVATE ENTREPRENEURS

CONTENTS

PUBLIC FUNDING OPPORTUNITIES FOR PRIVATE ENTREPRENEURS

Introduction

This book is oriented toward two types of technology companies, start-ups and innovative firms. The technology start-up is an about-to-be company or a newly formed firm. The innovative firm is an established company that wants to innovate within the company. This innovation could be either a new technology or an upgrade of an older technology (such as a new manufacturing process). In either event, a technology entrepreneur is usually faced with the problem of how to finance the new technology.

How do you obtain the money to get started? There are two roads to follow—the private and the public. There are many intersections and crossovers along the way so it is not a matter of choosing one route exclusively. Because it takes so long to arrange outside financing, it is important to determine the possibilities for your venture early on.

At the earliest stage, options include funding your venture yourself and/or borrowing from friends, neighbors, and relatives. Self-funding sometimes means using one's credit cards. Another possibility is to find a business partner. When you run out of money from friends, relatives, neighbors, and partners, what do you do next?

The Private Path

The private route is venture capital, either *angels,* individual investors willing to invest in the early stages of the firm's formation, or venture capital firms. Angels are people with money who are willing to invest in high-risk ventures. The most relevant angels for a high-tech firm are ones who are technically knowledgeable since they have a better basis to make a decision about the venture. Once a technically competent angel has committed to the project, other investors who are less technically knowledgeable may be more willing to invest.

The *venture capital industry* is a term that covers a wide variety of activities. Venture capital firms range in size from very large to very small and will consider activities from risky to quasi-banking type functions. For example, many of the larger firms now concentrate on *mezzanine financing*, funding firms just before they go public. However, there are still firms that will provide high-risk equity financing.

An important issue for the entrepreneur in accepting such funds is that angels and venture capital firms typically provide financing in exchange for a portion of the equity in a company. Even if you are willing to give up equity, a venture capital firm may not be willing to consider your project. The market niche may be judged too small; the time to market may be considered too long. The venture capital decision makers may lack confidence about the success of the project or they may fail to gain an understanding of its significance.

The Public Path

The public route is complex, comprised of a variety of grant, contract, loan, and subsidized assistance at the federal, state, and local levels. In this book, we deal primarily with the federal level and with joint federal and state programs. Over the past half-century, the federal government has developed a series of programs to assist technology entrepreneurs, either in start-ups or innovative, established firms. While these programs are not coordinated from above, the entrepreneurs using this book can maximize their chances of finding the right program(s) for their firms.

For projects that qualify, assuming they have a sufficient read-time government offers a good alternative. The concept is that public money is available with few, if any, strings attached. The government's objective is to generate jobs for future economic growth. Firms do not have to give up equity and, in most instances, will retain their intellectual property rights. The downside appears to be the long time frame from the preapplication inquiry to receipt of funds if successful.

Often, entrepreneurs are not successful on the first try. However, this is really not so much different than the traditional venture capital route because it too can have extended time frames. Most proposals to venture capitalists do not get a hearing or feedback. By contrast, government programs typically give feedback and encouragement to reapply if a good idea has been introduced without being sufficiently developed.

Government Dollars and Why Government Has Funds Available

Through its Small Business Innovation Research Program (SBIR), the federal government gave out $1.2 billion in fiscal year 1999 in research and development (R&D) funds. These funds were targeted directly at small firms. An additional $250 million in precompetitive research funds was available through the Advanced Technology Program (ATP). Small business has been successful in winning approximately half of the ATP funds in the recent past. The Small Business Administration (SBA) guarantees several billion dollars in loans to small firms each year, although technology firms have problems in accessing these funds. Through the Manufacturing Extension Partnership (MEP), government provides funding for subsidized consulting services to small businesses, delivered through regional and local offices.

Through the Cooperative Research and Development Agreements (CRADAs), approximately 700 government laboratories are available as partners on R&D projects to which government can make in-kind contributions of researchers' time and equipment. However, 70 laboratories actually undertake most of the partnerships. The Defense Advanced Research Projects Agency (DARPA) spends $2 billion each year on developing advanced technology with military relevance.

There are also various programs, primarily in the Department of Defense (DOD), such as Act II and ManTech, that provide other funding opportunities to take completed R&D work the next step toward production. The National Science Foundation (NSF) currently has an experimental program, SBIR 2b, that provides matching funds, two parts private to one part government (the current maximum is $100,000), for successful Phase 2 awardees who qualify. Dual use programs in various R&D agencies in the DOD offer opportunities to demonstrate the usefulness of civilian technologies to the military and vice versa.

It has been proven over time that the major growth in our economy and employment has come from small business and that much of this growth arises from advancement in technology. Because of a shortfall of funds, there is often a gap, sometimes called "the valley of death," between what technology entrepreneurs can and cannot do to bring new technology to the market after a prototype is developed.

Filling the Gap

The federal government has done a remarkable job of having funds available at the early stages of commercializing a technology. However, a persisting problem today is how to take a technology from a successful prototype through production and finally to market. State governments have acted to fill this gap in recent years, making $3 billion in funds available in a variety of programs, typically oriented to the state's existing and projected industries.

Nevertheless, the gap remains large. Federal government, venture capital industry, and joint public–private initiatives like SBA loans have yet to address many of the issues facing technology entrepreneurs and innovative firms. For example, SBA loan guarantees have difficulty taking into account the requirements of technology-based firms whose assets are typically in intellectual property rather than in fixed assets or inventory that can be used as collateral.

Who Should Apply

Although the topic of this book is technology programs, you do not have to be a technology expert to be successful in winning one of these grants. On the other hand, being an accomplished scientist or technologist is not a guarantee of receiving an award either.

Thus, if you are a scientist or engineer without business experience, you may wish to consider finding a consultant with business experience in technology to help you with the commercial side of your project. Conversely, if you are a businessperson and have an idea for a product or process that requires a technological component, it may be helpful to seek out a scientist or engineer whose experience is relevant to the technical side of the project.

The reason why a combination of business and technical skills is essential for success is that government technology programs are directed toward putting science and technology to use, not to pursuing research solely for the advancement of knowledge. Of course, there are a number of government research programs for this latter purpose, most notably at NIH, NSF and the Department of Defense. Indeed, some people think that this is the only purpose for which government provides, or should provide, research funds. However, we are not discussing how to apply to pure research programs in this book.

Rather, we deal here with a relatively new set of programs. These new programs have been created: (a) to take research results or original ideas a step or two closer to the market; (b) to take commercial problems and find relevant technology (from government, academic or from other industrial sources) to address the problem; and (c) to apply technology to solve government problems, whether civilian or military in nature. While the government will not usually pay for the final stages of product development and marketing, many of these programs will come quite close in helping you take research to the market or solve a production problem.

Public technology programs can help a firm extend its research capabilities. Indeed, some small firms have built their entire research programs on a succession of government grants. As companies grow in size they typically became less dependent upon government support. Nevertheless, access to public technology programs was essential to stimulating that growth.

The Application Process

The programs described in this book differ significantly. However, when it comes to topic areas, shared funding, and size of awarded amounts, there are several similarities in the application process. These are described in further detail below.

In general, the process of obtaining grants or contracts from one of the federal technology programs has several phases, including:

1. Announcement/Call for Proposals
2. Deadline
3. Screening
4. Technical and/or Business Review
5. Final Decision/Payment

The agencies that participate in the technology programs will, in most cases, issue a so-called *solicitation*. This is an announcement or call for proposals. Most of the programs, such as SBIR and ATP, do not accept unsolicited proposals, that is, applications that are received outside of the time limits described in the solicitation.

This call for proposals is most often made once a year (for one *fiscal year (FY)*), although some of the larger programs might issue more frequent solicitations. For instance, the SBIR program in the Department of Defense calls for proposals twice and the Department of Health and Human Services/National Institutes of Health issues solicitations three times every year.

You will discover that the solicitation is usually a thick document. Although most agencies still make paper versions, they are almost always available on the World Wide Web (WWW). Some agencies, such as the National Aeronautics and Space Agency (NASA) and the Department of Transportation (DOT), only make electronic versions. They can be downloaded, usually in a number of different formats (e.g., HTML, Microsoft Word, Adobe Acrobat) and, in some cases, ordered on diskettes through regular mail.

In the solicitation, you are likely to find the following:

1. A general description of the program, its basic mission, organization and previous history.

2. A general description of the agency that has issued the solicitation, including its mission and its goals related to the SBIR (or other) program.

3. Application deadlines and information about what should be included in the application. Certain forms that should be completed, and added as appendices, are available on the World Wide Web and can in most cases be submitted electronically.

4. Criteria that the application has to meet in order to be eligible for review. This not only has to do with the contents of the application, but also its length (including font sizes, etc.).

5. The technical and/or commercial criteria that will be used when reviewing the proposal, and the relative weight put on each criterion.

6. General and specific advice on "how to succeed" for potential applicants who want to submit an application.

7. An in-depth description of the technical areas, the so-called *topics* that are the focus of the current solicitation. Note that the agencies will only accept proposals that are linked to their current topics unless they specify otherwise.

8. Other information, such as upcoming program conferences or points of contact.

After the solicitation is released (made publicly available), you usually have from eight to ten weeks to complete the application, including getting all the documentation you need. If this is too short a time frame, you should be on the lookout for *presolicitation announcements*. These are preliminary descriptions of topic areas in upcoming solicitations. The Small Business Administration issues a presolicitation document for the whole SBIR program, and there are several such preliminary solicitations in the Department of Defense. They are made available on the World Wide Web and announced in the *Commerce Business Daily*.

Perhaps the most important reason to be on the lookout for the presolicitation announcements does not primarily have to do with gaining more time, but rather access to technical sources of information. The presolicitations will include contact information for the technical personnel within government who define the program topics. Discussion with them in advance of the issuance of the solicitation might give you a good indication of the kind of technologies and proposals they are looking for. In some cases, this can also be a way of influencing their process of selecting topic areas. You have the opportunity to bring your technology before decision-makers. They may see it as worthy of inclusion in the topics they generate. Note that once the official solicitation is released, in most cases you will *not* have another opportunity to talk to them until the awards are made. Because the technical staff often act as reviewers on proposals, they will not answer questions once the call for proposals is made public.

The agencies put much work into the solicitations, especially on topic descriptions and advice for applicants. Our experience is that they mean exactly what they say! Thus, the text in these documents should be taken literally. For example, if they say that 20% of the weight when reviewing will be put on the technical background of the applicants, this will actually be done. It is, therefore, probably wise to read the application advice carefully, especially the criteria for screening and review, and then write according to their specifications. Good proposals are balanced—they contain sufficient but not too much information on all the aspects that are to be reviewed. We emphasize this because many applicants discover that writing a good proposal is very difficult, especially because the number of pages is limited. A 25 page maximum is common in the SBIR program.

After the deadline, proposals will be screened. In this phase, the program managers determine if the applications meet the formal criteria described in the solicitation. Some have to do with the applicant, such as: Is the applicant really a small, independent firm? Will the majority of the work be done by the small company? Does the principal investigator devote most of his or her time to the project? Other criteria have to do with the application, for instance: Does it contain a plan for the research and commercialization phases? Does it contain resumes for all the key people involved? Have all required questions been answered?

If the application meets these formal criteria, it will be evaluated for technical or scientific merit and most often the commercial potential of the project as well. One, two, or more reviewers, either from the agency's own laboratories or technical divisions, or from external organizations like a university or a private firm, are selected to judge the proposal in accordance with the criteria described in the solicitation. Note that in the SBIR program, the reviewers are mainly technical personnel (scientists and engineers), so the technical criteria will be the most important. There is not a focus on a strict risk/return ratio, but rather on whether the project has commercial potential. Thus, it might be assumed that the SBIR is willing to take a greater business risk than most other government programs.

CHAPTER 2 • USING THIS BOOK

CONTENTS

CHAPTER **2**

USING THIS BOOK

Introduction

This book has multiple purposes, including:

- Helping entrepreneurs find money from government programs (Part IV)
- Helping entrepreneurs compete successfully for available government funds (Part I)
- Describing the government programs as they are today (Part II)
- Describing how these programs evolved (Part III)

You can enter the book at many points; it does not have to be read from beginning to end. One way to approach the book, of course, is to begin with Part I, which orients readers to the topics and suggested ways to proceed. Another way is to start in Part V, the Science and Technology (S&T) Preference Index. The S&T Preference Index is meant as a sample index rather than a complete index of topics, contacts, and programs available. At this time, this index primarily includes references to the Small Business Innovation Research (SBIR) program and the Advanced Technology Program (ATP). Find your topic area first and then find page references to (1) people with whom you should begin making contact (in Part IV) and (2) program descriptions (in Part II).

For those of you who are not sure where you fit in, here is yet another way to get started: Think in terms of using a compass and a map to guide yourself in uncharted territory. You need to (1) find the right program and (2) learn how to approach the program.

Finding the Right Program

The programs described in this book target different types of firms in different stages of their life cycle as well as firms with various products and technologies. For many firms, there is a natural sequence in the programs, moving from research to product development. They start out with a Small Business Innovation Research (SBIR) Phase I and Phase II award, then move on to the Advanced Technology Program (ATP), Cooperative Research and Development Agreements (CRADAs) or Dual Use, and then move to manufacturing-oriented programs. Others firms have experienced a different process, such as starting out with support from the Defensive Advanced Research Projects Agency (DARPA) or with a cooperative agreement with a national lab. The following table will help you find your match, based on different starting points in the innovation process.

Starting Point	Program
I have a good scientific/technical idea with economic potential, but I need to prove its feasibility.	SBIR (Phase I) (even if you have done a feasibility study, it is rare to start out in Phase II)
I have a new advanced technology and I can document its commercial potential.	ATP
I have a new technology with potential in both the military and civilian markets.	Dual Use
I need a loan and/or advice to get the firm started and/or to write a business plan.	Small Business Administration (SBA)
I have a good product/market idea, but I need to find the right technology.	CRADAs (or search SBIR for relevant technologies)
I need to test and evaluate my technology/idea, but I don't know how and I don't have the right equipment.	CRADAs
I have a commercially available technology/product that could be adapted innovatively to military use.	Commercial Operations and Support Savings Initiative (COSSI)
I have proven the feasibility of my military-useful technology/ product, but I need help to start manufacturing.	ACT II, ManTech
I have a good product, but I need to improve its manufacture.	Manufacturing and Extension Program (MEP)

Starting Point	Program
I work in a university or government lab and have a good idea, or I know somebody else working in a university or government lab who has a good idea.	Small Business Technology Transfer Programs (STTR)

Small firms (again, usually defined as those with fewer than 500 employees) can apply to any program and service. Larger firms can use all programs except SBIR, SBA, and MEP.

When you have found your match (or if you just want to browse and find out more), the book contains the following sections directly related to the programs.

Part II: User's Guide to Government Programs for Technology Entrepreneurs and Innovative Firms

Here you will find background information on each program, including technology and business criteria (where applicable), how to apply for funding, what the selection criteria are, and how and where to find information on the World Wide Web.

Part III: The Evolution of Public Venture Capital

Part III provides an in-depth analysis of the past 50 years of the government's encouragement of technology entrepreneurship, which had its origin in the patent clause of the Constitution. A series of programs has developed that deals with every phase of the technology development process, from testing the feasibility of a new technology to reviving a mature technology, and everything in between.

Part IV: Quick Reference Guide to Current Government Programs

In this part we have listed condensed information on the programs covered in this book, including contact information (address, phone, e-mail, Web page), type of program, technology and business preferences, type of financing, maximum amounts, deadlines, and special considerations. For the largest programs—the SBIR in the Department of Defense (DOD) and the National Institutes of Health (NIH)—we have also listed points of contact for different technical areas and/or in different labs, institutes, directorates, and more.

Part V: Indexes

The Science and Technology Preference Index is a sample index, rather than a complete index, of the main science and technology areas, primarily in the SBIR and ATP programs at this time. This index points to the pages in Part V where you will find more information about the agency that supports that area. There are also Name and Program indexes.

Learning How to Approach the Program

We will use SBIR as an example, because it is the largest and most complicated program, with ten participating agencies. Each agency issues a detailed description; collectively, they generate around 1,000 technical topics each year. Calls for proposals are issued by the ten agencies at various times throughout the year.

The first step in SBIR is to find where you belong, either scientifically or technically. Many entrepreneurs will know this already through previous contact with federal research agencies such as the National Institutes of Health, the National Institute for Standards and Technology, and other government organizations supporting research and development.

Note that general technological areas can be found in almost all SBIR subprograms. If you are working in electronics, materials, computer science, environmental technology, etc., most of the SBIR's participating agencies will have topics that may be relevant to you. Indeed, if your idea or technology is at a stage where it could be developed in several directions and towards several practical uses, then it may be worthwhile to get in touch with more than one program manager. Although you should not apply for funding for the same project from several parties, discussing the idea with different agencies could increase your chances of finding a good match and, eventually, of winning an award.

Being creative in finding applications for your technology may be worthwhile, especially since the military aspect of SBIR is so large. Some examples: a technology for wireless communication is useful both for military and civilian purposes; software to train students can also be used to train soldiers; and improving health in the general population can also be used to improve military personnel's health. If you develop an idea that is useful to both military and civilian purposes, there are additional chances of getting more funding connected to different "dual use" initiatives in DOD.

The table below indicates the different ways of approaching the SBIR program by using this book, based on different points of entry.

Starting Point	1st Step/Part	2nd Step/Part
I know where my idea/ technology belongs.	Find contact inform- ation in Part IV.	Read the SBIR information on that agency in Part II.
I need to find out where my technological area belongs.	Go to the Technology Preference Index, Part V.	Refer to Part IV (and possibly Part II).
I have a very concrete idea and want to find out if this has previously been focused on in the SBIR.	Use the CD-ROM that comes with the book; search the solicitations.	
I want to know if anyone has previously received SBIR funding in my area.	Go to Part IV and find the relevant Web page addresses.	Search previous awards on the Web.
I want to know if someone is focusing on my particular technology in the present award competitions.	Go to Part IV and find the relevant Web page addresses.	Scan the open solicitations.
I need to learn more about the SBIR.	Read the general SBIR section of Part II.	Read about the various SBIR participants, and use the references in Part IV to go further.

For all other programs, the process is much simpler. Part IV will give you a brief overview and points of contact, if you want to get in touch with a program official right away. If not, Part II will give you more in-depth information about each particular program.

CHAPTER 3 • WINNING AWARDS ON THE WEB

CONTENTS

WINNING AWARDS ON THE WEB

Introduction

This chapter is about the Internet, mainly the World Wide Web (the Web), where almost all the information that you will need to know about federal technology programs can be found.

You probably already have an e-mail account. If not, get one! Many of the federal technology programs require you to send in forms and applications by e-mail, so you will not get far without it. Most likely you also have a *Web browser*, a program that locates and displays Web pages for you. This will be necessary to download solicitations and other documents that announce award competitions. Still, everyone who has used a browser knows how difficult it can be to sift through hundreds, or even thousands, of pages of irrelevant information.

In this chapter, we discuss how the Web can be used most efficiently to win federal technology grants (or other grants, for that matter). The first section:

- defines the Web,
- identifies what is needed to conduct searches, and
- describes how to start.

The next section addresses how to:

- scan the information,
- improve the search specifications, and
- judge the quality of the information.

Finally, we examine some of the concrete ways that technology programs use the Web to communicate with their applicants and award winners.

Searching the World Wide Web— the Basics

Basically, the Web is a collection of publicly available documents, most often called *pages*, with information, text, pictures, sound, and more. The pages are located on computers all over the world, but each has its unique *address* or *URL* (Uniform Resource Locator). Computers with Web pages are often called *sites*. The address of a site most often has the general form www.site.suffix. Suffixes are based on what sector of society the site belongs to (at least in the United States; in other countries the suffix is a country code, for instance .au in Australia and .no in Norway). In federal technology programs, you will encounter many sites whose addresses end with .gov (government). Other suffixes you will encounter are .com (commercial), .mil (military), .edu (education), and .org (various noncommercial and nongovernment organizations). Thus, site addresses are very logical. If you want to access the Web pages of Columbia University or Microsoft Corporation, you will probably get lucky with www.columbia.edu and www.microsoft.com.

Most Web pages will have links to other pages. Click on the link, and you will be transported to a new page and often a new site as well. Some sites and pages are little more than large databases of links. It is useful to know some of these—they can be good places to start a search for information. Among the most frequently used are www.yahoo.com and www.altavista.com.

To search the Web, you need a computer with a modem, a browser program, and a subscription to an Internet provider. If you are going to do serious searching and downloading of the competition announcements (these files can be huge), you will need the appropriate modem. We would suggest that a modem with a transfer speed of 33.6K (Kilobits per second, or Kbps) is a minimum. By turning off the automatic loading of graphics, Web searches will take place more efficiently and quickly.

The pages of the federal technology programs can usually be read with any browser. Netscape Navigator, Microsoft Explorer, and lesser-known alternatives, will work well provided you have a relatively new version of the browser you choose. Many Web pages have menus and other relevant information, as well as links, written in a programming language called Java. Older versions of the browsers do not understand Java. To be safe, you should acquire version 4.0 or newer of Netscape Navigator or Microsoft Explorer (for other browsers, check with their supplier).

One final thing is needed to avoid as much frustration as possible: You must have some idea of what you are looking for—the more specific, the better. If you just want to "see what you can find out about a subject" (for instance, the Small Business Innovation Research program), chances are you will spend hours and hours sifting information, reading things you do not really need, or reading similar pieces of text over and over again. It is always an advantage to know what you are looking for or to know a good deal about the subject before you start your search on the Web.

Starting the Search

Finding the best information can be tricky if you do not know where to start. Fortunately, federal technology programs have their own Web pages. Most often subprograms in individual agencies, as well as centers that offer various kinds of advice and help, have their own pages, too. You will find links to technology programs and subprograms in the references section of this book. These pages offer fact sheets and brief advice, as well as long documents describing technical focus areas in detail, previous award winners, and much more. Many of them offer possibilities for doing text string searches if you are interested, for instance, in finding out if your technology is relevant for a specific agency.

In many cases, you will have other reasons for searching the Web. Are there any other small firms out there with ideas and technology similar to mine? Can I find a larger firm that is interested in certain applications that can help me get a prototype developed? Where are the leading experts within my field? Are there any venture capital companies that specialize in my technological area? Often, the goal is to find somebody to communicate with, not to get written answers to a few questions (at least not right away). The Web pages of the federal technology programs might be a relevant starting place even for questions like these. Program officers can help you along, and some of the Web pages offer lists of award winners, possible "mentor firms," experienced venture capitalists, and more. Still, chances are that you have to do a more general Web search to find the answers you need.

Yahoo! (www.yahoo.com) is a general search engine which is organized as a type of encyclopedia, not unlike the "yellow pages." Links to firms within a large number of industries can be found here, categorized in a hierarchy of themes that are easily accessed. This is often the best place to start. For instance, you can obtain an alphabetical list of Web addresses to venture capital firms or university departments in a certain field. The major problem is that, most likely, not all relevant firms or departments will be listed. Yahoo! may not know that they exist, or they may be among the few who do not have Web pages (this is becoming less common). Text string searches in Yahoo! are also possible.

AltaVista (www.altavista.com) is another general search engine that regularly and automatically scans a huge number of Web sites all over the world. The pages are not categorized as specifically as in Yahoo!, but you have the possibility of searching for any word on any of the pages in this enormous database. The advantage compared to Yahoo! is that you will probably get more hits, or links, to more pages than on Yahoo!. This is also AltaVista's major disadvantage—the number of hits is frequently too large to handle. But this can be dealt with in most cases.

For example, let us assume that you are interested in the Advanced Technology Program. You enter the search string "ATP." The result is more than 200,000 hits! You discover that ATP is also the abbreviation for the world ranking in tennis, so you enter a new search string "+ATP +program." The "+" means that both words must be in the document for it to be returned as a hit. Again, the result is extremely large—links to more than 68,000 pages are returned in response to your query.

You decide next to try the full name and enter "Advanced Technology Program." You are now down to fewer than 2,000 hits, but you notice another problem. The first link on your list is now to a political interest group that wants to terminate the ATP program, and the next nine links are all to the same small company in Kentucky, proudly announcing its receipt of an ATP award.

You have to find a way to make the search even more specific. Let us say you work in robotics, and you want to find out if any ATP awards have been given or if competitions have been announced in this field. You enter the search string "robotics "advanced technology program." The result is only 93 hits. This short list of links can be gone through quickly and irrelevant hits discarded.

Scanning the Information

Many of the Web sites of federal technology programs, firms, help centers, and other organizations, are organized in a similar manner. There is a heading (usually an image), a menu (almost always in a column on the left), and a main area where the selected information is shown. Some pages have a text only version, but not all. It may be necessary to load at least some of the graphics to select items in the menu.

Almost all sites have some kind of "fact sheet," often simply called "About Us..." or "About the Program." These contain brief and general information. Annual reports, which are commonly published on the Web, will give you similar data. Furthermore, several documents and pages are usually available to give you additional information about the program, office, agency, etc. Some of these can be very large. Note that the chapters about the federal technology programs in this book are, in fact, a compressed version of the information available on the Web, along with experiences and advice from applicants, program directors, officers, and others.

Most Web sites have a document called a FAQ. This stands for "frequently asked questions," and is a good place for a beginner to start. Although it is advisable to contact program directors or officers for the best and most updated advice and information, it is a good idea to check first if answers to some of your questions can be found in the FAQ. On the pages of the different Small Business Innovation Research subprograms, the FAQs will give basic information about who can apply for grants, maximum amounts, and deadlines for proposals. In addition to the FAQ, the page called "Points of Contact" (or a similar title), will be useful. The reference section in this book contains the necessary e-mail addresses, phone numbers, and fax numbers to get you started.

Some of the larger documents will not always be available in hypertext format (the Web "document language"). Instead, they are available for downloading in another format. A few of the solicitations (invitations to apply for funding, including long and in-depth descriptions of the relevant technology areas for that particular round of grants) are available in Microsoft Word format. Most large documents, however, are downloadable in Adobe Acrobat format. Adobe Acrobat Reader is a program with advanced formatting features that lets you read and print out documents. The program might be installed on your computer already and started automatically by your browser whenever needed. If not, it can be downloaded for free from the Web (www.adobe.com).

Finally, Web sites contain links to other Web sites. This is one of the best ways to find more information about a certain technology area, type of funding, or other resource.

The quality of the federal technology program sites is generally very good. Pages are usually updated continuously, and the information is correct and relevant. You may find that some sites have too much information, graphics, or links, but there is not much one can do about that (apart from reading the relevant chapters in this book). Most pages have the last update of the site listed at the bottom of the document. If not, "upcoming deadlines" and similar information will give you a lead if the data are recent. Links that do not work are frustrating, but fortunately they are rare in the government Web sites you are likely to encounter related to the technology funding programs.

Still, changes in the relevant information do take place: Budgets are rarely definite until the last minute. Most of the federal technology programs depend upon votes in Congress, and there is always a certain amount of "horse trading" or negotiating before the final budgets are settled.

After scanning the information on relevant sites, it is time to recap what you know, do not know, and want to know more about. We have found that the good old pen and paper is the best tool here. One of the best ways to narrow the search for information is by writing down questions and relevant answers as they are discovered. At the end of a search session, you will probably have a short and highly specific list of questions—perfect for getting in touch with that program manager, venture capitalist, or university professor.

Using the Web to Win Grants

Paper documents are used less frequently than in the past. It is costly to print and send them out; and new ones have to be printed next year, although only a small proportion of the text is changed. Electronic documents are easily updated, printed documents are not. Some of the information brochures and leaflets on technology programs now exist only in electronic form. More importantly, solicitation documents are increasingly produced in electronic versions only, rather than paper. This means that in order to participate in a grant competition, you will need to download the relevant documents.

Heretofore, grant applications were usually forms that needed to be filled out and sent, often by regular mail or private delivery service. It is increasingly common for programs to offer their forms electronically, making them available for downloading from the Internet. In most cases the applications have appendices, forms that require some financial and ownership information about your company. These appendices are now, with few exceptions, submitted electronically (even though the main application is mailed). Many programs now offer the option of submitting the entire application electronically.

This has an important consequence, especially if you are applying for grants from one of the larger programs, such as the Small Business Innovation Research programs in the Department of Defense. If more than 1,000 entrepreneurs are applying for grants and submitting certain information electronically, additional traffic is created on the relevant servers. Because deadlines are usually very strict, it would be immensely frustrating to miss a deadline due to server trouble or slow file transfers. In other words: Do not wait until the last minute!

One final issue that should be mentioned here concerns security. Some individuals may be reluctant when it comes to sending financial and other information over the Internet. "Secure transmissions" are offered by some servers; hopefully all will offer this capability soon. As electronic applications become more common, this issue will be addressed. As far as we know, there have been no exceptions in the requirement for electronic submission of appendices. However, if you are concerned about security, these matters can be discussed with the program officer.

CHAPTER 4 • LEARNING THE ROPES

CONTENTS

CHAPTER **4**

LEARNING THE ROPES

Introduction

Like anything else, applying for government technology funds is something that can be learned by trial and error. You can simply put in an application and see what happens and then learn from that experience. If successful, you may want to stop there and just repeat what has worked in the past when the time comes to apply again. If unsuccessful, you may wish to seek additional information from successful applicants, from program managers, and from professional colleagues before trying again.

This book is written for both prospective applicants and successful awardees who believe they may have something more to learn about the technology granting and contracting process from other peoples' experience.

Discussion of these issues is based on an analysis of government program materials and guidelines, as well as interviews with managers of technology programs and applicants to these programs. Program managers were asked what they think applicants need to know in applying to the programs and were asked to share their experiences in dealing with applicants. On the other hand, applicants were encouraged to share their experiences with programs and any advice they would give prospective applicants.

Think Like a Business Person; Think Like a Scientist

To meet the requirements for a successful application to a government technology program, you will need to "learn the ropes." As one successful awardee summed it up, you need to do two things: "Think like a business person; think like a scientist." To help you reach this goal, the experiences of persons on both sides of the process have been analyzed: the awarder and the awardee.

The "ropes" are guidelines to effective action in the government technology world. They are the rules of the game—both explicit and implicit. As discussed in this chapter, they are the suggested behavior patterns in dealing with public technology programs distilled from the advice of those interviewed. By knowing "the ropes" and accessing resources, you can turn the application process to your advantage.

Knowledge of the informal as well as the formal side of government technology programs can help you interpret program guidelines and find the best fit for your project ideas. The most important first step you can take to enter into the informal side of the award process is establishing a dialogue with a program manager in your area of interest. Initial contact can be made by a telephone "cold call," e-mail, or introducing yourself in a "one-on-one" session at a regional or national conference held by one of the many government technology programs.

A good investment of time and resources is attending one of the program meetings and establishing personal contact with program managers in your area of interest. When interviewed, a technology entrepreneur from California, who spent $1,200 to participate in an SBIR meeting in Washington, DC, said that the opportunity to meet program managers, successful applicants, and representatives from established firms who were looking for new technology was well worth it. The Web lists upcoming meetings (see sections III and V for addresses). The *Commerce Business Daily (CBD)* is the most complete source of current information about government business opportunities. Presolicitations, solicitations, calls for white papers, and conference announcements are listed in the *CBD*. This is, perhaps, the earliest notice you can get of upcoming opportunities.

The meeting section of *Technology Access Report (TAR)*, a newsletter (info@techaccess.com), also has information about SBIR, ATP, and other government program conferences. *TAR* also has a section that lists typical awards of these programs; the listing includes brief descriptions and amounts of the awards. Program managers run workshops and participate in panels at a wide range of industrial, professional, and technical conferences. It is useful to check the upcoming programs of meetings in your field of interest and either make an appointment in advance or introduce yourself at a session.

Advancing Science; Commercializing Technology

Most of the "ropes" discussed below relate in one way or another to the dual goals of government technology programs. Despite different degrees of emphasis, each program is dedicated both to advancing science and technology and to promoting its commercialization. Attention must be paid to both, giving each its due, and of course, the relationship between the two must be made clear. If your project is purely a business proposition, without technological advance or transfer, you should look to the private sector or perhaps state programs for support.

Conversely, if your project is wholly concerned with advancing science and technology, there is another set of federal programs from which to choose. For example, in National Institutes of Health (NIH), a so-called RO1 grant may be appropriate. On the other hand, some researchers have found that reviewers of their RO1 proposal, or similar applications for research support to other agencies, have criticized them for being too focused on the practical implications of their research. If you feel that you fall into this category or have been advised that you do, then one of the programs discussed in this book may provide a home for your project.

You do not necessarily have to be incorporated in order to apply to all of these programs. For instance, SBIR requires only an Employer Identification Number (EIN) at the time of application. Indeed, some awardees find that they do not subsequently incorporate until much later, if ever.

Some programs are larger than others. If it can be assumed that all other attributes are equal, you might want to "go where the money is." For example, the U.S. Air Force funds several times as much environmental-related research as the Environmental Protection Administration (EPA), an agency officially and overtly devoted to this objective, does.

Moreover, some programs have follow-on funding arrangements that take you further along the road to a market or a customer, even if it is the agency itself. For example, the Army has the ManTech and Act II programs to move technology into production.

The National Science Foundation (NSF) has an experimental SBIR Phase 2b, which provides matching funds to selected Phase 2 awardees to help them take the next step to the market by providing selected awardees with additional matching funds. A wide variety of funds, including support from state agencies, are acceptable to meet the match. Typically, there is a rush over a few months to line up your contribution to the match and get the money in the bank before the deadline.

Rope 1. Learning the System: People, Documents, and Deadlines

People

There are three key types of people in public technology programs usually referred to as the point of contact, listed and described here.

1. The initial point of contact is usually a *program manager* who has responsibility for dealing both with the external world of prospective applicants and awardees and the internal world of the agency. A program manager typically has input into the award decision, formally or informally, but the final decision is made elsewhere.

2. Sometimes, there is also a *technical point of contact*, a government scientist or technologist who is responsible for a particular technical field in a given agency. This is especially true in the Department of Defense (DOD). The term *technical point of contact* (POC) denotes a government scientist or technologist who has responsibility for 1) finding useful technologies or ideas from the outside world to meet the mission of the lab and 2) generating topics for the agency's solicitation. Thus, the POC is a potential customer for any given technology that can be shown to further the lab's or agency's objectives. Although this term is used in its generic sense in this book, most scientists in other agencies interact with their counterparts in industry and academia without any formal designation.

3. A *contracts and grants administrator* has the responsibility for seeing that the terms of an award are met. This person also arranges disbursement of funds and is available to answer questions about the terms of an award, problems in receiving funds, and so forth. If the project is administered as a contract, there most likely will be negotiation to specify the work plan and expected results more precisely.

The roles above sometimes overlap and a single person may fill more than one of the three. Moreover, the first two types of officials likely will be met initially during the application process, while the third is more likely to be encountered only after an award is made.

The program manager is the public face of the organization, attending conferences and presenting information about the program to prospective applicants. The technical point of contact is more likely found in a government laboratory, although, of course, such persons participate in technical conferences in their fields as researchers rather than as representatives of a public technology program.

The DOD encourages people to be in touch with its in-house researchers to discuss ideas. On the other hand, the National Institutes of Health (NIH) prefer that potential applicants draw upon their own contacts for technical advice. Nevertheless, you may already have, or can readily make, contacts with relevant government scientists and technologists at professional conferences.

The program manager, who has direct oversight responsibility for a program, is the most important contact person for both applicants and awardees. Program managers take individual approaches to their jobs. Indeed, most programs are decentralized, allowing a range of management styles. One SBIR program manager said, "I demand things of my grantees that I know others do not. I am a stickler for details." She follows up with them regularly and mentors them. If things do not work out, she encourages those who have not received an award and talks to the so-called *principal investigators* (PIs) to see how they can make it work. She also demands that her awardees do effectiveness testing and try to get a potential marketer relatively early in the project rather than waiting until it is close to completion. Other program managers are less stringent and more *laissez-faire* in their management style.

Documents

Just as there are different types of personnel, there are different types of documents. You will encounter different documents, depending upon when you get into the process. At first, you may see a brochure or Web site outlining the purposes of the program and a contact point.

One type of announcement directly asks you to submit a full-scale proposal while another type of announcement proceeds in two steps. A first step might be a presolicitation where the specific technical topics for an upcoming competition are listed. When a presolicitation is released, the technical people in a lab are available for discussion so that you can see where you fit best and ask them what they really want.

Yet another type of announcement takes a more elaborate staged approach, asking for a white paper, presolicitation proposal, or abstract first. White papers can range from a brief three to four page outline of a particular idea to a comprehensive document detailing a strategic approach for the entire program.

There are different ways of conceptualizing a white paper. The approach you take to the white paper process will depend in great measure on the scale and capabilities of your organization and the range and scope of your interest. You may wish to present a "big picture" of how to advance an entire area, a technological focus with great future potential, or a specific innovative idea that fits an existing category. Any of these formats, if done well, can capture the interest of a program officer and lead to special encouragement to continue on to the next stage.

In all cases, the final step is the issuance of a solicitation, an invitation to respond to a request for proposals. It is usually a comprehensive document; the largest part of which is a description of technical topics. It is here that you will either find a place for your project or not, enabling you to determine whether it is worth proceeding. The solicitation will also provide you with the criteria by which your proposal will be evaluated.

Deadlines

It is important to note the deadlines listed on the solicitation. Some deadlines are very short (one month) while others are long-term (six months or more). Of course, once the deadline is past, the solicitation is only of interest if you wish to get a feel for the program. Solicitation deadlines are absolute. People have broken down in tears upon arriving at the agency with their package a minute after the deadline and having it refused. Typically, overnight deliveries increase precipitously as the deadline date approaches.

It is important to note that some programs may require some of the information to be submitted electronically. An Internet server site may be down or the network may be overloaded, so it is best to try to submit before the last minute. Also, some programs require as many as 15 bound copies of 40 pages each, so be sure to leave time for production.

Rope 2. Get to Know the People

Some program managers take the traditional role of the venture capitalist, going well beyond the basic requirements of their job in dealing with applicants and becoming informal advisors and mentors to the entrepreneurs with whom they work. Many program managers welcome being kept abreast of a firm's progress, and some call their awardees regularly for this purpose. In addition to guiding the awardees through the stages of a federal program, these managers may make helpful suggestions, such as a possible firm from among the program officer's portfolio of awardees with which to collaborate.

There are different ways of getting to know relevant program managers. This can take place through a telephone call or e-mail to someone identified on a Web site, in a directory, or at a formal session or informal gathering at a conference.

There may also be an opportunity to interest a government scientist or technologist, particularly in the DOD, in a research area that is not yet part of a program, and have it added to the solicited topics. The initial step most likely would be to find the best fit between a government program and your idea. This also may depend on its stage of development, whether it is closer to the research front or product development and whether it is oriented to a government or commercial market, or both.

Programs are interested in a variety of research topics and industrial sectors but often have different views on the stage and phase of research and development (R&D) that they are willing or able to support. Through discussion at a meeting or follow up on the phone, you may be able to find a place for your project idea in a government technology program.

As one experienced applicant to DOD put it, "Take advantage of the presolicitation period and start a dialogue with the technical POC and let them give you a focus or direction. Look to them for advice as to whether you fit or not or should tweak your idea to [get a] better fit." It is also possible that through ongoing discussions the topic may be refined or a more relevant topic might be introduced into the program later.

On the other hand, another applicant reported a mixed experience saying that, "Some program managers really understand how the program operates, others are not so knowledgeable." In this case, new applicants will have to rely more on written materials available from the agency, often posted on the Web, and contacts among successful applicants to the program to learn about its nuances.

Some successful applicants are willing to share their experiences and, in a form of payback, participate in seminars and otherwise advise new applicants on how to pursue an award. Other successful applicants are less open. Some simply feel they do not have the time as a small firm to deviate from a 100% concentration on their work. Others are fearful that by discussing their experience they are only creating more competitors for themselves, making future awards more difficult to obtain.

An alternative possibility is that "proposal pressure," an increase in the number of good proposals for which there are insufficient funds to make an award, will encourage expansion of government technology programs. Indeed, since its official inception in 1982, the SBIR has been expanded from $1/2$ of 1% to 2.5% of the research budgets of federal agencies that conduct more than $100 million of research per annum.

Rope 3. Dual Goals: Good Research and Good Commercial Potential

Public technology programs are designed to achieve identifiable commercial and public goals. Technology programs should not be viewed as a substitute for basic government research programs. The purpose of public technology programs is not to fund research as an end in itself. Nor should such technology programs be seen as a means to gain supplemental funds for a basic research project unless it is to explore a practical possibility that has emerged from a curiosity driven investigation.

It is irrelevant whether a project starts from a product idea or results from research. The key is for the project to involve *research* that will in the foreseeable future lead to a *commercial result*. As one SBIR program manager put it, "You can have a neat idea but you have to know what you are going to do with it. The most successful proposal is when you say here is a specific product or service that you will develop."

Various programs have different time frames for expected results. What they all have in common is a close connection between research and commercialization. There must be an apparent path to a clearly identified product or technological advance that can be expected to result in an array of future products.

The government's twin goals of *technological advance* and *commercial success* have a different emphasis in comparison to the private funding process. In the private sector, the main emphasis will be on business potential although a technical advance may be an important factor in reaching that goal. In the public process, a technological advance that will extend beyond the particular project will also be an important goal for government, even if the entrepreneur is solely concerned with the success of his or her own product.

Rope 4. Collaborate, Collaborate, Collaborate

Government technology programs usually require a combination of expertise which is typically some mix of scientific, technical, business, and entrepreneurial skills. The dual nature of government technology programs that combines research and business objectives, suggests that some, but by no means all, applicants will have both sets of skills—thus, the importance of collaboration. Entrepreneurs who have business backgrounds and others with technical backgrounds have both been successful in gaining awards. Both types of persons have found it useful, even necessary, to partner with persons whose skills complement their own.

Technical people should identify a person with business skills to work with and vice versa. The person with relevant, complementary skills may be someone in your social network. For example, a cardiologist with a software project thought of a patient who had just sold his business as a possible collaborator. Furthermore, individuals with professional skills such as TV producers, accountants, and lawyers who are not researchers themselves, may be able to initiate collaborations with researchers and make successful applications. However, it sometimes takes more than one try to find the right collaborator.

Program managers may be helpful in initiating new applicants to the government technology award process and pointing them in the right direction. A currently successful applicant, whose earlier proposal had been rejected, recalled her initial reaction to the SBIR solicitation. She said, "It looked like 300 pages of tax forms." She described her experience contacting an SBIR program manager. She said, "[my program manager] is great. I landed on Mars and she translated. She works well with the layman." The applicant learned about the program at a professional conference where she participated in a workshop on the SBIR She had no previous knowledge of SBIR, and she concluded from the presentation and printed material that although "SBIR is usually for academics, it could also be useful to me." She had applied for grants before but not to programs with a research component. The SBIR program manager assured her that her "TV expertise was perfect." For the medical side of the project, the applicant recruited a National Cancer Institute (NCI) designated Cancer Center. However, she recalled that the social scientist she collaborated with initially did not have the appropriate skills for her project. SBIR reviewers made it clear that she needed a better methodology. "Everything else was OK. But it needed to be more scientific." Her program manager handwrote her a note after the initial failure. "There is a lot of potential there. This is what you have to do." She offered to look at a draft.

This applicant looked at her program manager as a coach. She found the SBIR "a great learning process. In '98, I succeeded because I failed in '95. They give you a written critique. I then went about fixing it. They said 'it was a good failure' but they did not even score it. You need perseverance to find the correct academic talent. It took a year to find the right academic. It takes persistence to read the solicitation and to apply properly." After an initial failure due to lack of a sufficient research component, she made cold calls and identified an appropriate social scientist.

Rope 5. How Topics Are Selected

A topic is a description of a specific technology area that a program focuses upon in an award competition.

The ideas for topics come from several sources including:

1. Program managers and technical personnel within an agency
2. Discussions between agency representatives and entrepreneurs
3. Three-way brainstorming sessions among representatives of government laboratories, universities, and firms

The general orientation of particular programs, whether to meet agency mission objectives or to assist external clients such as industry, determines where the primary emphasis is placed in generating topics. Thus, SBIR, whose official objective is encouraging small firms to participate in government sponsored research programs, selects its topics with the purpose of meeting the research needs of the various participating agencies. Nevertheless, this criteria allows considerable leeway to demonstrate that a technology meets government's needs and has commercial potential—the ideal combination!

On the other hand, the Advanced Technology Program (ATP) of the National Institute of Standards and Technology (NIST) in the Department of Commerce (DOC) has the mission of fostering innovation in industry and thus generates its topics collaboratively with industry, encouraging interested companies and industrial groups to take the lead. Indeed, in its most recent competition, ATP did not list any special topics in advance and instead grouped successful awards together by topic area after the selections were made.

ATP program officers hold regular meetings at technical conferences, industry meetings, and its own biannual regional gatherings to encourage participation and brainstorming. Topics that fit ATP's mandate support precompetitive R&D, bringing significant benefits to other companies in an industry and/ or across industrial sectors. These sessions also provide an opportunity to meet ATP program officers in your area of interest.

The SBIR topic generation process, while taking place more within government, also varies, depending upon the extent to which decision making is decentralized. At NIH, each institute makes its own decisions, leaving choice of topics as close as possible to agency subunits and is thus quite decentralized.

Alternatively, in DOD, topic selection is relatively centralized, coordinated among different parts of an agency. For example, the Army sets priorities following a "bottom up" approach. Topics are suggested at the technical point of contact level, screened by program managers and their advisors, and finally selected further up in the agency. Thus, program slots are allocated according to the Army's overall needs.

Topic generation is a complex process that goes in different directions in various agencies. Nevertheless, it usually includes some combination of the following steps, although it may begin from either end or even from the middle. The process first goes down the line within the agency and then laterally, within and without the agency, for advice on internally generated topics or to solicit ideas from industry and academia. It then goes up the line, within the agency for prioritizing.

Indeed, depending upon the agency and its priorities, the topic generation process can start from any of these standpoints. For example, the Army looks inside first, relying initially on its own laboratories for ideas to make into SBIR topics. By contrast, NIH SBIR looks first to the academic individual investigator and high-tech firm community. Thus, NIH tends to have generic topics, broadly related to the mission of each Institute, while the Army focuses more tightly on specific topics, prioritized across its technical units. On the other hand, the Defense Advanced Research Projects Agency (DARPA), which takes a broad DOD-wide approach to innovation, relies heavily on its program officers' assessment of technological trends and capabilities and begins from an internal, "top down" perspective.

There is usually some point of entry, depending upon the agency, where the entrepreneur can suggest topics that can then filter in or up, influencing the topic selection process. If you get to know a technical person in an agency or a program manager, you may be able to propose ideas of interest and gain input over time on the topics that are chosen for future solicitations.

Indeed, some agencies make such input the focus of their topic generation efforts. As discussed, the ATP relies on group discussions with potential proposers in a technical area in advance of a solicitation and the proposal evaluation process itself to produce a final set of topics after the fact.

Rope 6. Preparing a Proposal: Getting It Right

The two essential ingredients of public technology programs are that they combine scientific and technological aims with commercial goals. Thus, a successful proposal must address both sides of the equation. As a reviewer for NIH SBIR said, "The common thread is that there has to be a testable hypothesis, and a commercializable product."

When these criteria were met, she "saw a lot of companies adding a project and leveraging their company. The best submissions were high risk/high gain." On the other hand, "The worst ones were handwritten. It was clear they had not read the solicitation. They had no planned experiments, no detail, and no test of feasibility. They did not research if it belonged to someone else (for example, by conducting a patent search) and therefore could not be commercialized."

Thus, it is important to follow solicitation guidelines, complete all parts of the proposal, and carefully edit the text. It is also a good idea to have others review the proposal. Possible candidates to provide this assistance are consultants you have used, fellow collaborators, or professional colleagues familiar with the award process. All should review the proposal, with the guidelines in mind, to make sure you have all the pieces in hand before preparing a final version.

Be aware of whom you are writing for. While one or more reviewers may be experts in your special area, it is more likely that at least some of the reviewers will only have general expertise related to your specific project. Thus, it is important to explain in a coherent way what you plan to do and how you plan to do it. Another reviewer, who was also a successful applicant, said, "Keep in mind that applications are for the most part reviewed by people with general expertise in an area. So write for an educated nonspecialist. Be aware that a reviewer may get as many as 20 to 30 applications, so make it good-looking, clean, and error free."

Conform to the specs in the solicitation in a logical manner. Another reviewer said, "Avoid poorly reproduced copies, and don't use 10pt font—it is too hard to read." In SBIR applications especially, you need to be sure in the specific aims section and in experimental procedure that there is a test of feasibility in the Phase 1 application so you know if you can go on to Phase 2. Demonstration of feasibility in Phase 1 is a requirement for succeeding in winning a Phase 2 (a much larger sum) award. This is often a problem with academic entrepreneurs who may not include a test of feasibility.

The abstract of the grant application is the format that the greatest number of people will see. You must capture the essence of your proposal in the abstract, which should be carefully framed. On the one hand, it goes on the Web, so you do not want to put in anything you wish held proprietary. On the other hand, some reviewers may not get much past the abstract due to time constraints, so you want to give them as much specific detail as possible.

There may be as many as 15 persons on a review committee. Indeed, one interviewee reported that a large number of the people on the review committee might only see your abstract given the number of proposals they must review. The reviewer said, "You only have 25 pages or whatever the specific number of pages allowed by the particular program. Don't waste 10 pages on résumés and descriptions of your facilities. The emphasis should be on the science or technology and the path toward their commercial utilization. Keep the bios short. A lot of people don't disclose things because they want to keep it confidential, but you won't be funded unless you tell people what is going on."

Secrecy is a double-edged sword. On the one hand, prospective applicants would like to see successful proposals so that they can have a model to work from. On the other hand, they may not wish to make their own proposal public out of concern for giving up a competitive advantage.

Once SBIR makes an award, the front two pages of the application go on the Internet site. This contains the name of the PI and a 200 word abstract, but the rest of the proposal remains proprietary and is not disclosed unless you give permission. It is our understanding that those involved in the review process, including program managers and reviewers, sign nondisclosure agreements.

An abstract, of course, only gives an indication of the type of work being done. It does not take you through the thought process of the applicant or show you their work. Some people might not wish to even let that much information out and therefore might not apply. Some program managers request permission from awardees to put the best proposals in their entirety on the agency Web site so that prospective applicants can see what a good proposal looks like.

Rope 7. Evaluation Criteria

The weighting of the evaluation criteria will change significantly depending on which government technology program you are applying to. A common set of criteria can be identified. The background of the reviewers who are going to evaluate your proposal typically depends upon the emphasis within the program between technical and business risk. If the orientation is in one direction or the other, the reviewers, whether inside or outside of government, will be drawn more from the technical or commercial side, or their judgements will be given greater weight.

Proposal evaluation basically follows the twin goals of *technical advance* and *commercial potential* with the additional and significant criteria of the ability of the applicant to perform the work. For example, the three criteria for scoring proposals, and their relative weights, in the DOD SBIR program are:

Technical soundness—40%

Qualification of staff and facilities—30%

Potential for commercialization in private or public sector—30%

An NIH program manager defined the categories and weighted them slightly differently than DOD, reflecting differences in the cultures of the two agencies.

Scientific merit—50%

Qualification of staff and facilities—25%

Potential for commercialization—25%

Note the respective orientations toward technology in the DOD and science in NIH, as well as the somewhat greater attention to utility in DOD. Although emphases may differ, these are the basic criteria used in all programs. Each criterion must be met at some level to gain an award. If a proposal does not seriously address all three issues, the chances of success are slim.

Thus, business potential or research advance by themselves will not lead to an award in these programs. Research by itself is appropriate for other government or private foundation grants designed for this purpose. A good business idea, by itself, may also find support from a private venture capital firm or "angel," an individual investor in early stage companies. Government technology programs are appropriate for applicants who can bring together technical and business expertise to solve a technological problem that has commercial potential.

The evaluation criteria are always listed on the Web site and in the solicitation itself. The criteria are usually explained in several paragraphs, giving in some detail the program view of "scientific merit" or "commercial potential."

The main reasons people fail are as follows:

1. The proposal is not specific. It is not clear what the proposal is going to do. There is too little about the project and too much about the key people;

2. There is a lack of innovative ideas;

3. Finally, and perhaps most distressingly, many applications fail not because the idea is bad but because it is not well presented

The biggest problem is often communication skills. As one program manager commented, "50%, if better written, would have gotten funded."

Many programs make proposal preparation handbooks available to try to teach people to write proposals. An initial injunction is do not leave anything out; give them everything they ask for. A missing section, such as a lack of a commercialization plan when one is requested, can kill an otherwise excellent proposal. Allocate the pages wisely, according to the review criteria. For example, if the researcher's background counts for 10%, then devote approximately that much of the proposal to the issue, leaving sufficient space for more heavily weighted topics.

Rope 8. Differences between Public and Private Funding: Why Seek Government Support?

Differences between Public and Private Funding

The public and private technology funding processes differ in significant ways.

In the private venture capital process, you may be introduced personally or you may send in a business plan. If the private venture capitalist is interested, you may be called in for a meeting to see about working together. Assuming there is further interest, they may negotiate with you.

In the public venture capital process, access is more open. Program managers are available to take calls, and every submission is entitled to go through the decision-making process. Personal contact comes earlier in the public process but is excluded in the later stages while the application is being reviewed. In the private process, usually interaction is not extensive until after a business plan has been submitted and the venture capitalist expresses continued interest.

In the public process, once the proposal has been submitted, no further contact is permitted until an award decision has been made. Also, in the public process, there is typically a debriefing procedure. If you fail, a program manager will explain why and clue you in on areas to improve if you decide to reapply. Often, project ideas go through more than one round before succeeding.

Why Seek Government Support?

Government support should be viewed as one possibility with both advantages and disadvantages. The major advantages of many government programs are:

- their willingness to support the early stages of technology development;
- their willingness to accept long lead times from the initiation of an investment to the time of expected revenue; and
- that equity is left intact for the entrepreneur. A firm is not asked to give up stock in exchange for government money. As one awardee put it, "If I get an SBIR grant, there is no liability. It is free money."

In contrast, private sources want to see an almost guaranteed, short-term, large-scale revenue stream at the time of their investment.

The federal government takes the long-term view. In addition to meeting its technology needs, government sees the payback as:

- increased employment in the future;
- "spill-over effect" (technology useful to a broad range of firms, not only the original investigator); and
- additional tax revenues in the future.

Private sources take the short-term view. Most private investors require a return on investment that is sizable and near-term.

Another advantage of government support is that helpful advice is often available from program managers in meeting the program's requirements. For example, a DOD SBIR awardee said of his sponsoring agency, "It is a very friendly organization or customer compared to commercial industry. You need to have patience with the paperwork, but in return they are very helpful and very forgiving. The people who monitor the contract are technical people. They understand your situation and they help you. They give you free services and they won't steal it."

The major disadvantage of many government programs is the persisting gap between the end of most public technology funding programs and the introduction of a product to the marketplace. This has been termed "the valley of death." Government anticipates that private sources of capital will come in when the prototype is ready, but this is often not the case. An awardee noted that, "The SBIR is weak when you finish Phases 1 and 2. You have done your R&D work. You have a prototype. The prototype is great. It works. What do you do with it? You go to private industry and they say, ' Have you tested it in a factory?' No. They want a beta test before they will take it on. I don't have a production line because I am a small company." The solutions that government offers are few and far between at this time. This particular entrepreneur was able to find a solution in a DOD program. He said, "I go to ManTech" [a DOD follow-on program for their SBIR awardees]. Through the support of this program, unique to the DOD, he has a contract with a large defense corporation to take his proto-type into production. Most entrepreneurs with government awards are not this fortunate.

Rope 9. Make Sure You Are Comfortable with the Government as a Partner

It is important to be aware of responsibilities and requirements that may come with the receipt of government funds. For example, a successful awardee advised that you should "make sure you are comfortable with government as a partner; know the terms on which you are working with the government, whether work will be made public or held confidential."

Another issue is intellectual property rights, whether potential patents that result will be owned by the company and what special rights, if any, the government retains by virtue of having made the award. Typically, only a limited portion of the information that you divulge in a proposal is available to the public. With the exception of the abstract and first two pages, SBIR has an exemption from the Freedom of Information Act and your proposal remains confidential unless you give permission for it to be publicized. Other programs have similar exemptions. Some proposals made to the DOD may be kept entirely confidential on the grounds of national security.

Another matter of concern is who owns intellectual property rights resulting from collaboration, whether through provision of funds as in SBIR or ATP or carrying out joint work as in a Cooperative Research and Development Agreement (CRADA). In an SBIR or ATP award, the company owns any intellectual property rights that come out of the project. An SBIR awardee has five years to patent any results. If they do not do it within that time period, they lose it. The SBIR encourages starting patent protection as early as possible. It should be noted that government retains a license free agreement in perpetuity.

There are also issues of timing to be considered. If the window of opportunity for the project is short, SBIR or other government programs may not be appropriate because the process is too slow. In deciding to access government programs, an entrepreneur said, "They have to assess if they have a quick time to market technology versus time to develop the technology and then go to the market. SBIR is appropriate for the latter. SBIR drags out the time to market." On the other hand, the clear positive side of the government technology funding process is that the entrepreneur does not have to give up equity.

Finally, government programs are continuously being revised. Many past problems have been successfully addressed, and some complex procedures have been simplified.

For applicants who have dealt with government procurement previously through Federal Acquisition Regulations (FAR), be aware that things have changed. Many of the funding programs for technology entrepreneurs and innovative firms discussed in this book have greatly streamlined their procedures. Indeed, some have instituted fast track submissions over the Internet and reduced time gaps between program phases.

Rope 10. Appropriate Behavior

There is an etiquette to dealing with public technology programs that may differ from the private sector experience. There are times in discussions with venture capitalists when anger, openly expressed, may bring positive results in turning around a failing negotiation by calling sharp attention to a product feature or market that the potential funder may have missed. The structure of the public technology award process makes such a tactic difficult, if not impossible. The time gap between proposal submission and award notice prescribes a clear "before" and "after" to the decision making process. Thus, there is little or no point in vociferously protesting an adverse decision.

Rejection should be taken calmly, at least in dealing with the program. As one technology entrepreneur who has experienced both success and failure and served on review committees put it, "If you are rejected, do not come back with a scathing response. Address the issues brought up, no matter how trivial they may seem to you. Remain polite. Address the issues raised and resubmit. Sometimes what comes back may seem bizarre but the chances are that next time the people will be different so you will have a second shot. It is so disappointing because you are losing six months to a year." From his experience on review committees, he noted that "the ones who got funded were those who stayed focused. They addressed the issues raised by the review committee, no matter how absurd they thought the comment was."

The possibility to resubmit is a contrast to the private negotiation process where there is little possibility of repeating the process, at least in the short-term, once a negotiation has failed. You cannot go back to the same people under most circumstances. You must start again with someone else. The upside of the public technology funding process is that resubmission in the next round is not unexpected and it is often encouraged as a follow-up to a negative decision. Indeed, in many programs an initial rejection is an intermediate stage and a normal part of the eventual funding of a proposal.

Sometimes it is a good idea to resubmit to the same program; at other times, if the problem appears to be lack of fit with agency interests, it is best to look for another agency. Keep in mind that there are a variety of government technology programs, many of which have overlapping interests. Thus, there is more recourse on the public side.

Following the private sector model of seeking another source upon rejection is not necessarily applicable to the public sector. To fail to resubmit may be to give up too soon.

When asked "What do you need to succeed?", a recipient of 15 SBIR awards replied, "Stamina and perseverance." A successful awardee from both DOD and NIH reiterated that "If you go the SBIR route, you have to have a thick skin and perseverance."

To improve your chances of success, whether in an initial application or reapplication, an awardee advised that it is best to "Get involved before the topic comes out in the presolicitation phase or even earlier. Network early." If you get rejected in one place, change the form and resubmit to fit the new problem statement. For example, change the point of contact (e.g., Army to Air Force or Air Force to Army).

PART II
USER'S GUIDE TO GOVERNMENT PROGRAMS FOR TECHNOLOGY ENTREPRENEURS AND INNOVATIVE FIRMS

In this section, programs of potential interest to technology entrepreneurs and innovative firms are reviewed. The opportunities offered in several programs made available by federal agencies, as well as some joint federal and state programs, are also discussed. In addition, the organization of the program, who is eligible to qualify for funding, how to access the program, the expectations that the program has of applicants, and helpful hints on how to match your objectives with program goals are explained.

Many entrepreneurs are skeptical of government programs and have an innate distrust of government. As one skeptical entrepreneur asked, "Isn't the government hard to work with?" Some are pleasantly surprised when they overcome their initial skepticism and start an interaction with a program manager. Another skeptical entrepreneur indicated how surprised he was when he found willing help from government employees every step of the way.

The government programs discussed below are meant to help entrepreneurs develop their concepts in the hope of eventually expanding the number of jobs in the economy. Just as venture capitalists realize that although many companies fail, the successes more than make it worth their while to fund venture companies, the government likewise realizes the same. Government is willing to step up to the plate at an earlier stage in the funding process than most private venture capitalists. The discussion of relevant government programs begins with perhaps the largest and most available to the individual entrepreneur, start-up firm, or small company, the Small Business Innovation Research Program (SBIR).

This part of the book is split into three chapters. In chapter five, we describe the SBIR and STTR programs. They provide funding for an early phase of scientific and technological development, and the technical authority of the proposals is given very much weight. SBIR—the Small Business Innovation Research Program—is perhaps the largest and most available to the individual entrepreneur, start-up firm, or small company.

Chapter 6 describes funding sources that put more weight on commercial criteria, which means that they are likely to fund projects that are closer to the market. The Advanced Technology Program (ATP) and its military equivalent, the agency DARPA, both target new technologies with high potentials but also unusually high risks. Dual Use programs in the Air Force, Army , and Navy can be a source of funding for the development of a project that has both military and civilian use. In fact, most of the programs that are relevant for technology entrepreneurs and innovative firms have both a military and civilian side. The broad range of facilities, activities, and technologies in the Department of Defense implies that the military will be interested in many products and technologies that also have a potential nondefense market.

In chapter seven, we describe a number of programs and agencies that are smaller and/or have targets that are more specific. ACT II is a military program oriented at mature technologies, while CRADAs are contractual arrangement with the federal laboratories. Many small firms have successfully used CRADAs, for instance related to testing and validating their product and technology. ManTech and MEP are both manufacturing-oriented programs while the Small Business Administration (SBA) had a number of services to offer the small business community, including help centers and loan programs.

CHAPTER 5 • EARLY PHASE: THE SMALL BUSINESS INNOVATION RESEARCH PROGRAM

CONTENTS

EARLY PHASE: THE SMALL BUSINESS INNOVATION RESEARCH PROGRAM

Introduction

In fiscal year 1998, the total budget for the Small Business Innovation Research (SBIR) programs exceeded $1 billion. Presently, around $1.2 billion is awarded annually. More than 9,000 small firms and 40,000 projects have received awards from the SBIR program since its start in 1982. The firms come from all 50 states and from a wide range of technology areas. The application process is relatively simple and straightforward.

The competition for funding is strong. Nevertheless, if you are an individual or a company with less than 500 employees that is able to conduct research and development (R&D) of high quality, you are eligible to win an award for research and development. The founder of the program, Roland Tibbetts, says that, "SBIR projects should be high-risk but also have large potential for economic benefits if they are successful."

In this section, the following will be described:

1. Background of the SBIR Program
2. The SBIR System
3. What It Takes to Qualify for Participation
4. The Awarding Process and Criteria
5. The Three Phases of the Program
6. The Small Business Technology Transfer Program (STTR) Program: A Variant of SBIR
7. Advice Before Submitting Proposals
8. SBIR and STTR on the Web

Purpose of the SBIR Program

The premises of the program are laid out in the Small Business Innovation Development Act of 1982 (PL 102-567) and 1992 (PL 102-564). The four purposes of the act are to:

1. Stimulate technological innovation;

2. Use small business to meet federal research and development needs;

3. Encourage the participation by disadvantaged and minority persons in technological innovation; and

4. Increase private sector commercialization derived from federal research and development.

The SBIR System

This is where the funding comes from. Each federal agency with an external research and development budget of more than $100 million must establish an SBIR program. The agencies are required to set aside 2.5% of their total research budgets for the program (originally the percentage was lower, but it has gradually increased until it reached the current 2.5% requirement in 1997). Some advocates in Congress have proposed that the percentage be increased to 3% when the law authorizing SBIR comes up for renewal in 2000. It is said that the entrepreneurial sector is where most innovation and innovators thrive, thus, this sector is the target of the SBIR. By reserving a specific percentage of federal research and development funds for small business, SBIR protects small business interests and enables small business to compete effectively for some federal research and development funds.

The federal departments and agencies that participate in the program are listed below (the number in parentheses denotes an approximate estimate of the current SBIR budget in millions of dollars). The total SBIR budget, for instance, was around $1.1 billion in fiscal year 1997.

1. Department of Agriculture (10 to 15 million)

2. Department of Commerce, including the National Institute of Standards and Technology (10 to 15 million)

3. Department of Defense, with several large suborganizations participating (greater than 500 million)

4. Department of Education (5 million)

5. Department of Energy (75 million)

6. Department of Health and Human Services, including the National Institute of Health (greater than 300 million)

7. Department of Transportation (10 to 15 million)
8. Environmental Protection Agency (10 to 15 million)
9. National Aeronautics and Space Administration (100 million)
10. National Science Foundation (50 million)

Since the SBIR is based on a set-aside of an agency's research and development budget, the final SBIR budget is determined by Congress every year when it decides each agency's overall research and development budget. Recent years have seen strong political support for large increases in funding for health-related research and development. This recent increase is in part due to recognition of the role of health-related research and development in the creation of a strong U.S. biotechnology industry. This has in turn led to a dramatic increase in the SBIR budget at the National Institutes of Health and other Department of Health and Human Services (DHHS) participants. In fiscal year 1995, the DHHS SBIR budget was $179 million; in fiscal year 1999, it is expected to be $307 million.

In addition, the U.S. Small Business Administration (SBA) plays an important role in SBIR. Most important is perhaps its role as an information link. Much material, both to get you started in the application process and to help you when you have completed the SBIR phases, is available on-line. Furthermore, the Small Business Administration is formally the coordinating agency for SBIR. It directs the agencies' implementation of SBIR, reviews their progress, and reports annually to Congress on the program's operation.

What Does It Take to Qualify for Participation?

To be able to participate in the SBIR program, small businesses must meet certain criteria:

1. The company must be American owned and independently operated. Allowable company types are sole proprietorships, partnerships, joint ventures, associations, and cooperatives.

2. The company must be for-profit (nonprofit organizations are not eligible).

3. The primary employment of the *principal investigator* must be with the small business. He or she must spend more than half of his or her time employed by the firm at the time of award and during the conduct of the effort.

4. The company size is limited to 500 employees. However, according to the SBIR founder Roland Tibbetts, most of the award winners are small high-tech, start-up firms.

The Award Process

Through its SBIR program, each participating agency develops topics (technology areas, etc.) and releases *solicitations* describing those topics. SBIR solicitations are specific Requests for Proposals (RFPs) released by the federal agencies that may result in the award of SBIR funding agreements. The Small Business Administration releases a *presolicitation announcement* that is a single source for the topics and anticipated release and closing dates for each agency's solicitations. The presolicitation, agency solicitations, and application material are all available on-line (see the Quick Reference Directory in Part IV for Web addresses and people to contact).

An overview of the different solicitation release dates and proposal deadlines can be found below. See also the descriptions of the various agencies' SBIR programs below for particular information about the proposal process.

Agency	Solicitation Release	Proposal Deadline
Department of Agriculture	Jun	Sep
Department of Commerce	Oct	Jan
Department of Defense	Oct	Jan
	May	Aug
Department of Education	Feb	Apr
Department of Energy	Dec	Mar
Department of Health and Human Services (including National Institutes of Health)	Jan	Apr
	May	Aug
	Sep	Dec
Department of Transportation	Feb	May
Environmental Protection Agency	Sep	Nov
National Aeronautics and Space Administration	Apr	Jul
National Science Foundation	Mar–Apr	Jun

Proposals from firms are submitted to the agency where they are reviewed and evaluated on a competitive basis. Each agency makes its own awards using contracts, grants, or cooperative agreements. All agencies are active in more than one technology area. A summary of awards in different broad technology areas is given in the table below.

Technology area	Total awards 1983–95, dollars in billions
Computer, information processing, analysis	1.87
Electronics	2.49
Materials	1.63
Mechanical performance of vehicles, weapons, facilities	0.79
Energy conversion and use	1.09
Environment and natural resources	0.64
Life sciences	1.52

Note: Some awards are assigned to multiple technology areas, the sum of the right column would thus be larger than the actual total of awards.

The largest subareas, measured in total awards from 1983 to 1995, are advanced materials, optical devices and lasers, information processing and management, biotechnology and microbiology, computer and communication systems, electronics device performance, medical instrumentation, and electromagnetic radiation/propagation.

After the proposals have been submitted, the agencies in general make SBIR awards based on these criteria: small business qualification, degree of innovation, technical merit, and future market potential. In practice, the reviewers will look at various specific criteria like the following ones used by the Department of Defense:

1. Soundness and technical merit of the proposed approach;
2. Potential for commercial (government or private sector) application and the expected benefits from commercialization;
3. Adequacy of the proposed effort for fulfilling requirements of the research topic; and
4. Qualifications of the proposed principal investigator or key researchers, supporting staff, and consultants (including the ability to perform the research and development and to commercialize the results).

Due to the advanced technological nature of most projects, a heavier weighting is usually put on the scientific and excellence of the proposals as compared to the weighting placed on commercialization issues. The reviewers themselves normally come from a research and development organization.

The Three Phases of the Program

Small businesses that receive awards or grants then begin a three-phase program.

Phase I

Phase I is the start-up phase. Awards are given up to $150,000 (but less in many agencies) for approximately six months to support exploration of the technical merit or feasibility of an idea or technology. The purpose of Phase I is to show (1) that the proposing firm can do high quality research and development, (2) that the proposed effort is technically feasible, and (3) that sufficient progress had been made to justify a much larger agency investment in Phase II. A minimum of two-thirds of the research and/or analytical effort must be performed by the proposing firm during Phase 1. The rest may be used for consultants or subcontractors. Nevertheless, despite these formal requirements, it is quite possible to operate as a virtual firm, hiring workers on a part-time, as needed basis.

It is difficult to get a Phase I award. In most agencies, only ten to twenty percent of the submitted proposals are granted awards. But in comparison with private venture capital, this is not a bad ratio. As one early stage venture capitalist recently said, " We fund one out of a hundred proposals submitted to us." Also, as discussed in Chapter 4, "Learning the Ropes," entrepreneurs often are encouraged to revise and resubmit their unsuccessful Phase I proposals and eventually become successful SBIR Phase I awardees the second or third time around.

Phase II

Once you get a Phase I award, however, it is easier to get to Phase II. Typically, 40% of Phase I awards go on to become Phase II awardees. It is important to stress that only Phase I award winners are considered for Phase II. (There is a significant exception to this rule. Some agencies have a fast track procedure in which Phase I and Phase II are awarded simultaneously. Note that this fast track procedure should be considered only if you can demonstrate proof of feasibility at the outset.)

In Phase II, the firm gets an award of up to $750,000, for as long as two years, to expand Phase I results. During this time, the research and development work is performed and the awardee evaluates commercialization potential. During Phase II, at least half of the research and analytical work must be performed by the proposing firm. Although many firms are operating formally in their own space and with full time employees by Phase II, some firms in Phase II continue to work virtually, conserving resources for research and development.

The award criteria for Phase II are the results of Phase I (i.e., how well you met the proof of feasibility test), the scientific and technical merit of the Phase II proposal, as well as its commercial potential. A highly encouraged way of meeting the commercial potential test is to provide evidence of a subsequent commitment by a funding or purchasing source. Examples of this include another firm willing to manufacture or market, a venture capital firm willing to invest, or a government agency interested in purchasing the technology or product.

For many firms, the waiting time between Phase I and II (evaluating Phase II proposals might take up to six months) can be frustrating. Several agencies such as the Department of Defense and The National Institutes of Health under the Department of Health and Human Services have initiated policies to help speed up this process. In the Department of Defense, the fast track policy gives Phase II applicants funds sooner if they meet certain special criteria. These are mainly concerned with the success of Phase I. The advantage is that fast track speeds up the award process.

The downside of fast track versus the normal process is that applicants must provide a match of around half of the Phase II funding with money from a private investor or another government program. Jonathon Baron, the SBIR program manager in the Department of Defense, reveals that apart from speeding up the award process, the fast track policy is also meant to increase commercialization and get more projects into Phase III. Baron said, "Around 10% of our present projects come under the fast track rule."

Phase III

Phase III is the period during which Phase II innovation is commercialized. No SBIR funds support this phase. The small business must find funding in the private sector or other non-SBIR federal agency funding. Possible help can be found in the Small Business Administration. This agency has developed a Commercialization Matching System, a way of assisting SBIR awardees in their efforts to locate sources of funding to help them get their technology or product to the market. Thus, SBIR funds the critical start-up and development stages. In order to get Phase II funding in many of the participating agencies, you need to have a funding commitment for Phase III from a private or public investor. Even where this is not required, it is definitely seen as an advantage and as an indication of the commercial viability of the project.

An overview of the maximum awards in the different phases, as well as the known success rates, can be found in the table below. The award sizes mainly follow from the total size of the participant's SBIR program, although there are exceptions. For instance, in the Department of Transportation, the award sizes are similar to those of the larger participants. Note also that success rates can vary. It seems that at the present, it is easier, relatively speaking, to get a Phase I award from the National Institutes of Health, while a Phase II award is more within reach in the Environmental Protection Agency (but here the Phase I rejection rate is among the highest).

Agency	Ph. I Max. Award ($K)	Ph. II Max. Award ($K)	Ph. I Success Rate	Ph. II Success Rate
Department of Agriculture	65	250	NA	NA
Department of Commerce	75	300	NA	NA
Department of Defense	100	750	15%	40%
Department of Education	50	300	18%	37%
Department of Energy	100	750	12%	45%
Department of Health and Human Services (including National Institutes of Health)	100	750	23%	41%
Department of Transportation	100	750	NA	NA
Environmental Protection Agency	70	295	10%	58%
National Aeronautics and Space Administration	70	600	15%	40%
National Science Foundation	100	400	NA	NA

The Small Business Technology Transfer Program: A Variant of SBIR

The Small Business Technology Transfer (STTR) program was established in 1992 and was implemented in the participating agencies from fiscal year 1994. The main difference between the two programs is that the STTR requires the company to cooperate with a nonprofit research institution (e.g., university, research center, national laboratory). This is also allowed in the SBIR, but is not mandatory. Darryl Gorman, the STTR program manager at the National Science Foundation (NSF), says that the idea behind the program at NSF is to tap into a different source of ideas—the ideas that can be found in universities and federal laboratories.

The main purposes of the STTR are the same as those described above for the SBIR, to move research and development towards commercialization. Whereas SBIR focuses on the commercialization of research and development performed within a small firm, STTR focuses on the commercialization of research and development performed with federal research and development dollars in universities and government laboratories. Basic program features are the same: some agencies set aside a percentage (0.15%) of their external research and development budget and use a three-phase approach. The maximum Phase II STTR award is a bit lower, $500,000. Five federal departments and agencies participate in the STTR.

The following list shows STTR participating agencies in order from highest research and development budget amounts to lowest . (These agencies are the ones with the highest research and development budgets).

1. Department of Defense
2. Department of Health and Human Services
3. Department of Energy
4. National Aeronautics and Space Administration
5. National Science Foundation

These agencies designate research and development topics and accept proposals in the same way as described above for SBIR. Proposals must respond to the solicitation as published by one or more of the participating agencies. SBA is also the information link to STTR. SBA collects solicitation information from all the participating agencies and publishes it periodically in a presolicitation announcement. To qualify, the small businesses must meet the same eligibility criteria that were explained above. There is a major exception to the SBIR size limit of 500 employees or less. The nonprofit research institution can be of any size but must meet certain criteria:

1. Located in the United States
2. Meet one of three definitions:
   a. Nonprofit college or university
   b. Domestic nonprofit research organization
   c. Federally Funded Research and Development Center (FFRDC)

The small company and the research institution must develop a written agreement prior to a Phase I award, which for instance can be a CRADA. This agreement must be submitted to the awarding agency if requested. A company may participate in both SBIR and STTR simultaneously (through the same or different agencies), but it may not perform the same or essentially similar work under more than one contract or grant.

It is clearly stated by the Small Business Administration that collecting funds more than once for the same work is fraud. To avoid such potential problems, many agencies require the companies to list all previous awards when applying for SBIR and STTR funding so that the reviewers can judge the similarity. The small business concern is the prime contractor, and it can change research institutions in Phase II. It must perform at least 40% of the work and research institutions must perform at least 30% of the work.

Separate solicitations are issued for the STTR program by each participant, although the total budget is quite small (around $50 million). Frequently, due to the small size of the program, only a few key technological areas are focused upon every year. For example, the National Science Foundation focused exclusively on "Nanotechnology" and "Sensors in Harsh Environments" in 1998. The STTR solicitations, as well as the proposal documents, contracts, and so on, are very similar (or identical to) those of the SBIR.

Since STTR is very similar to the SBIR, questions have been raised whether there is need for another program at all. A preliminary study by the General Accounting Office indicates, however, that the quality of proposals is high and that there are no negative effects on the SBIR.

Proposal Advice

There is a well prepared, extensive Proposal Preparation Handbook available on-line at the Web page of the Small Business Administration's Office of Technology (for SBIR-related Web addresses, see the paragraphs on SBIR/STTR on the Web below). The following is, to a great extent, based on that handbook and advice from previous awardees. A computer science entrepreneur, who had received two Phase I and one Phase II awards, said that "the application process is relatively simple and straightforward and relies much on technical information that most will have readily available."

When planning to get an award from the SBIR/STTR programs, there are three important steps: (1) gather information, (2) consider relevant projects and their technologies and markets, and (3) prepare the proposal. These three steps are discussed in the following.

Gathering Information

SBIR/STTR programs may be an excellent way to do the research and development necessary for a small firm to enter a new area. Applying for federal funding, however, can be a long and costly process. The first thing to do is to consider if you or your firm have the research and development capabilities (including staff) to do the advanced type of work that is required in these two programs. The Small Business Administration (SBA) recommends that firms interested in the SBIR and STTR programs start by drawing up a business plan. The plan can be an instrument to help you decide what program you want to compete in (which department or agency). In addition, most venture capitalists and other potential investors require a good business plan in order to provide funding. As a minimum, the SBA's Proposal Preparation Handbook lists the following topics:

a. Summary of what your company's objectives are and what business you are in;

b. Description of the specific products and/or services that you are or will be providing;

c. Description of the markets you are in or plan to compete in;

d. Description of your competition and your advantages *vis-a-vis* the competition;

e. Biographical information on the principals and key personnel;

f. Purpose(s) for which you are seeking funds and an estimate of the funds you will receive; and

g. Financial statement which includes both the past few years (if any) and projections for the next three to seven years.

Many Small Business Development Centers give free courses and other free help to entrepreneurs on writing good business plans. See the section on the Small Business Administration for more on these centers.

Networking is a key word in the information gathering phase. You should try to talk to relevant representatives from federal, state, and local government, companies, universities and nonprofit institutions, and also with independent consultants. Lists of previous awards are available on-line. You might want to try to get in touch with firms in your state or city that have already been successful in obtaining SBIR/STTR funding. For many, SBIR conferences are important meeting points. These are held several times every year. At these, you not only meet others in the same situation, but also program managers from the various agencies who can be valuable contacts in the future. Experts in your field can naturally offer valuable insights to the company and its staff, and the STTR program requires, as mentioned previously, a formal link between the company and a nonprofit research institution.

Considering Relevant Projects

To improve your chances of success, the SBA recommends that you meet the following criteria:

a. Respond to agency needs, problems, or mission area;

b. Carry out a quality technical effort that will make a significant impact; and

c. Market and sell a technological innovation resulting from the research and development effort.

You probably have an idea that you would like to work on. Possibly, you are interested in a project that will be important to the future of your company. It is important to find an agency solicitation topic that matches the technology that you want to develop. Bear in mind that, broadly speaking, some agencies focus on solving specific, targeted problems that are associated with the mission of their agency (i.e., education, transportation, etc.). Others are more oriented to technology arising from scientific and technical disciplines in general (e.g., the National Science Foundation). This means that the two kinds of agencies are likely to judge originality or innovativeness (which are important quality criteria) differently. Problem-solving research and development agencies tend to emphasize a new approach to solving a problem, while more research oriented agencies tend to emphasize technologies that demonstrate the practical usefulness to society of the scientific and technical disciplines that they support. Both will, however, select the projects that are most likely to meet their needs. The agency can also turn out to be a demanding and crucial first customer for your firm.

Remember to look at the SBA's presolicitation announcement, which provides summary information on solicitation topics by agency. It also contains opening and closing dates of agency solicitations, who to contact for a copy of specific solicitations, and estimates of the number of awards to be made under each solicitation. The presolicitation announcement is only available on-line and is updated quarterly. It is searchable, for instance, by topic.

The agency solicitation itself is the most important document you will need in order to apply. It outlines rules for submission in each agency, topics on which proposals may be submitted, criteria for awards, information to be included in proposals, evaluation criteria, procedural criteria (such as length limits on proposals, schedules for submission, evaluation, awards, and so on), and budgetary guidelines (such as total funding, limits, number of proposals funded, and whether profit is allowed). The solicitations are available on-line from the program office at each agency.

When considering projects to propose, remember also that, in general, all potential SBIR projects are evaluated along three dimensions: agency relevance, commercial importance, and technology leadership. The projects should be tailored so that the firm is able to meet the federal research and development needs, the results can be commercialized in some way, and the firm is able to play a leading role in developing the relevant scientific and technical base. If your score along one or more of these dimensions is very weak, there could be little chance of success.

Preparing the Proposal

The reviewers look for three essential questions to be answered in a proposal:

a. What problem are you going to solve (or what are you going to produce), and what difference will your efforts make (significance of the problem)?

b. How you are going to go about solving the identified issue? What are your specific technical objectives and what are their roles in the proof of feasibility? How do you plan to accomplish the objectives?

c. Why are you the right firm to perform the work? What evidence can you provide to establish your firm's or your own credibility, including previous experience in the conduct of related research and development and the qualifications of key personnel?

The most important issue for the reviewers, however, is the *scientific and technical quality of the proposed project*, which is communicated throughout the proposal. When evaluating proposals, agency reviewers assign points to criteria that generally parallel the above components. The agencies' solicitations often state the weighting of various criteria, so again, read them carefully. According to the SBA, each of the above three components accounts for about 20% of the total score in most agencies. The remaining 40% is assigned to the overall scientific and technical quality, innovativeness, and originality of the proposed project. As mentioned previously, this should be addressed throughout the proposal rather than in any special section.

SBIR proposals are restricted in length to 25 pages. Thus, you must be cautious when selecting material for inclusion. A common mistake is said to be overemphasizing the credibility enhancers such as qualifications of personnel. Many losing proposals have wasted valuable space by including detailed resumes of anyone related to the effort, long lists of the firm's clients, previous work and products, etc., which in most agencies count for only 20% of the total score. It is important to show that you are qualified, but pay heed to the different components and their scoring.

If you have managed to get SBIR or STTR funding, use it in your marketing. Because the competition for awards is so strong, especially Phase I, this is certainly a stamp of approval and a sign of excellence and credibility. SBIR/STTR awards are, of course, powerful leveraging tools for attracting other kinds of funding. The SBA has also developed a computerized matching system which will bring together potential funding sources with SBIR winners. This system will match Phase I and II winners with capital sources in light of technical interests, dollar amounts, geographical locations, and time frames. (For a description of SBIR Web sites, see the next section.)

Finally, it must be mentioned that many successful SBIR/STTR winners have gone through the application process more than once, using the rejection(s) and the technical evaluations as a learning experience. You should not be discouraged if you do not win, but try to draw lessons from the process and the comments from the reviewers. A two-time, Phase I award winning entrepreneur from computer science said that she had sent both her applications twice before they were accepted. 'The first one I didn't change at all, because I was certain that the proposal was good and the evaluation basically said so too, and it got funded when I applied again. When the second proposal was rejected, I saw that the technical evaluation pointed at some central weaknesses in it, so I changed the proposal accordingly and got the award when I reapplied."

SBIR and STTR on the Web

All the participating agencies have their own SBIR Web sites. Most often these cover the STTR program, too (if applicable). On the Web pages, you are likely to find information on the programs, lists of previous awards (most often searchable), success stories, and information about ongoing award competitions. Solicitations are available on-line for download and usually for viewing as well. The trend seems to be that more and more of these documents are made in hypertext format, making it easy, for example, to incorporate technical links.

An important advantage to having the solicitations in electronic form is that they are often searchable. This means that scanning the present or last solicitation from all agencies for a particular scientific or technological specialty is much easier. The addresses of the agencies' SBIR Web pages are given below. Moreover, most of them have links to the others; if you find one central SBIR site, the others are within easy reach.

Some nice features have begun to develop, linking the different Web pages even closer. For instance, the Environmental Protection Agency has started to link to other agencies' SBIR pages that also offer support for projects related to environmental science and technology. The Ballistic Missile Defense Organization maintains an on-line database of all SBIR-related resources in the different states. This could be a good place to look for follow-on or "in-between phases" funding that frequently can be obtained at the state level. Hopefully, increased collaboration and cross-agency coordination of technical topics will be even more prevalent in the future.

http://www.sba.gov/sbir

This is the central SBIR/STTR page of the Small Business Administration, which has overall administrative responsibilities for the programs. They issue general guidelines to the participating agencies and report to Congress. Annual program reports are not available on-line, but can be requested.

This comprehensive site is a good starting point to introduce yourself to the SBIR and STTR programs. It has a good, general introduction and links to all the participating agencies, as well as to other sites of interest to small businesses. Two things should be particularly useful. First, there is the presolicitation announcement that, in broad terms, describes the agencies' technical topic areas that have been selected for this fiscal year, as well as the relevant release dates for solicitations. Second, a thorough on-line "Proposal Preparation Handbook" can be found here. Note that the main SBA Web site is a large one with lots of information about starting, financing, and expanding a small business. See the separate section on the SBA for more information about the various services offered and what can be found on the Web.

http://www.zyn.com/sbir

This site is the general Web page for the SBIR conferences. Future meetings, conferences, and so on can be found here (the site is sponsored by the National Science Foundation).

A nice feature is the "Solicitation Finder" that lists all solicitation release dates and proposal deadlines for the coming year. A complex "Topic Finder" was also recently established on the Web at the above address. Here, using keywords to describe your technology and ideas, you can either search all open solicitations (where you can still compete for grants or awards) or the most recently closed solicitations.

http://www.inknowvation.com

This web site belongs to a private firm that has gathered a lot of information about the SBIR program. The web site, which is under construction, also includes various bulletin boards and advice for potential applicants. However, the site is not free. You have to register and pay around $200 a year or $60 for three months to gain access to the sections that contain more than publicly available information. A free guest membership might give you an indication of what to expect. (It should, however, be mentioned that the public web site www.zyn.com (described above) is very comprehensive and includes all the information necessary to participate in SBIR conferences and more. Its newest and most impressive feature, the topic finder, is also free to use.)

http://win-sbir.com

This is the site of a private company that sells software and consulting services tailored to the SBIR program. We do not have any third party information about these products and services, but if you are applying for an SBIR award, this could be a place to check out (at least after you have tried the official conferences and program officers, not to mention the advice in this book).

Federal Agency SBIR Programs

This section deals with special characteristics of the SBIR and STTR programs in the various participating agencies. Although some basic program features are similar as described in the preceding text, there are also important differences between the agencies. The size of the programs, the size of the awarded amounts, application requirements, and reviewing procedures are just some of the elements that may vary. For instance, the amount you can receive in Phase II ranges from less than $300,000 up to $750,000, depending on where you apply.

In addition, the agencies have very different missions, and technical topics in the programs are most often closely tied to these missions. Although the same technical topic can be found in more than one subprogram, some of them would be more likely to fund a close-to-market project, while others have a more basic research orientation. Hence, a fundamental

Summary Table—SBIR Budgets, Maximum Awards, Success Rates, and Deadlines

Agency	SBIR Budget ($M)	Ph. I Max. Award ($K)	Ph. II Max. Award ($K)	Ph. I Success Rate	Ph. II Success Rate	Solicitation Release	Prop. Deadline
Department of Agriculture	10–15	65	250	NA	NA	Jun	Sep
Department of Commerce	10–15	75	300	NA	NA	Oct	Jan
Department of Defense	>500	100	750	15%	40%	Oct	May Jan Aug
Department of Education	5	50	300	18%	37%	Feb	Apr
Department of Energy	75	100	750	12%	45%	Dec	Mar
Department of Health and Human Services (including National Institutes of Health)	307	100	750	23%	41%	Jan	Apr Aug Dec
Department of Transportation	10–15	100	750	NA	NA	Feb	May
Environmental Protection Agency	10–15	70	295	10%	58%	Sep	Nov
National Aeronautics and Space Administration	100	70	600	15%	40%	Apr	Jul
National Science Foundation	50	100	400	NA	NA	Mar–Apr	Jun

Note that all numbers are approximate, based on the latest available information.

understanding of the participating agencies is necessary to improve the chances of winning an award.

United States Department of Agriculture

In the United States Department of Agriculture (USDA), the SBIR program is oriented towards research proposals that address important scientific problems and opportunities in agriculture. The objective is to achieve significant benefits from the research both for the firm and for the public. The agency is the sixth largest SBIR participant and does not make STTR grants. The program is administered by the Cooperative State Research, Education, and Extension Service.

One solicitation is released every year, usually in the beginning of June. The closing date is approximately three months after that. Phase I successful applicants get a maximum grant of $65,000 for a project with a six month duration. The following topics were part of the 1999 solicitation, and the USDA states that these will be continued in the next solicitation:

1. Forests and Related Resources
2. Plant Production and Protection
3. Animal Production and Protection
4. Air, Water, and Soils
5. Food Science and Nutrition
6. Rural and Community Development
7. Aquaculture
8. Industrial Applications
9. Marketing and Trade

Under these headings, several subtopics are indicated and the scope of the research is described. USDA emphasizes that the subtopics are only examples, and should not be treated as exclusive. Note that the last topic allows for funding of projects like assessments of marketing opportunities, development of marketing systems, and development of information systems.

On their Web pages, the USDA indicates what elements are common to successful (Phase I) proposals. These proposals:

1. Are well written, succinct, and logical;
2. Reflect thorough literature review;
3. Address an important problem;
4. Present an innovative approach;
5. Outline a well-designed and detailed experimental plan; and
6. Demonstrate good commercial potential, if successful.

On the other hand, common proposal criticisms made by the USDA reviewers are that:

1. The proposal is poorly written and presented;
2. The principal investigator lacks the necessary technical expertise;
3. There is insufficient literature review;
4. There is insufficient technical information;
5. It cannot be completed within six months;
6. There is inadequate bibliographical information;
7. It lacks letters from consultants;
8. The research was already done by others;
9. It is too vague and unfocused;
10. There is a failure to indicate where the project would go in Phase II;
11. The commercialization potential is poor;
12. The economic prospects are doubtful;
13. There is inadequate detail in the experimental plan;
14. Too much of the research will be done at a university; or
15. It will require consultants to be engaged to add expertise in areas where the principal investigator is deficient.

Although the idea by itself is naturally important, it can be seen from this list that the way the idea is presented in the proposal is vital to receiving an award.

http://www.reeusda.gov/sbir/

The USDA SBIR Web site is not very large, but contains the most important program information, as well as solicitations and forms available for download in different formats. Firms that apply for SBIR awards from the Department of Agriculture find the list of other funding sources for agriculture-related research and development to be relevant. An overview of technical and scientific information sources can be found in the solicitation.

Department of Health and Human Services

The Department of Health and Human Services (DHHS) has a broad purpose—basically, everything that could benefit public health falls under the mission of this agency. DHHS, where the SBIR and STTR programs are administered by the National Institutes of Health (NIH), is the second largest SBIR and STTR participant. NIH made SBIR grants in fiscal year 1998, totaling more than $265 million. This amount is expected to exceed $300 million in fiscal year 1999. Due to increased funding for medical research, the program has seen a steady and significant increase in recent years. Annual STTR awards total around $18 million.

Normally, support for Phase I SBIR projects is provided for six months in the amount of $100,000, while a Phase II award can be for as much as $750,000 in up to two years. The amounts are a bit different in the STTR program. Here, the applicants take as long as one full year in Phase I (but get the same dollar amount). The amount for Phase II, however, is limited to $500,000 for a two-year period. NIH emphasizes that applicants may propose even longer periods of time and greater amounts of funds if it is necessary for completion of the project. It is probably wiser to be realistic and not propose research that is too ambitious for a six-month period.

The mean success rate for Phase I SBIR applications has been 23.1% for the last seven years and 40.8% for Phase II. These rates differ greatly from year to year, from 17% to 30% for Phase I and 29% to 51% for Phase II. The STTR program has slightly higher success rates, but the variance is even larger there.

Of course, only small firms may apply for money as in all SBIR programs. Nevertheless, an SBIR award can extend an academic research program and add value to the intellectual property generated from it by taking it several steps toward commercialization. Thus, it is not unheard of for a faculty member or graduate student to apply for an SBIR award, with a view toward founding a company, if the award is granted. One member of a research group might then decide to move wholly or largely into the firm while others remain in their positions in the university, acting as consultants to the firm. In such cases an SBIR award can become the bridge between academia and industry, a bridge that is built out from the university, with government support, and then later finds its footing on the other side, with private sector funding. If the process is successful and repeated, the university is surrounded by a group of firms that have a close relationship to academic research, having originated from the university itself.

NIH topic areas basically follow the organization of the NIH Institute system. SBIR proposals are currently sought by the following organizations:

1. National Institutes of Health (NIH)
   a. National Institute on Aging (NIA)
   b. National Institute on Alcohol Abuse and Alcoholism (NIAAA)
   c. National Institute of Allergy and Infectious Diseases (NIAID)
   d. National Institute of Arthritis and Musculoskeletal and Skin Diseases (NIAMS)
   e. National Cancer Institute (NCI)
   f. National Institute of Child Health and Human Development (NICHD)
   g. National Institute on Drug Abuse (NIDA)

    h. National Institute on Deafness and Other Communication Disorders (NIDCD)

    i. National Institute of Dental and Craniofacial Research (NIDCR)

    j. National Institute of Diabetes and Digestive and Kidney Diseases (NIDDK)

    k. National Institute of Environmental Health Sciences (NIEHS)

    l. National Eye Institute (NEI)

    m. National Institute of General Medical Sciences (NIGMS)

    n. National Heart, Lung, and Blood Institute (NHLBI)

    o. National Human Genome Research Institute (NHGRI)

    p. National Institute of Mental Health (NIMH)

    q. National Institute of Neurological Disorders and Stroke (NINDS)

    r. National Institute of Nursing Research (NINR)

    s. National Center for Research Resources (NCRR)

    t. National Complementary and Alternative Medicine (NCCAM)

    u. National Library of Medicine (NLM)

2. Trans-NIH Research Programs

3. Centers for Disease Control and Prevention (CDC)

    a. National Institute for Occupational Safety and Health (NIOSH)

    b. National Center for Injury Prevention and Control (NCIPC)

    c. National Center for Infectious Diseases (NCID)

    d. National Center for Chronic Disease Prevention and Health Promotion (NCCDPHP)

    e. National Immunization Program (NIP)

    f. National Center for HIV, STD, and TB Prevention (NCHSTP)

4. Food and Drug Administration (FDA)

The dates for receipt, review and award, are as follows:

SBIR application receipt date	STTR application receipt date	Scientific Merit Review	Secondary Review	Earliest Award
Apr 15	Apr 1	Jun–Jul	Sep–Oct	Nov
Aug 15	Aug 1	Oct–Nov	Jan–Feb	Mar
Dec 15	Dec 1	Feb–Mar	May–Jun	Jul

As you can see, three solicitations are released every year, providing many opportunities for both SBIR and STTR funding. Note that there is a minimum seven month period between receipt of application and award decision.

There are some special features of the applications in NIH. First, there is a salary cap for the primary investigator (PI), which is currently $125,000 per year. This could be a problem for highly paid scientists. Second, the application has sections concerning the use of human subjects and vertebrate animals in the proposed research. If the research involves living persons, samples from living persons, or live vertebrate animals, the proposed use must be approved by an institutional review board prior to funding. There are also guidelines concerning the inclusion of children, women, and minorities in the subject population. If these issues are not addressed, the application might be labeled "incomplete" and will then have to wait until the next review cycle. The solicitations (which are also available on the Web) will have more information. For scientists who have applied for grants from NIH for other purposes, such rules should be familiar.

The NIH SBIR emphasizes seeking a broad range of proposal ideas from applicants following the culture of its investigator-initiated RO1 extramural award program. This is in contrast to the approach of generating specific topics internally which is commonplace in DOD and through interaction between the researchers in its laboratories and potential applicants. NIH prefers to have applicants discuss their ideas during the presolicitation phase with SBIR program officers rather than with in-house NIH researchers. This local difference between NIH and DOD in interpreting the SBIR mandate illustrates the decentralized nature of a program that is conducted in all the leading federal research and development agencies. On the other hand, the following general guidelines are applicable to any application.

An abstract and a list of specific aims should be written for every proposal. This should be written carefully—proposal reviewers are selected on the basis of this information only (along with the project title). If these sections are unclear, chances are that you will be assigned reviewers who are not appropriate. A clear, well-written abstract and list of aims might also get more people than just the primary reviewers interested in reading the proposal. You can also request in a cover letter to have appropriate primary and/or multiple NIH institutes or centers review your proposals. This might be especially relevant if your research crosscuts scientific interests or several institutes.

Applications are reviewed by a "scientific review group" composed of scientists from both academic and for-profit organizations. The members may change from one review cycle to the next. This means that if you submit a revised application, the reviewers are likely to be different from the previous ones. However, the new ones have access to prior summary statements. However, note that all abstracts for SBIR/STTR proposals become public information if funded. Hence, do not include proprietary or confidential information here.

NIH states that the most common reasons for not scoring a Phase I application are:

1. Lack of innovative ideas
2. Unfocused, diffused, or superficial research plan
3. Lack of sufficient experimental detail
4. Absence of acceptable scientific rationale
5. Lack of knowledge of published relevant work
6. Lack of experience in essential methodology
7. Questionable reasoning in experimental approach
8. Overly ambitious

For Phase II applications, the main reason is an inability to demonstrate that the goals of Phase I were accomplished.

NIH Fast Track

The SBIR and STTR programs have a fast track review option. This has two advantages. First, there is single submission and evaluation of both Phase I and Phase II applications. Second, there is a minimal funding gap between the phases (or none at all).

To be eligible for Fast Track, applications must satisfy three criteria in addition to the regular ones:

1. The Phase I application must include measurable milestones that will be used to judge the success of the Phase I research. Correspondingly, the Phase II application must include a discussion of these milestones and their implications (in place of a progress report).
2. The Phase II application must be accompanied by a concise product development plan appendix (maximum of five pages).
3. The Phase II application must be accompanied by a Commitment Appendix that specifies the amount of company, partner, or other funds or resources to be dedicated to activities directly related to the SBIR/STTR project.

Note that both a Phase I and Phase II application form must be completed, following all the instructions for each one of them. Fast Track is intended for "high quality applications with sufficient preliminary data to clearly define milestones for proof of feasibility." If your application does not meet the above criteria, it is probably wiser to apply for the ordinary Phase I SBIR/STTR funding.

If you manage to get an award, there is certain documentation you will have to provide. This is the case in all agencies. A "Welcome Wagon" memorandum will inform you of this, if your application is successful. Note that the NIH Web pages include a "model application" that has been developed by the program staff, as well as other information relevant for making a good application.

http://www.nih.gov/grants/funding/sbir.htm

The Department of Health and Human Service SBIR/STTR is found on the Web pages of the National Institutes of Health. This site contains much information and advice, as well as relevant links for medical research projects. The most recent solicitations are available on-line (in Hypertext format). A model SBIR Phase I application has been developed for download (Adobe Acrobat format).

The Department of Defense

Improved military strength is the common denominator underlying all Department of Defense (DOD) programs, but increased U.S. economic strength is an important mission of the DOD SBIR/STTR programs as well.

DOD is the largest SBIR and STTR participant, providing more than half a billion dollars for SBIR alone. As a rule of thumb, half the total SBIR funding comes from the DOD research and development budget. In fiscal year 1997, 1,526 SBIR and 111 STTR Phase I awards were made, along with 639 SBIR and 54 STTR Phase II awards. The Air Force is the largest DOD participant in SBIR and STTR, followed by the Navy, the Army, the Ballistic Missile Defense Organization, the Defense Advanced Research Projects Agency, the Office of the Secretary of Defense, the Defense Special Weapons Agency, and the Special Operations Command. The latter three are all relatively small and do not participate in the STTR program.

Success rates vary greatly, but around 15% of proposals for both programs are awarded a Phase I contract and 40% of successful Phase I awardees subsequently receive Phase II Awards. A statistical profile is available on-line. Phase I awards are between $60,000 and $100,000 for a six-month project, while Phase II awards range from $500,000 to $750,000 for a duration of two years.

Projects that are funded fall inside a vast range of science and technology areas. Two solicitations are released every year for the SBIR program, while there is only one for the STTR. Note that not all DOD program participants take part in both SBIR solicitations. See below for more details on the individual programs and their special characteristics.

SBIR Solicitation 99.1 was made available to the public October 1, 1998, with proposals accepted from December 1, 1998, to January 13, 1999. The second SBIR solicitation was made available May 1, 1999, with proposals accepted from July 1 to August 11, 1999. In future years, the dates will probably be similar to this. STTR solicitations are released in the beginning of January; proposals are accepted from the beginning of March and closed in mid April. The solicitations are available both in hard copy and on the World Wide Web.

These release dates are important for more reasons than getting an application finished on time. In the two-month interval between release of the solicitation announcement and the initial date for submission of proposals, all "topic authors," those scientists and engineers who have come up with the topics for that round of reviews, are available for questioning. Their names and telephone numbers are posted on the DOD Web site. After the agencies start accepting proposals, the topic authors will not answer further technical questions! Note also that the DOD and the Small Business Administration release presolicitation announcements. These include full descriptions of topics, including points of contact, so that possible applicants have longer than two months to ask technical questions of the topic authors. The laboratories of the Air Force, for example, will even prerelease their own topics even before the DOD. These are announced in the *Commerce Business Daily*.

Still, there is another option for acquiring technical information when you are working on the proposal. The DOD has an on-line interactive topic information system called SITIS (available on the DOD Web pages). Here, questioner and respondent remain anonymous and all questions and answers are posted electronically for general viewing until the solicitation closes.

DOD Fast Track

The DOD SBIR/STTR programs have also featured a fast track process the last few years. Similar to such policies in other agencies, the main purpose is to speed up the reviewing process and reduce the funding gap between Phase I and Phase II. If the project qualifies for Fast Track, the company will receive interim funding of $30,000 to $50,000 between Phase I and Phase II, will be evaluated for Phase II under a separate, expedited process, and will be selected for Phase II award provided a certain "technically sufficient" threshold is met or exceeded. So far, including the first 1998 solicitation, 94 Phase I projects have qualified for the Fast Track. The success rate here is exceptionally high. Eighty-seven of these (93%) have been selected for Phase II award. This is more than twice the ordinary success rate. So far, it seems that these companies experienced no significant gap in funding.

To qualify for the fast track, certain procedures must be followed:

1. Toward the end of a company's Phase I SBIR or STTR project, the company and its investor must submit a Fast Track application. Here, they state that the investor will match both interim and Phase II funding, in cash, contingent on the company's selection for a Phase II award. For companies that have not received a Phase II award before from any agency, the matching rate is twenty-five cents for every SBIR/STTR dollar. For all other companies, the matching rate is one to one.

2. The applicant must certify that the outside funding qualifies as a Fast Track investment, and the investor qualifies as an outside investor.

The rules are relatively strict; the investor should not be related to key people in the company, should not be owner or part owner of the business, and should not be an affiliate firm. Internal funds from the company do not qualify either, and the money should not be a loan. Another government program, like the Advanced Technology Program, would be a valid outside investor, along with banks, venture capital firms, state programs, and so on. All the rules, along with questions and examples, are available on-line.

http://www.acq.osd.mil/sadbu/sbir

This is the main page of the SBIR and STTR programs in the Department of Defense, and probably the best place to start. All solicitations, presolicitations and other documents and announcements are made available here. There are links to all the defense participants.

On this Web site there are also many statistics, success stories, sample proposals, model contracts, lists of upcoming events, and other relevant information for small firms. The site is frequently updated.

Below, some special characteristics of the DOD subprograms are described.

Air Force

The Air Force SBIR/STTR programs are managed by the Air Force Research Laboratory, Wright-Patterson Air Force Base, Ohio. In total, the budget for the SBIR is now more than $200 million and the STTR budget is around $12 million. Nearly 50% of Phase I contract recipients are selected for Phase II. Note that Phase I contracts generally last nine months in the Air Force program.

Topics come from a large number of Air Force laboratory sites, product centers, program offices, test centers, and logistics centers located across the country. To be able to market your proposal in the best possible way, it is important to identify the specific organization(s) that is working in the company's basic line of research. Previous solicitations constitute handy references in this respect. The Air Force only participates in the first DOD SBIR solicitation (released in October).

A list of topics would be too extensive to list here—in the 1997 solicitation, the Air Force alone developed 260 topics! One important feature can be mentioned, however: The topics touch on many areas that may not seem to be immediately connected to military purposes. Environmental issues are a good example. This is an area that has seen dramatic growth in recent Air Force solicitations, and is closely coordinated with the Environmental Protection Agency (EPA). Note that even though the EPA has its own SBIR program, the Air Force SBIR set-aside for environmental issues is more than twice the total EPA SBIR budget.

http://www.afrl.af.mil/sbir/index.htm

This is the Air Force SBIR and STTR Web site. It contains an introduction to the programs in the Air Force, including several information brochures and a downloadable guide. Considerable space is reserved for specific technical topic descriptions, including links to Air Force laboratories and others where the technical personnel who suggest topics and evaluate proposals are found.

Army

In fiscal year 1999, the Army SBIR budget was approximately $100 million and was expected to fund around two hundred Phase I and one hundred Phase II projects. The Army participates only in the second DOD SBIR solicitation (opening in July and closing in August).

In contrast to the highly complex Federal Acquisition Regulations (FAR) familiar to large firms, the DOD follows a pared down and highly simplified version of its procurement model in seeking research and development from small firms through the SBIR process. The DOD also places a strong emphasis on involving its own technical personnel in defining agency research and development needs. Moreover, the DOD generally encourages interaction between its research and development personnel and potential applicants.

An Army SBIR program manager described the approach as one that first goes down to the technical personnel in the Army to solicit their ideas. It is at this point that the discussions between entrepreneurs and technical points of contacts, researchers in the Army labs, bring ideas from outside the Army into the process when technical personnel include entrepreneur's suggestions in the topics that they recommend. For example, in the Army Research Lab (ARL), the SBIR program manager solicits seven sources, five directorates and two Centers, for topic recommendations. In one year, in the ARL alone, there were over 80 proposals for approximately 25 approved topic slots.

http://www.aro.ncren.net/arowash/rt/sbir.htm

The Army SBIR/STTR Web site is comprehensive and seems to be frequently updated. It has more about the following topics:

1. General program descriptions
2. Special features of the Army SBIR process
3. Descriptions of recent awards and technical topics; past awards are searchable
4. Solicitation news
5. The Quality Awards Program

6. Phase III accomplishments

7. Points of contact

8. Conference schedules

9. Links to other SBIR sites and other relevant Army programs. There are many research and development programs in all the military agencies/services that could be worth a closer look, although an SBIR grant could be a good place to start to get to know the technical installations and people.

A special feature in the Army SBIR program is their Quality Awards program. Each year, the five most exceptional Phase II projects are selected and presented awards at a formal banquet. Although this does not necessarily imply more funds, these quality awards can be a crucial marketing source as well as a source of recognition. Winners are selected on the basis of three criteria: originality and innovation of the research, relevance of the research to the Army mission, and immediate commercialization potential.

Navy

The Navy SBIR and STTR programs are almost as large as those of the Air Force. Thirty-three different science and technology areas have been identified as the ones that are necessary to meet the mission responsibilities. These are very broad ("Materials," "Chemistry," etc.), but more detailed topics are developed for each solicitation.

Phase I and II proposals have some unique Navy requirements. Most important is that several appendices must be submitted over the Internet, through the Navy SBIR/STTR Web site. If this is not done, the proposal will not be accepted. Because traffic on the net tends to increase when a deadline is approaching, applicants are advised not to wait until the last minute but submit appendices early.

http://www.onr.navy.mil/sci_tech/industrial/sbir.htm

The Navy SBIR/STTR Web site contains the following information:

1. About SBIR/STTR

2. Submission

3. What's New

4. Solicitation

5. Search Database

6. Points of Contact & Links

7. Success Stories

8. FAQs (Frequently Asked Questions)

Ballistic Missile Defense Organization

The Ballistic Missile Defense Organization (BMDO) is the fourth largest defense participant in the SBIR and STTR programs. Its mission is broadly to provide a defense system against all kinds of missiles. Basically, any innovative technology that makes things lighter, faster, stronger, or more reliable, are of interest. However, it should have some relevance to ballistic defense systems. A much-improved fire extinguisher is an example of a project that might satisfy criteria of innovativeness and potential commercial market, yet has no BMDO relevance.

BMDO develops a number of technical topics for each solicitation. They participate in the DOD winter solicitation only, the one with a proposal deadline in January. Many of the topics fall within electronics and computer science. A special feature of the BMDO SBIR program is the topic area called "Surprises and Opportunities." As the title suggests, this area is held open for any new and unique advanced technologies that do not fit into the others topics of the solicitation. The specific technology should be described in detail, including a discussion of why it offers special opportunities for ballistic missile defense systems. Unless your technology is unquestionably new and advanced, you should probably go for one of the other topic areas.

Phase I grants normally do not exceed $100,000. Indeed, usually less than $65,000 is awarded for a merit or concept examination. Proposers may themselves suggest technical reviewers in a cover letter that should include name, organization, address and phone number, and rationale for each suggestion (of course, someone else might be selected in the end).

Phase II proposals may be awarded up to $750,000, or $500,000 under the STTR program. Note that BMDO puts considerable weight on the commercial potential of the technology when deciding what Phase II proposals to fund. This means that getting another sponsor (a venture capital firm, etc.) to share some of the Phase II costs can improve your chances of winning. The same applies to having follow-on funding for Phase III.

Another point to note is that principal investigators who are also tenured faculty will not be considered primarily employed by the small firm if they receive compensation from the university while performing the SBIR contract. Waivers can be requested explicitly with a justification pointing to a "compelling national need," but the BMDO expects to grant no such waivers.

http://www.winbmdo.com/

The SBIR/STTR Web site of the BMDO contains all the usual program information, awards statistics and descriptions, solicitations, and a powerful search engine for past awards. It also has a frequently updated list of venture capital firms that are potentially interested in funding innovative firms that have been successful in the SBIR/STTR process. There is also a page of advice on writing a press release, telling people how to do the first marketing of an SBIR/STTR contract and a new product or technology. Two of the proposal appendices can be submitted electronically through this Web site. BMDO also maintains an on-line database of all SBIR-related resources in the different states. This could be a good place to look for follow-on or in-between-phases funding that frequently can be obtained at the state level.

Defense Advanced Research Projects Agency

This agency, DARPA, is the fifth largest DOD SBIR and STTR participant, slightly smaller than BMDO. Its mission is to advance state-of-the-art defense technology, and it is in many ways the Department of Defense agency that is closest to both the academic basic research and industrial technology frontiers. DARPA participates in both the annual DOD solicitations. It is one of the most competitive SBIR agencies that participate with only around 10% of the proposals being funded.

Awards in Phase I and two can be up to $100,000 and $750,000, respectively. It is more common, however, that $375,000 is awarded for the development phase, and that additional funding might be available for "optional tasks." As with BMDO, a potential for follow-on funding is an advantage when applying for Phase II funding. Not only can this signify increased commercial potential, but it also proves that the company is willing to go all the way through a commercialization phase. There are no special deadlines for submission of Phase II proposals. Applicants that have received a Phase I grant are invited to apply by their program manager.

Note that DARPA administers programs that offer support for so-called dual use projects—technology development projects that have both a military and a civilian commercial application. Hence, some program managers in DARPA might be able to give good leads about where to get additional funding for Phase II and III.

http://www.darpa.mil/sbir/

This is the "DARPA Small Business Support Center" on the Web, containing significant information on a number of programs and information sources. The main sections deal with the SBIR and STTR programs.

Other DOD SBIR Programs

In addition to the five large services/agencies described above, there are three other SBIR participants in the Department of Defense. These are:

1. Defense Threat Reduction Agency [DTRA, formerly the Defense Special Weapons Agency (DSWA)]

2. Special Operations Command (SOCOM)

3. Office of the Secretary of Defense (OSD)

None of these participate in the STTR program. OSD is the largest with 59 Phase I and 23 Phase II awards made in fiscal year 1997 (out of 211 and 59 proposals). This is also a relatively new participant in the program. The reason is that OSD has been given responsibility for topics related to chemical and biological defense. Still, the topics are also developed by research and development personnel in the Army, Navy, and Air Force, and it is the Army SBIR program that is responsible for evaluating and selecting the proposals. SOCOM and DSWA are much smaller (with a total of 19 and 25 awards made in 1997), and the latter is the only one without its own Web site promoting certain topics and giving special information. The DOD solicitation gives more information about these participants.

Although the Special Operations Command has its own Web site, it is currently under reconstruction. The DOD central Web site (see above) will contain all the information you need on the small SBIR programs in the Defense Department.

Department of Commerce

The Office of Research and Technology Applications runs the SBIR program in the Department of Commerce (DOC), which is part of to the National Oceanic and Atmospheric Administration (NOAA). DOC is not a large participant in the program. In fiscal year 1998, 45 Phase I and 19 Phase II awards were made. The maximum amounts are $75,000 in Phase I and $300,000 in Phase II. Topics come from NOAA and the National Institute for Standards and Technology (NIST). NIST is in fact larger than NOAA, and has its own program staff. As in all other SBIR programs, the topics are described in detail in the solicitation. In fiscal year 1999, the NOAA topic headlines were:

1. Atmospheric sciences

2. Ocean Observation Systems

3. Living Marine Resources

4. Ocean Science

5. Cartography and Photogrammetry

The same fiscal year, the NIST topic headlines were:

1. Adaptive Learning Systems

2. Advanced Building Materials and Systems

3. Advanced Detection and Suppression of Fire

4. Combinatorial Discovery of Materials and Chemicals

5. Condition-based Maintenance

6. Intelligent Control

7. Intelligent and Distributed CAD

8. Infrastructures for Distributed Electronic Commerce

9. Measurement and Standards for Catalysis and Biocatalysis

10. Measurement and Standards for Composite Materials

11. Measurement and Standards for Membrane Materials

12. Microelectronics Manufacturing Infrastructure

13. Microfabrication and Micromachining

14. Organic Electronic Materials Technology

15. Photonics Manufacturing

16. Supporting Technologies for Semiconductor Lithography

17. Integration of Manufacturing Applications

Naturally, these topics can change from year to year. However, they do indicate some of the general fields and interests of the technical and scientific groups in NOAA and NIST. One solicitation is released every year. Expected release date for the fiscal year 2,000 solicitation is October 1, 1999, with an indicated closing date mid January 2000. If the Phase I application meets the formal requirements of size, length, format, and such, it will be reviewed by two independent scientists or engineers from NOAA or NIST. These individuals are most likely the ones that are behind the definition of topics as well. The Phase II application undergoes a stricter evaluation by three reviewers, some of whom may come from outside the participating DOC organizations.

http://www.rdc.noaa.gov/%7Eamd/sbir.html

http://www.oar.noaa.gov/orta/orta.htm

http://www.nist.gov/sbir

The first of these addresses is for the general DOC SBIR Web site, and the second is for the NOAA SBIR pages. The third URL is for the NIST SBIR program and is the most comprehensive. At this site, the full solicitation can be found (including topics from NOAA), along with some other background information on the SBIR program in the Department of Commerce.

Department of Education

The Department of Education is the smallest SBIR participant. In fiscal year 1998, their program budget was around $5.1 million, resulting in 41 Phase I and 18 Phase II awards. Success rates are average: 18 percent of the Phase I applications and 37 percent of the Phase II applications got funded in 1998. The maximum award amounts are $50,000 and $300,000, respectively.

One solicitation is released every year in the beginning of February, and applications are due in early April. Seventeen different topics were developed for the 1999 solicitation. Some of these are likely to change, but the names of the offices behind the topics can give some indications as to what their interests are:

1. Office of Special Education and Rehabilitative Services, which has the most topics, and in general displays interest in technologies with relevance for people with disabilities
2. Office of Vocational and Adult Education
3. Office of Educational Research and Improvement

http://www.ed.gov/offices/OERI/SBIR

Note that the Web server of the Department of Education is case sensitive, with regard to capital and lower case letters. You have to write the last part of the SBIR Web site address (OERI/SBIR) in CAPITAL LETTERS.

Given that this is the smallest SBIR participant, the Web site is well structured and contains considerable information, including an electronic version of the solicitation in Microsoft Word format. The usual pages that give an introduction to the program, overview of past awards, and links to other sites of interest can also be found there.

Department of Energy

The Department of Energy (DOE) is the fourth largest participant in SBIR and STTR after the Department of Defense, the Department of Health and Human Services, and the National Aeronautics and Space Administration. DOE's SBIR budget is expected to be around $75 million in fiscal year 1999, funding approximately two hundred Phase I and seventy-five Phase II projects. Maximum awards are $100,000 in Phase I and $750,000 in Phase II. Success rates are typical of the larger participants. Only 12 percent of the Phase I applicants have on average succeeded, while 45 percent of the Phase II applicants have been successful.

DOE's annual solicitation contains topics in technical areas such as:

1. Basic Energy Sciences
2. Biological and Environmental Research
3. High Energy and Nuclear Physics
4. Fusion Energy Sciences
5. Computational and Technology Research

6. Energy Efficiency and Renewable Energy
7. Nuclear Energy
8. Fossil Energy
9. Environmental Management
10. Nonproliferation and National Security

Each year about 40 topics are allocated among the technical areas in proportion to their contributions to the budget. The solicitation is usually released in the beginning of December, and it closes in the beginning of March.

http://sbir.er.doe.gov/sbir

The Web site of the DOE SBIR program contains the basic information about the program, past awards, and an on-line solicitation.

Department of Transportation

The Department of Transportation's (DOT) SBIR program is administered by the VOLPE National Transportation Systems Center in Cambridge, Massachusetts. As one of the smallest program participants, it is twice the size of the Department of Education and about the same size as the Environmental Protection Agency. Maximum awards are the same as in the larger agencies, however—$100,000 in Phase I and $750,000 in Phase II.

Mid February is the usual release date of the solicitation. Starting in 1999, the DOT SBIR solicitation will only be available electronically. It can be viewed on the DOT Web site, and it can be downloaded as a Microsoft Word file. On the Web page, you have the possibility of registering your name to receive a notification of when the solicitation is available. This has to be repeated every year. The closing date is early May. Applications should still be submitted in paper form. Topics change from year to year. If your project is relevant to the DOT but not to the current topics, there is an opportunity of getting in touch with technical personnel through the Department's Web site.

There are several closing dates for receipt of Phase II applications (five every year). Award criteria are the same as for the other agencies, although special consideration can be given to proposals that have obtained commitments for follow-on funding from state or private sources for Phase III. You should also note that subunits of the Department of Transportation might themselves provide follow-on funding if the products or processes that are under development are of special interest to them.

http://www.volpe.dot.gov/sbir/

The Web pages of the DOT SBIR program contains all the usual information. Be advised that solicitations are only available electronically (in Word or hypertext format).

Environmental Protection Agency

The Environmental Protection Agency (EPA) is another small SBIR participant, about the same size as the Department of Transportation. Maximum awards are $70,000 in Phase I and $295,000 in Phase II. The competition is high in Phase I with only around one out of ten applicants getting funded. However, the success rate is relatively high in Phase II—over the past six years 58 percent of these applicants received awards.

EPA's annual SBIR Phase I solicitation opens in September and closes in November. A separate Phase II solicitation is released in the spring. As might be expected, the aim of EPA's SBIR program is to spawn commercial ventures that improve the environment and quality of life. The EPA's Office of Research and Development's strategic plan is the starting point for topics.

Independent peer review of all topics is carried out. Topics are oriented towards helping companies comply with stringent emission standards, allowing firms to avoid the use of toxic and hazardous materials in production, enabling companies to recover and recycle materials, and providing companies with the option of selecting environmentally friendly products. Some of the other topic headings are:

- Air Pollutants
- Indoor Air
- Global Change
- Drinking Water
- Waste Site Risk Characterization
- Waste Management
- Site Remediation

EPA states that some of the topics that will be emphasized over the next few years include:

1. Drinking Water Disinfection
2. Particulate Matter
3. Human Health Protection
4. Ecosystem Protection
5. Endocrine Disruptors
6. Pollution Prevention and New Technologies
7. Technologies for Prevention and Control of Air Emissions
8. Waste Reduction and Pollution Prevention Techniques
9. Drinking Water Treatment Technologies
10. Technologies for Municipal and Industrial Wastewater Treatment and Pollution Control

11. Treatment, Recycling, and Disposal of Solid Wastes, Hazardous Wastes, and Sediments

12. Technologies for In Situ Site Remediation of Organically Contaminated Soil, Sediments, and Groundwater

13. Technologies for Treatment or Removal of Heavy Metals at Contaminated Sites

14. Technologies for Prevention and Control of Indoor Air Pollution

15. Biosensors and Immunoassay for Pesticide Residue Identification and Monitoring

16. Technologies for Wet Weather Flow Treatment and Pollution Control

17. Innovative Monitoring Technologies

If you have a technology relevant for one or more of these areas, you should note that several of the other participating SBIR agencies release topics related to the environment. For instance, the Air Force alone funds more environmentally oriented SBIR projects than the entire EPA. In addition, the maximum awards are higher in the Air Force. Note also that EPA has provided some of the winning companies with Phase III funding.

http://es.epa.gov/ncerqa/sbir/

This Web site has an unusual and interesting feature: It has links to other agencies that make awards in similar scientific and technological areas. The pages contain the following:

1. EPA's SBIR Program

2. SBIR Solicitation

3. SBIR Factsheet

4. Non-SBIR Solicitation of Potential Interest to SBIR Audiences

5. List of Awards, Project Abstracts, Project Abstracts from Other Agencies

6. EPA's SBIR Program Success Stories

7. Guide to Technology Commercialization Assistance for EPA SBIR Program Awardees

8. Environmental SBIR Awards by Other Agencies

9. Links to Other Federal Agency SBIR Sites

National Aeronautics and Space Administration

In the National Aeronautics and Space Administration (NASA), the SBIR program is administered from the Goddard Space Flight Center, although topics come from all NASA field installations. Each of the field installations have defined certain "Centers of Excellence" that represent a focused leadership responsibility for a certain technology or knowledge. The STTR topics come directly from some of the centers.

NASA SBIR grants were set at maximums of $70,000 and $600,000 in the two phases in fiscal year 1997. Maximum STTR awards are the same across all agencies—$100,000 in Phase I and $500,000 in Phase II.

The annual NASA SBIR solicitation is released in late April, and closes ten weeks later. For the STTR program, the closing date is in mid May and the release date in early March. NASA does not have separate Phase II solicitations. The review period for Phase II applications is the summertime for SBIR and late fall for STTR. Note that the solicitations are only available in electronic form, either the World Wide Web or other electronic services. If requested, NASA also sends the program information on diskettes.

A large number of scientific and technological areas are relevant to NASA. Specific topics are likely to change from year to year. As an example of topics, the following general headings were found under the STTR program in 1998:

1. Human Operations in Space
2. Launch and Payload Processing Systems
3. Structures and Materials
4. Turbomachinery
5. Space Propulsion
6. Rocket Propulsion Test

http://sbir.nasa.gov/

This is a comprehensive Web site with substantial information under the heading of "Info Central." In addition to the usual overviews, lists of awards, solicitations, outside links, etc., there is an on-line feedback form, a newsletter, and an Electronic Handbook for submission of forms and proposals over the Internet.

National Science Foundation

The National Science Foundation (NSF) is the fifth largest participant in the SBIR and STTR programs (and the smallest STTR program since only the five largest agencies participate in this program). It was actually people in NSF that initiated the SBIR program as an in-house experiment in the late 1970s. The program staff is experienced in selecting proposals with both high technical quality and commercial potential. The program is administered by the Division of Design, Manufacture, and Industrial Innovation in the Directorate for Engineering. Maximum SBIR amounts are $100,000 in Phase I and $400,000 in Phase II.

NSF's mission is in many ways different from most of the other agencies (with the possible exception of the National Institutes of Health under the Department of Health and Human Services). Instead of having specific tasks related to issues such as transportation and energy, the main task of NSF is to support the best fundamental research and technology in a large number of fields and specialties. Commercial criteria do play a role when selecting among SBIR applicants, but the proposed technology does not have to relate to an agency technology mission as in the departments of Transportation and Energy. However, NSF is especially likely to fund projects on topics that it has already funded that move the research through its investigator initiated projects toward commercialization. These are generally "cutting edge" technologies. In addition, NSF's SBIR program goals are intended to contribute to develop intellectual capital, strengthen the physical infrastructure, integrate research and education, and promote partnerships.

The SBIR solicitation closes in the beginning of June, while the STTR solicitation closes in the beginning of December. Both are released two to three months before the closing date. As a starting point, SBIR applications are accepted across all fields of science and engineering, but some suggested subtopics are developed by the foundation's subdivisions each year. In fiscal year 1998, some "critical technology areas of national importance" were emphasized.

1. Applied Molecular Biology
2. Distributed Computing and Telecommunication
3. Integrated, Flexible Manufacturing
4. Materials Synthesis and Processing
5. Microelectronics and Optoelectronics
6. Pollution Minimization and Remediation
7. Software
8. Transportation

Note that NSF STTR focuses on only one technical topic (or at most a few) every year due to the program's small size. In 1998, STTR proposals were accepted in the areas of Nanotechnology and Sensors in Harsh Environments only. As with some of the other agencies, NSF looks favorably upon applicants that have commitments for follow-on funding in the commercialization phase. Nevertheless, NSF has recognized the gap between Phase II and private sector funding by establishing Phase 2B, an experimental program that offers follow-on funding to selected awardees. NSF will match 50% of a private investment up to $100,000.

http://www.eng.nsf.gov/sbir/

These Web pages contain the same information as most other SBIR Web sites. Solicitations and program information are available on-line, along with lists of program staff, previous awards, and links to other relevant programs and sites.

CHAPTER 6 • LATER PHASE: DARPA, ATP, AND DUAL USE

CONTENTS

LATER PHASE: DARPA, ATP, AND DUAL USE

DARPA—The Defense Advanced Research Projects Agency

The Defense Advanced Research Projects Agency is a major player in the military research and development system, and is the broadest ranging of the military research and development agencies that work closely with industry and universities. Well-known firms like SUN Microsystems and Silicon Graphics received early funding from DARPA, and the Internet actually started in this agency. The dual use research and development programs were also established here first. DARPA has an annual research and development budget of $2 billion dollars, much of it within reach of innovative firms not part of the traditional military-industrial system. It is fair to say that DARPA is the military version of ATP; and it is ten times as big as its civilian counterpart. (Of course, DARPA came first and ATP is its civilian daughter.) See Part III for a more complete account of this relationship.

In this section, the following will be described:

- DARPA in brief—organization and technological focus
- Features of projects
- Getting in touch with DARPA
- DARPA on the Web

DARPA in Brief—Organization and Technological Focus

When the Soviet Union launched its Sputnik in the 1950s, it came as a shock to the United States. An early response was the establishment of DARPA in 1958 with a mission to ensure that the United States maintains a lead in applying state-of-the-art technology for military capabilities and to prevent technological surprises from potential adversaries. This mission remains unchanged. Although DARPA was and still is coordinated with the military research and development establishment, it is completely independent of it.

The agency does not do the research and development work itself. It mainly develops new technological topic areas, generates ideas, and selects projects for funding. Scientists and engineers coming from industry, universities, government laboratories, and other federal research and development centers act as program managers. DARPA has a small, flexible, and flat organizational structure. Support personnel (technical, contract, and administrative) are hired on a temporary basis to get into and out of an area without the problems of maintaining a permanent staff. In total, 240 people (of which around 140 are technical) work in the agency, currently making up a budget of $2 billion. In many ways, DARPA is a unique research and development organization, a type of flexible technological research council probably seen nowhere else in the world. DARPA has the special ability to support a technology area from academic research project through to commercial success, without gaps, as long as there is a clear defense objective.

Technically, DARPA focuses on ideas, technologies, and approaches that the traditional research and development community finds too unconventional or risky. The specific focus of attention changes constantly, but a list of the technical offices gives some indications of the agency's preferences.

1. *Defense Sciences Office*, seeking to identify the most promising new ideas within the basic science and engineering community, and develop them into new military capabilities

2. *Electronics Technology Office*, aiming to produce smaller, lighter, and more mobile information systems

3. *Information Systems Offices*, providing technologies and systems to allow battlefield awareness and force management to the commander

4. *Information Technology Office*, seeking to advance the frontier of computing systems, information technology, and software

5. *Sensor Technology Office*, investigating applications of advanced sensor technology

6. *Tactical Technology Office*, engaging in high-risk, high-payoff advanced military research, emphasizing the "system" and "subsystem" approach to the development of air, land, and naval systems technologies

7. *Discoverer II*, a joint initiative with a mission to develop an affordable space-based radar

It can be seen that electronics and computer science are main areas of the agency. The Internet actually started out several decades ago as the

ARPANET (DARPA was then called ARPA). In the last decade, DARPA has focused on technologies and solutions that are relevant to all the military services (joint-service systems and problems) as well as technologies with both civilian and military applications (dual use).

Each technical office has its own Web page. This is a good source of information on ongoing projects and areas of interest, as well as various outreach activities. For information on current invitations to send in proposals, see "getting in touch with DARPA" below. A quick way to get an overview of some of the current focus of DARPA is to look at the DARPA topics in the two to three most recent SBIR solicitations from the Department of Defense. These topics change completely from one solicitation to the next, but are always connected to areas of interest of the technical offices.

Features of Projects

According to DARPA, the typical technical project is structured as follows:

1. $10 million to $40 million over four years
2. A single DARPA *program manager* with direct control over efforts and funding
3. *Contractors* to support the Program Manager in the management of efforts and the representation of the program with Congress, the Office of the Secretary of Defense, the military services, and others
4. An *agent* in a military research and development lab to provide technical and contracting support
5. Five to ten *contractor organizations* and two universities executing tasks focused on a specific aggregate goal

Of course, the size of project varies—from less than $1 million to several hundreds of millions—but the basic organization remains the same. The main difference is the number of contractors involved. One way to enter the DARPA world is to become a subcontractor to an organization with an existing DARPA award.

DARPA has legal authority to enter into contracts and grants. In addition, DARPA has developed a lot of other and more innovative agreements to support research and development activities. They are often oriented at dual use technologies, consortia, or multiparty agreements, and work supported by multiple funding sources. Cost-sharing or joint funding is often not only encouraged, but also required.

A typical selection process for a smaller contract (a few hundred thousand dollars) is for the program manager to solicit proposal abstracts and white papers. The program manager, who provides nonbinding feedback to the proposer, then reviews proposal abstracts. Then the program manager and additional procurement officials review full proposals according to the criteria described in the solicitation. Selected proposals are examined for potential impact on achieving the DARPA program goals (described as an "inner product" between scientific quality and relevance to the program and agency mission). Although scientific quality and mission or program relevance is what counts, proposals should also include a plan for technical success and a transition plan to get the developed technology and products into the market place. Finally, a subset of the selected proposals are selected according to the technical and scientific review and are funded.

The success rate in DARPA is actually quite high compared to SBIR Phase I or ATP. In DARPA, around one out of three preproposals (proposal abstracts or white papers) are funded in the end. Nevertheless, each program manager receives a large amount of proposal material during the year, so it is important to have a good abstract or introduction to the proposal, where the key technical idea is highlighted.

Getting in Touch with DARPA

There are basically three ways of getting in touch with DARPA. First, there is the opportunity to respond to specific solicitations. Second, you can participate at one of the industry briefings that are frequently arranged. Third, you can get in touch with a program manager.

Solicitations (calls for proposals) are always announced in *Commerce Business Daily (CBD)*, the Department of Commerce publication in which all federal procurements over $25,000 in value are listed in brief. *CBD* is available in paper format, and it can also be found in a searchable format on the Web. Most solicitations will also be available through the home pages of the different technology offices of DARPA.

Solicitations can be broad agency announcements, requests for proposals, sources-sought announcements, or special research announcements. The first two types differ in how specifically they describe the desired proposals, and the two latter are advanced notices of DARPA's interest in a particular area of technology. These are often used to survey the market to find potential participants.

Industry briefings are used whenever possible to outline problems within specific technology areas and to request submission of technical solutions to the problems. During the briefings, all potential proposers are provided with identical information and should therefore have an equal opportunity to respond. The home pages of the different DARPA technical offices will often have information on upcoming industry briefings. All briefings are in any case announced in *CBD*. This process of outlining problems is very similar to the white paper process connected to focus areas in the Advanced Technology Program.

Program managers are central in DARPA. One of their major tasks is to create new projects, often relying on input from industry. Historically, about half of the new project ideas are proposed from outside DARPA.

According to the agency, the best time to influence new project ideas is in the spring. It is advisable to check with program managers (or on the Web) to see if there are projects in your area of interest, and not to submit "blind proposals" (submission without any prior discussion with a program manager). Such submissions rarely reach the right customer.

A final remark is that if you are an entrepreneurial type, innovative, and have an excellent in-depth knowledge of your technical or scientific field, maybe a program manager position in DARPA is an option for you. These positions, usually lasting four years, give you much responsibility and possibly a unique opportunity to develop your field.

DARPA on the Web

The DARPA home page can be found on http://www.darpa.mil/. There are good, general—and not too long—descriptions of DARPA, its history, and organizational structure. All the technical offices have their own home pages where the more concrete information on solicitations and industry briefings, as well as ongoing projects and technological focus areas, can be found. The DARPA SBIR program also has its own home page.

To access DARPA solicitations and announcements on the *Commerce Business Daily's* Web page, do the following:

1. Enter at http://cbdnet.access.gpo.gov/
2. Click on "Browse the CBD"
3. Click on U.S. Government Procurements
4. Click on Services, Class Code A, for DARPA solicitations

Another possibility is to enter the CBD and use the simple search feature to find all documents containing the term "DARPA" (or the name in full).

The Advanced Technology Program

There are three good reasons for taking a close look at the ATP. First, the size of awards for a single applicant can be up to $2 million, about three times as much as the maximum SBIR Phase II awards. Second, the chances of getting an award are about the same as in SBIR. Third, ATP awards often lead to collaboration with (1) other firms, both large and small; (2) university research groups; and (3) government laboratories.

For most ATP competitions, the percentage of award winners out of the total applicants is not much lower than for Phase I of the SBIR. Also, the ATP welcomes ideas for technical topics from individual firms. The ATP's preferred mode of topic generation is through discussions among firms in related areas of interest at meetings held around the country. Indeed, ATP encourages groups of firms to propose such meetings to the agency to which it will send program managers.

However, more work is typically required for filling out the application forms for the Advanced Technology Program than for SBIR. The greater effort is due primarily to the ATP placing greater weight on the nontechnical portion. In addition, it is important to be aware that there are two parts to the ATP application process. The first round is a written application, roughly similar to the SBIR except that greater weight is placed on commercial potential.

Approximately 20% of the authors of the best proposals from the first round are invited to ATP headquarters in Gaithersburg, Maryland, for a second round. The second round is comprised of a face-to-face session with experts knowledgeable about the general technology area and market sector of your proposal. A final award decision is made on the basis of both the oral and written presentations.

The following themes will be presented in this section:

1. Background and facts of the program
2. Small firms and the ATP—why you should consider applying
3. How can personnel from universities and federal laboratories participate?
4. The project proposal process
5. Submitting program ideas
6. Competitions in ongoing and planned program areas
7. ATP on the World Wide Web
8. Points of contact

Background and Facts

In 1991 the ATP started operation after a $10 million appropriation in 1990. The Clinton administration made this program the centerpiece of its civilian technology initiative and encouraged Congress to substantially increase funding for the ATP. The administration intended the ATP to become a $750 million program by 1996. Although the ATP reached a height of close to $350 million, a backlash in Congress against government funding of research and development at large corporations led to a reduction in the level of ATP funding to the current level of about $200 million. Nevertheless, ATP was not eliminated, as some in Congress proposed. Instead, it was reoriented from projects primarily involving collaborations among large corporations to projects emphasizing the contributions of smaller firms. Large firms are still welcome but they play a lesser role in the revised ATP.

The goal of the program is "to benefit the U.S. economy by cost-sharing research with industry to foster new, innovative technologies." ATP concentrates "on promising, but high-risk, enabling technologies that can form the basis for new and improved products, manufacturing processes, and services." ATP is especially interested in encouraging "spill-overs" (broad implications for a wide range of technological and industrial areas) from particular projects that it supports. Its expectation is that the research and development projects that it funds should lead to improvements in processes and products, upgrading existing fields and possibly creating new ones as DARPA did for the Internet.

The ATP is organized under the National Institute of Standards and Technology (NIST), and has its own program staff. A list of the staff members and their phone numbers, e-mail addresses, and such can be found on the ATP Web page on http://www.atp.nist.org. Contact information is also available in Part IV of this volume.

Product development is not funded directly. However, the scope of the ATP is still broad in theory. It ranges from developing new technologies that introduce new capabilities and features to improving the quality and performance of technologies by enabling improved productivity and lower costs just up to the point where market-oriented product development starts. It includes developing know-how that can lead to new products and services. ATP is also especially interested in projects that utilize new technologies, such as artificial intelligence, to upgrade the level of older technologies in mid-tech industries.

In practice, the ATP parameters are such that projects that interest venture capitalists are not (or should not be) funded by ATP on the grounds that they are too close to product development. On the other hand, ATP is precluded from project areas that can also be considered too far away from technology, for instance, by being too close to basic research. The difficult balance to be managed is between the program's focus on both commercial potential and high-risk technologies.

The appropriations for ATP showed a sharp rise until 1995, but were cut from that year. However, most people connected to the program seem to be optimistic about its future. The total annual appropriations are as follows (numbers in millions of dollars):

Year	Appropriation
1990	10.0
1991	37.0
1992	49.9
1993	97.3
1994	199.0
1995	341.0
1996	221.0
1997	223.0
1998	192.5
1999	203.5

Note that much of the annual budget goes to projects that won awards in previous years. In fiscal year 1999, around $66 million were available for first-year funding of new projects. In recent years, ATP has funded between 50 and 100 new projects every year.

Like other public programs, private firms compete for awards by responding to competition announcements. Unlike the SBIR program, where ideas for topics and program areas mostly come from the participating agencies, the ATP relies much more on input from industry. Industry is the major source of ideas for new program areas, which are developed in collaboration with the program staff. Program areas under the ATP still change over time. From 1994 to 1998 there were several award competitions, one general award and six in focused program areas. These included motor-vehicle manufacturing technology, information infrastructure for healthcare, digital data storage, technologies for the integration of manufacturing applications, component-based software, and tissue engineering in the latter years. In 1999, however, this was changed. Applicants are now invited to submit proposals within any technological field. The ATP now plans to form its focus areas on the basis of grouping sets of related awards. Although the ATP continues to develop certain special areas of interest and may announce focus competitions in the future, at present it is inviting all innovative ideas.

Small Firms and the ATP—Why You Should Consider Applying

Some have the impression that the ATP is oriented mostly toward large firms. This is not the case. A look at the statistics (1991–1998) reveals that more than half of the awards to single applicants have gone to small firms.

Single applicants:	285	Small business:	190
Joint ventures:	146	Led by small business:	48
Total:	431	Total:	238

Small firms, even tiny start-up companies, have received a larger share of the total grants in the latter years. For instance, in 1997 the majority of the awards (48 out of 64) went to small businesses either for single-company projects or as the lead company in an industry joint venture.

Small firms do not receive any extra points or credits in the competitions. However, there have been signals that small firms may be given more priority in the years to come. The proposal preparation kit makes the point that the participation of small firms in a joint venture project is viewed favorably. The participation of large firms in such collaborative projects is also important, especially for their dissemination and marketing capabilities. Not-for-profit research and development organizations are also encouraged to participate in ATP collaborations. In the past, they have been known to bring special systems expertise to a project, integrating the contributions of diverse participants.

The ATP emphasizes cost sharing. On average, the awardees pay more than half the total costs of research and development. This functions a bit differently for single applicants and joint ventures. The single-applicant requirement for cost sharing is that the company covers its indirect costs. Most start-ups and small companies have low, indirect costs, so this requirement is not prohibitive. Direct costs of single applicants are 100% reimbursable up to $2 million.

The large award size is attractive to small firms. However, there is more paperwork required for an ATP application than for an SBIR application. An applicant from computer science who made it to the semifinalist round stated that "compared to the SBIR, it is much more costly to complete an ATP application. You have to come up with a lot of market and business-related information that I didn't have readily available. Of course if you do get an award, the large size of it will justify the effort, but you should carefully consider your chances of winning."

Although oriented mostly toward the "middle ground" between basic research and product development, both market-oriented and research-oriented small firms use ATP funding. The former can become interested in developing a new technology to gain a unique competitive advantage, and the latter in taking their know-how closer to product development and commercialization.

Some small firms have felt "too small" to apply for funds on their own and have created a joint venture with a much larger company. The small firm then acted as a subcontractor to the large company. This is not necessarily a wise strategy unless there are already relatively close ties between the two firms. Instead, joint ventures between small firms with different focuses (market or research) can be considered, and the ATP award statistics reveal that many small firms gain awards on their own.

On the ATP Web site, firms have the possibility of locating other firms who might be interested in forming a joint venture. See the section "ATP on the Web" that follows for more information.

In summary, these are some of the central points to consider before applying for an ATP award:

1. How much effort do I have to put into making a good application?
2. What are my chances of winning (see selection criteria that follow)?
3. What difference can a $2 million award make for the firm?
4. Can the project benefit by subcontracting or forming a joint venture?

How Can Personnel in Universities and Federal Laboratories Participate?

Universities play a central role in many ATP projects although they are not allowed to receive awards directly. In general, both small, medium, and large (for-profit) companies, and joint ventures led by two or more companies are eligible for direct funding. Universities, federal laboratories, and independent nonprofit research organizations participate in many ATP projects as subcontractors or as members of joint ventures. If they are members, the joint venture is required to have at least two companies that are substantially involved in the work. Still, an independent, nonprofit research organization may submit the proposal and administer the project provided that the joint venture is industry led (i.e., the commercial members formally define the research agenda and plans) and has at least two for-profit members.

If subcontracting to a single applicant (not a joint venture), a university or federal laboratory can recover both direct and indirect costs from the ATP because this is regarded as a direct cost to the ATP applicant. As mentioned, the direct costs are 100% reimbursable up to $2 million, but note that tuition for students participating in university subcontracts cannot be paid for.

Out of the 431 projects selected by the ATP since its inception, 234 of the proposals included plans to involve one or more universities. More than 400 instances of university participation have been recorded in the ATP projects (e.g., as subcontractors brought into a project after its inception). The large participation of universities and other nonprofit research organizations is notable, according to the ATP legislation, since to date they cannot retain title to patents from ATP-sponsored research and development. However, they can receive mutually agreed upon payments. Nevertheless, this is a continuing legislative struggle. The universities would like to make the intellectual property theirs and the ATP would like to continue the orientation of the program toward firms.

The Project Proposal Process

Just as for SBIR proposals, scientists and engineers who are experts in the subject area review each. The first cut is done by reviewers who usually are federal and academic experts. This avoids problems connected to conflict of interest and helps to protect proprietary information. But ATP proposals that score well in this technical review go on to a further evaluation. Considerations are the potential economic impact, the level of commitment to the project on the part of the proposer, and other business-related factors. This review is primarily conducted by experts from the private sector who have agreed to abide by nondisclosure requirements and agreed to avoid conflicts of interest.

The director of a small medical firm who won a $2 million ATP grant in 1997 says that the application process was very difficult, but that focusing the project in such an exacting process *should* be difficult. "The application is a combination of a business plan and scientific plan, which is good. Putting the science part together was easier, but the most useful part for us was the business side. The increased weight on business criteria in the ATP, compared to the SBIR and STTR that we also have received grants from, forced us to build more economic value into the project."

Based on the technical and economic reviews, some of the proposals will be selected as semifinalists. All semifinalists receive in-depth oral reviews. They are ranked, and funding is awarded on the basis of this ranking.

The oral interview is described as a "tough, dissertation-like session" with 20 to 30 people in the room. You do not have to face this test alone. You are invited to bring two associates with you. Ideally, the team should consist of the best individuals to address key aspects of an ATP proposal: the technology itself, its commercial implications, and potential spill-over effects. This oral examination is quite thorough. You should prepare carefully with mock sessions in which colleagues or consultants grill your team about all aspects of the proposal before you meet with the ATP. The actual session can take the better part of a day. A semifinalist from computer science said that you have to be well prepared and also bring several people to the interview that can answer the different kinds of questions. "The questions are fair but tough, and the people know both the technical and the business side very well. My technical side was fine, but you also have to do a strong business case. But with the development that has been done in the company now, I think we have better chances of winning an award the next time we apply, and they told me that, too." An award-winning small medical firm also had to apply twice, but made it to the semifinalist round the first time. The second time they applied in a focused area rather than the general competition, and they worked more on the business and economic part of the application.

When applying, the same advice that was mentioned for the SBIR is as valid here. It will be important to gather as much information as possible before proposing, especially on the relevant program area. Relevant white papers should be studied carefully, and the program manager(s) will most likely be an important contact. The program manager can later, if you are successful in getting an award, function as a gatekeeper to expertise in the different NIST laboratories.

A proposal preparation kit is available on-line, and can also be sent to you in paper form upon request. Here, the different formal requirements are spelled out in detail. For instance, the numbers and types of official forms that need to be completed. The kit is described in further detail in the section below. Note that you should provide an original signed proposal and 15 copies, each separately bound, in addition to completing a form (different for single applicants and joint ventures). The proposal should not exceed 40 pages (50 for joint ventures), including everything but the official forms. It is not possible to submit proposals by e-mail or fax. Also note that joint ventures should enclose the joint venture agreement, which should conform to the general characteristics that are defined in the proposal preparation kit.

The main section of the proposal, where the specific project is described, must contain the following five sections (numbers in parentheses refer to the relative weight of the section when ranking proposals):

1. Scientific and Technical Merit of the Proposal (30%), including when appropriate

   a. Quality, innovativeness, and cost-effectiveness

   b. Appropriate levels of technical risk and feasibility

   c. Coherency of technical plan and clarity of vision of the technical objectives

   d. Adequacy of systems integration and multidisciplinary planning

   e. Potential broad impact on U.S. technology and knowledge base

2. Potential Broad-Based Economic Benefits (20%), such as

   a. Potential to improve U.S. economic growth and productivity

   b. Timeliness

   c. Degree to which ATP support is necessary

   d. Cost-effectiveness

3. Adequacy of Plans for Eventual Commercialization (20%), for instance

   a. Evidence of a commercialization plan

   b. Degree to which potential applications are defined and plans for technology diffusion and protection of intellectual property are developed

4. Proposer's Level of Commitment and Organizational Structure (20%), including

   a. Level of commitment

   b. Type of organization structure

   c. Participation by small businesses (defined as less than 500 employees—involving one or more small businesses in a meaningful way in a joint venture has some chance of increasing your proposal's ranking)

   d. Subcontractor, supplier, and collaborator participation and relationships if applicable

   e. Project management plan

5. Experience and Qualifications (10%)

   a. Adequacy of facilities, equipment, design and manufacturing tools, and other technical, financial, and administrative resources

   b. Quality and appropriateness of staff

   c. Past performance (e.g., SBIR awards)

Although the same points apply, the evaluation was somewhat simplified for the competition in fiscal year 1999. Now it is stated that proposals are evaluated for their scientific and technological merit, and for their potential for broad-based economic benefits, with both parts weighed equally.

The SBIR proposal advice can be followed, although it requires a lot of work to make a good business case compared to the SBIR. Do not use too many pages for describing and documenting your experience and qualifications; this only counts as 10% of the total score. Furthermore, your credibility will be enhanced if you acknowledge any deficiencies and explain how you plan to overcome them, instead of letting the reviewers discover the deficiencies.

The director of the small medical firm that won an award in 1997 says that one should take everything in the application guide and brochure very literally. "The ATP means exactly what it says in the form and brochure. They were very good in explaining what they wanted. Attending seminars in advance and reading the ATP brochure over and over was extremely useful to us."

There are also some other formal requirements, such as a budget narrative. According to the ATP, the most common reason for failure when considering technical merit is the lack of a clear research and development plan. A good plan spells out the specifics of the innovation(s) being developed and provides enough detail to allow the reviewers to judge the degree of innovation. Success in getting ATP funds is a stamp of approval for the applicant, and should be used as such. A proposal, which has been turned down in one solicitation, may also become funded later if it is revised taking into account past reviewers' comments.

Submitting Program Ideas

It is important to understand the distinction between programs and projects. Programs have a fixed life span (usually three years per solicitation) and describe major research directions for the ATP. Projects are specific pieces of work that are proposed to the ATP in response to formal competitions.

Individual industrial firms (e.g., trade associations, professional societies, universities, and federal laboratories) can propose ideas for future programs at any time. This means that your firm can influence the direction of future funds from the ATP. The programs are selected based on four major criteria:

1. Potential for U.S. economic benefit, including the credibility of the program's proposed pathways to economic growth, the importance of the existing or potential sector(s) affected, and the probability of subsequent commercialization;

2. Good technical ideas that are "cutting edge," high-risk, strategically important, and based on sound scientific and technical concepts;

3. Strong industry commitment, including breadth and depth of interest and willingness to share costs and to work with the ATP and other partners; and

4. The opportunity for ATP funds to make a significant difference by supporting work that is unique or complementary to other industrial and government efforts, that offers timely and significant acceleration of research progress, and that requires a critical mass of funding that the ATP can provide.

A broad range of ideas is welcome, and getting in touch with the ATP program manager for your technology area is worthwhile. Often, firms are encouraged to send a "white paper." A white paper is a document that outlines information regarding the criteria above. Technologies and capabilities that are to be developed and achieved should be specified. Because submitted ideas will be shared with other companies and possibly discussed in working groups, it is important that no proprietary information is included.

Although experience shows that white papers range from describing major technologies that will influence large sectors of society, to technologies that are tailor-made to one specific purpose, all such papers should take a broad view. They should not depict a project that only your company would like to undertake. White papers should focus on broader program concepts in which many companies in your industry, or related industries, would want to participate. Alternatively, it could be a concept for the intersection of a new technological and industrial synthesis, such as biotechnology and computer science, or bio-informatics. The most common deficiency in white papers is that they have more of an individual project focus than a broad program focus according to the ATP.

Available on-line at the ATP Web site is a guide to submitting program ideas. The guide includes a more detailed description of the selection criteria and several examples of good proposals (see also ATP on the Web below). Bear in mind, however, that submitting a good white paper can be a comprehensive process that perhaps is better suited to large firms, industry associations, or not-for-profit organizations who can put together a team for this purpose. Smaller firms with an innovative concept could submit on their own or collaborate with others to submit a white paper, bringing their ideas to the attention of the ATP.

What happens after the ATP has received a white paper? First, the ATP's technical and economic staff reviews the ideas, often consulting outside experts. If there appears to be sufficient internal and external interest in a particular program concept, the ATP generally hosts a public workshop to discuss and further refine the idea. An ATP program manager will be responsible for this process. Informal meetings, data collections, analytical studies, and such can be relevant in addition to workshops. Naturally, not all program ideas are made or incorporated into programs, and not all planned programs are expected to be funded. This depends among other things on the available funds and how well the proposed programs meet the four selection criteria.

In summary, these are the major steps of the idea submission process, which is described in much more detail in the on-line guide (which can also be found on the CD-ROM accompanying this volume):

1. Draw up a letter or a short "white paper."

2. State technical and business goals related to the program, which should be seen as a broader concept that can include a collection of independent projects.

3. Discuss how the program meets the four selection criteria described above.

4. Do not include proprietary information.

5. Include a title page marked "Program Idea" with key information and send five copies of the proposal to the ATP program manager (see listing in Part IV).

Competitions in Ongoing and Planned Program Areas

Each year the ATP invites individual firms and joint ventures to send in proposals to compete for awards. Competitions are announced in *Commerce Business Daily*, by direct mail, and posted on the ATP Web page (see Part IV). Only project proposals submitted in response to a formal competition are considered for evaluation. Both technical and economic criteria are given weight (see below). In 1999 one competition was held, with a final deadline in the middle of April. This is likely to be repeated in the future.

Traditionally, there have been two types of competitions: general and focused. The *general competitions* have been open to all technology areas. Past general competition awards have covered a broad spectrum of technologies in agriculture, biotechnology, microelectronics and electronics manufacturing, machine tools, advanced automotive manufacturing, advanced materials, information and communication technology, chemical processing, and other areas. Not much money has been allocated to the general competition compared to the large number of applicants. In recent years there have been more than 300 applicants in the general competition, yet less than 10% of them have received an award.

In the past, the largest share of ATP funding has been tied to competitions in *focused program areas*, which are aimed at specific, well-defined technology and business goals. These are the result of ideas that have been submitted in white papers and assessed as discussed above. In general, the ATP tries to develop a suite of interlocking research and development projects that complement and reinforce each other in parallel.

In fiscal year 1999, this changed in part. The whole competition was made "general," implying that proposals from any area of technology could be made. Peer review of the proposals was done by one of five technology area boards—electronics, information technology, biotechnology, materials and chemicals, and manufacturing.

The development of focused program areas will continue, however. This means that when new projects are funded, they will be clustered in complementary groups for management and information sharing purposes. Some clusters will be part of existing focused programs, while other clusters might form new programs. How this will precisely function in practice in the future is still unclear, but it is still highly advisable to carefully read through the ongoing focus areas in search of a match with your potential project.

Another new feature of the 1999 competition was the possibility of submitting *preproposals*. These are abbreviated proposals that can be submitted at any time during the year but well before the final deadline if you want to make the upcoming competition. The ATP will provide feedback as to the suitability of the proposed project. Appendix E of the Proposal Preparation Kit (see the section of this chapter on ATP on the Web below as well as on the CD-ROM accompanying the book) gives detailed instructions on the submission of preproposals.

As of spring 1999, the following are ongoing focused program areas (all the programs have on-line overviews and most of them have separate white papers):

1. Adaptive Learning Systems
2. Catalysis & Biocatalysis Technologies
3. Component-Based Software
4. Digital Data Storage
5. Digital Video in Information Networks
6. Information Infrastructure for Healthcare
7. Manufacturing Composite Structures
8. Materials Processing for Heavy Manufacturing
9. Microelectronics Manufacturing Infrastructure
10. Motor Vehicle Manufacturing Technology
11. Photonics Manufacturing
12. Premium Power
13. Selective Membrane Platforms
14. Technologies for the Integration of Manufacturing Applications
15. Tissue Engineering
16. Tools for DNA Diagnostics
17. Vapor Compression Refrigeration Technology

Several new program areas are under development. These are based on ideas that have been submitted from a number of sources (these can also be found, with contacts for each area, on the ATP Web page; see also Part IV of this book):

1. Combinatorial Chemistry and Materials Research
2. Composites in Civil Applications
3. Condition-Based Maintenance
4. Genetic Manipulation in Animals: Advanced Transgenesis and Cloning
5. Initiatives in Healthcare Informatics
6. Intelligent and Distributed Engineering Design
7. Intelligent Control
8. Interoperable Infrastructures for Distributed Electronic Commerce
9. Microsystems and Nanosystems Technology
10. Motor Vehicle Manufacturing Technology
11. Nano and MEMS Technologies for Chemical Biosensors
12. Organic Electronics Technology
13. Semiconductor Lithography
14. Tissue Engineering
15. Tools for Engineered Surfaces
16. Wireless Communications

Descriptions and white papers are available on-line in all these areas. There are often possibilities of joining workshop discussions related to the technological area.

ATP on the World Wide Web

It is relatively easy to get a good overview of the ATP program, because all the information is gathered in one place: http://www.atp.nist.gov. The Web site is one of the best of all federal technology programs. There is considerable information here; it is well structured and relatively straightforward. An ATP CD-ROM is available, which is in fact a "snapshot" of the Web site as of February 1999. This can be ordered on-line. If you join the ATP mailing list, you will be notified when new competitions are announced or other things happen in the program.

Some sections on the ATP Web site can be found at most of the federal technology programs. These include news and publications, information about the program, links to other programs, and a presentation of past success stories. The site can be searched for certain text strings, which might be useful if you are looking for a particular technology.

In the "How to Apply" section you will find a guide to sending in program ideas, as well as a "Proposal Preparation Kit." An on-line form for requesting generic information about the ATP or to add your name to the ATP mailing list is also available here. The Proposal Preparation Kit consists of several medium-sized files that can be viewed with Adobe Acrobat or new versions of Microsoft Word. A zipped version of the kit (around 350 Kb) is available for download. The three main chapters of the Proposal Preparation Kit provide an overview of the ATP, detailed guidelines for preparing proposals, and administrative award requirements and procedures. In the appendices you can, for instance, find instructions for submitting preproposals and a sample joint venture agreement. A number of electronic forms are included in the kit.

There are also sections that give information about active competitions and focused program areas (main technology areas of the program). Most of the technology areas have moderately long, publicly available white papers that state, for instance, the technical and business goals of that particular area. This should be useful information to more precisely understand what the ATP wants. All technology areas have brief on-line descriptions and information, outlining what ATP officers are responsible for in a particular focused program.

"Funded Projects" contains a listing of all ATP projects so far with a brief description of each. "ATP Offices and Staff" provides links to the ATP program managers who have their own Web pages that describe what they do in further detail. The Web pages of the offices and individual staff members often contain relevant links within their particular area of technology.

A nice feature is the "Alliance Network." This part of the ATP Web site is designed to help firms to collaborate with others for application to the program. Alliances can be used whether firms are applying as single companies or as joint ventures. In the alliance network you will find an introduction to research and development alliances oriented toward explaining its pros and cons, and some statistics about the effects of collaboration on previous ATP awardees. There is also a link to the formal requirements to ATP joint ventures. On the "Collaboration Bulletin Board" you can search for possible alliance partners, and in the "Forum" you can exchange ideas with others about research and development alliances.

On the accompanying CD-ROM, you will find the following ATP related files (all are in hypertext format except the Proposal Preparation Kit, which is in Adobe Acrobat format):

1. Overview of the program
2. Guide to submitting program ideas
3. Overview of current and possible future technology areas
4. List of the ATP staff (with contact information) (also found in Part IV of this book)

5. Introduction to the Proposal Preparation Kit

6. Proposal Preparation Kit (both zipped and unzipped into many small files)

Dual Use Technology Programs

If you are developing a technology that has both a commercial potential and might be useful to the military, then it might be worthwhile to take a closer look at programs supporting such dual use technologies in the Department of Defense. Under these programs, private firms form partnerships with defense units, sharing costs to develop technology that is beneficial to both parties. Flexible contractual agreements, and frequently a large award size, make the program attractive also to small firms.

The following topics are discussed in this section:

1. The history of dual use
2. The Dual Use S&T Program
3. Selection criteria and the application process
4. The COSSI program
5. The future of dual use programs
6. Dual use on the Web

The History of Dual Use

Traditionally, the military has developed its own technologies, either in specially designated laboratories or in collaboration with firms that have developed the technology for defense use only. In the early 1990s, however, the concept of dual use appeared. Experience in collaborating with private industry and cuts in the defense budget led policy makers to think that there had to be a more efficient way to develop militarily useful technology than the traditional approach offered. It was also seen that in many technology areas, such as electronics and computer software, that the competence level and innovativeness was often higher in the civilian than the defense sector.

In brief, a dual use technology has both military utility and sufficient commercial potential to support a viable industrial base. Underlying the dual use concept is the assumption that it can be more efficient and useful both to the private firm and the military to collaborate in development projects. Through the shared and increased effort, the technology is expected to come into defense use earlier and reach the private market faster as well. Thus, both the military and the firms (and eventually the economy) benefit from it. Such "win–win" relationships are often the first objective of dual use contracts.

The first program based on dual use principles, the Technology Reinvestment Project (TRP), had its first award competition in 1993, with a second and third round the following two years. Around $500 million were awarded in these three competitions to technology development. On average, almost $6 million were awarded per project. The program was managed by the DARPA, belonging to the Office of the Secretary of Defense (OSD). DARPA developed solicitations and awarded grants in much the same way as is done for the ATP and SBIR programs. New contractual devices were developed that were flexible and non-bureaucratic, which also contributed to the program's popularity.

Preliminary assessments have shown that the Department of Defense has benefited from many of the projects, which have had commercial impacts as well. But the TRP had a high public profile and became very controversial. Some argued that the program was a misuse of defense money and an attempt at an industrial policy that "picks winners." When Congress changed from Democrat to Republican control in 1994, no more award competitions were held and the program came to a close.

After the controversy died down, there was, nevertheless, agreement that dual use technology is an important and useful concept although there was disagreement as to whether the TRP really was a dual use program. So out of the ashes of the TRP arose the Dual Use Applications Program (DUAP), which partly is still in existence. DUAP differed from the TRP in that the military services (Army, Navy, and Air Force) play a much more central role. The individual service agencies issue the solicitations and select projects themselves. This means that projects are to a larger degree tied directly to concrete defense needs and, in the long run, it is hoped that dual use collaboration will be a normal way of doing business in the Department of Defense.

DUAP has had a lower profile and less money than the TRP. In fiscal year 1997, the total budget was around $125 million. Of that, $75 million went to dual use science and technology development, while the rest went to a new initiative called the Commercial Operations and Support Savings Initiative (COSSI). From fiscal year 1999, COSSI has migrated to the Office of the Secretary of Defense, while DUAP has been renamed Dual Use Science & Technology (DU S&T). These two programs are described below.

The Dual Use S&T Program

The objectives of the DU S&T program are to partner with industry in advanced dual use projects that benefit both the military customer and the firm's competitive advantages. The goal is to make dual use development of technologies a normal way of doing business in the armed services. Program officials state that the benefits to industry include a leverage of science and technology funding, vehicles to form beneficial partnerships, access to advanced technology, and potentials for developing new markets.

In fiscal year 1999, it is expected that around $30 million will go to science and technology projects from the DU S&T program. The military services (Army, Navy, and Air Force) will spend around the same amount. This is half of what DU S&T was appropriated the previous year. In fiscal year 2000, it is again expected (or hoped—see the section titled "The Future of Dual Use" that follows) that $60 million in federal funds will be available for DU S&T. Total funding for dual use S&T projects in fiscal year 1998 was $294 million; $68 million came from the DU S&T program, the same amount from the military services, and the rest ($158 million) from industry through cost sharing. Ninety-five proposals were approved in 1998, resulting in an average award size of more than $1 million.

Universities and federal laboratories cannot compete for awards except as part of a consortium. But as in the Advanced Technology Program, participation by universities in joint ventures and as subcontractors is significant.

Technical topics or focus areas are developed and issued by the Army, Navy and Air Force. In fiscal year 1999, the headlines were:

1. Affordable Sensors
2. Advanced Propulsion, Power, and Fuel Efficiency
3. Information and Communications Systems
4. Medical and Bioengineering
5. Weapons Systems Sustainment
6. Distributed Mission Training
7. Advanced Materials and Manufacturing
8. Environmental Technologies

The solicitation describes in more detail what technology areas are focused on in the award competition, how to apply, and by what criteria projects will be selected. All projects must have

1. Defense relevance, as defined by the focus areas (although it has been possible to submit proposals under the heading "others" rather than the selected technology areas in that competition)
2. *Collaboration* between a military organization and one or several firms
3. *Cost sharing*—at least 50% should be paid by the commercial participants, and half the military cost by the military service or the agency that will eventually use the technology
4. The awareness that they will be selected on a *competitive basis*

Selection Criteria and the Application Process

A joint broad agency announcement is made each year starting in 1999 on topic areas for all three armed services, replacing the earlier separate announcements by each service. The fiscal year 1999 solicitation was released in August 1998, with industry proposals due by mid December and the selection process starting from February 1999. There is an opportunity to get feedback on an early version of the proposal, called a "white paper." (This white paper is not to be confused with the white paper process of the Advanced Technology Program.) DU S&T white papers are due about a month after the release of the solicitation. The white paper deadline was the end of September for fiscal year 1999. Full proposals, due in December, should be a maximum of 40 pages.

Proposals are ranked based on the following criteria, which are of equal importance:

1. *Quality of industrial cost share*   The proposer must bear at least 50% of the project costs, and 50% of the cost share must be of high quality (mainly money and materials). Low quality cost share are nonfinancial resources, typically wear-and-tear on in-place capital assets such as machinery.

2. *Military benefit*   The project should focus on technologies that will have a major impact on the cost, performance, or sustainability of defense systems.

3. *Commercial viability*   It is essential that a commercialization path for the proposed technology is identified. Technologies that would not be economically viable without significant military purchases will not be supported by the program.

4. *Technical & management approach*   This is common to most technological programs, and includes a technical description of the technology, objectives, statement of work, project plans, description of the project team, and so on.

These criteria are dealt with in several different sections of the proposal. Applicants are therefore asked to provide a one-page index showing the pages of the technical proposal on which each of the selection criteria is addressed.

If successful, you will find that the contractual arrangements are relatively simple. Ordinarily, contracts with the military are covered by Federal Acquisition Regulations (FAR), which are long and complicated. DU S&T projects use Technology Investment Agreements. These are non-procurement instruments that are covered by assistance regulations. Program officials describe these as relatively simple. These instruments offer a great deal of flexibility with regard to negotiating intellectual property rights.

It may be that during the proposal review and final stages of the selection process, some proposers are asked to provide clarification and oral presentations to members of the selection panel or to travel to Washington, DC (or elsewhere) for an interview.

The Commercial Operations and Support Savings Initiative

Although the Commercial Operations and Support Savings Initiative (COSSI) is no longer formally a part of the dual use program described above, activities still run in parallel in the two programs. While DU S&T projects focus on the development of new dual use technologies, COSSI projects are oriented toward encouraging adaptation of certain commercial business practices into military uses.

COSSI projects utilize commercially available civilian technologies. The goal is to reduce defense costs by introducing commercial products and processes into military systems. The projects must reduce costs of parts or maintenance, reduce the need for specialized equipment, or increase reliability and efficiency.

COSSI funds the nonrecurring engineering, testing, and qualification process needed to adapt a commercial item for use in a military system. Selected proposers develop, manufacture, and deliver prototypes to a military customer for installation into a defense system. Each prototype must consist of a commercial item (or combination of items) that are adapted, qualification-tested, and ready for insertion. All proposals must include a signed statement from the military customer. On the COSSI Web site there is a list of Department of Defense Procurement Offices and research and development activities which might help locate a relevant customer.

A two-stage approach is used. In Stage I, the prototype kit is developed and tested, with costs shared between the award winner and the military customer. Note that only currently available or "imminent" commercial products and processes are eligible for application in this subprogram. COSSI does not support research and development projects (such as the DU S&T program described above). If Stage I, which ordinarily lasts one to two years, is successful, the military customer may purchase reasonable quantities of the kit for insertion into the fielded system, which is termed Stage II.

At least 25% of the estimated Stage I cost must come from non-federal funds but not necessarily from the applicant. As with the DU S&T program, the amount and quality of the cost share is an important factor in the evaluation process. Proposals that include higher cost shares are viewed more favorably.

No competitions were held for COSSI in fiscal year 1999. Officials expect, however, that new federal funds will be available in fiscal year 2000 of approximately $90 million. Selection criteria in the last competition were:

1. Equivalent system performance (pass/fail), meaning that insertion of the new kit will not reduce the performance of the military system. Note also that projects should not be oriented toward military systems that are not yet operational or that are near the end of their useful lives.

2. Operations and support savings (30%)—how much the proposed kit will reduce costs within a 12-year analysis period.

3. Military customer commitment (25%)—strong support is necessary; this is shown in the customer support letter as well as the willingness of the customer to come up with additional funding.

4. Technical and management approach (15%)

5. Commercial leverage (15%) that shows the "core" of the kit is a commercial product or process. You will score better if the commercial item has wide commercial applications.

6. Non-federal share of project costs (15%)—if the company is willing to take a larger financial risk, there might be a better chance of gaining an award.

Even though defense relevance is important for both COSSI and the DU S&T program, it can be seen that it is measured in different ways.

A firm should ask itself whether the technology that is developed has important use in the military. A careful reading of the solicitations is a good idea to get an overview of what the defense units consider important. However, the technology (or item) must also have a civilian market, and the larger the ordinary commercial application possibilities are the better. If the technology is militarily useful, the company should also consider if a collaborative project would improve the chances for commercial success. Cost sharing might reduce development time, and both DU S&T and COSSI projects can provide the company with an important and highly competent "lead user."

The Future of Dual Use

Dual use technology is regarded as important at the political level. Congress has decided that a certain percentage of applied research projects in the Army, Navy and Air Force should be dual use. This percentage is furthermore expected to rise in the coming years, from 5% in 1998 to 15% in 2001. The total number of dual use projects has increased in recent years from 68 in 1997 to 95 in 1998.

The future of the programs themselves, however, is not that certain. It is expected that the programs will be completely transferred to the military services in the near future, making them less visible than they would be through a central office. In fact, there might be three slightly different programs, one in each service (Army, Navy, and Air Force), with its own solicitations and competitions. Some coordination is still likely, such as the Broad Agency Announcements, to avoid overlaps.

Finally, it should be noted that other departments and agencies may be willing to share costs of developing technology that is useful to them, for example the Department of Energy. Also, the Small Business Administration has several so-called federal procurement programs that aim to make it easier for small firms to win government contracts or acquisitions.

Dual Use on the Web

http://www.dtic.mil/dust/ is the Web site for the DU S&T program. This well-made Web site contains the following information:

1. Fact Sheet
2. Activities (For instance, information on various outreach activities. There are "Industry Days" oriented at presenting the program to potential applicants and helping them in their proposal preparation. The dual use personnel also travel to military lab sites and technical meetings for briefings).
3. Projects
4. Guidance
5. Points of Contact
6. Other Links

COSSI can be found at http://www.acq.osd.mil/es/dut/cossi/. Because there was no solicitation in 1999, the site does not offer very much information so far. The program description is thorough, however, including discussion of selection criteria. There is also a list of contact points in the various armed services.

CHAPTER 7 • OTHER PROGRAMS: DEVELOPED TECHNOLOGIES, MANUFACTURING, AND SMALL BUSINESS IN GENERAL

CONTENTS

OTHER PROGRAMS: DEVELOPED TECHNOLOGIES, MANUFACTURING, AND SMALL BUSINESS IN GENERAL

Cooperative Research and Development Agreements

There are more than 700 federally funded research and development centers in the United States, including the large national laboratories. They employ some of the country's best scientists and engineers. Private firms have the possibility to enter partnerships with these centers, which could be a good way to validate or develop the company's technology and products, or finding what you need to make the technology work. The most common type of partnership with the labs is called a cooperative research and technology agreement (CRADA), where the federal laboratory and the firm agree to collaborate on and share the costs and results of a particular research and development project.

The following topics are touched on in this next section:

1. What is a CRADA?
2. The federally funded research and development centers and getting in touch with the labs
3. How the agreements work
4. Types of projects—choose the right one and increase the chances of success
5. CRADAs on the Web

What Is a CRADA?

CRADAs are not particular technology or research and development programs, but rather a mode of interaction. In 1986, the Federal Technology

Transfer Act (PL 99-502) authorized government-operated laboratories to collaborate with non-federal parties, including private firms, to conduct specific research and development. Firms were allowed to access laboratory staff and facilities through joint research and development ventures, and the laboratories were allowed to use funds already in their budget for such cooperation. CRADAs are the most common collaboration mechanism.

Formally, a CRADA is a contractual agreement in which a federally funded research and development center and one or more partners outside the federal government agreed to collaborate on, share the costs of, and pool the results from a particular research and development program. The contract is standardized and regulates issues such as intellectual property.

A majority of CRADAs lasts for three years or more. Agreements between a single firm concerning a particular technology or research and development project, often valued between $1 million and $2 million, with industry paying on average between a third and a half of the amount. There are, however, several very large CRADAs involving many laboratories and whole industries that we will not describe further here. The project has to be relevant both to the firm and the lab. If the project does not enhance the federal lab's expertise, the firm must bear all the costs. On the other hand, if this criterion can be met, then the lab is allowed to contribute to the cost of the project.

Note that many small firms (and others) use funding from federal programs such as STTR and ATP to enter into partnership with national laboratories and other government research and development facilities. State programs are also often mentioned as a possible source of funding for CRADAs, not least from the state where the specific research and development center is located. Still, SBIR grants cannot be used to pay for a CRADA, although there might be possibilities of hiring lab scientists and engineers as subcontractors on an SBIR project.

The cooperative agreements have become popular. The first three years of CRADAs led to a total of 3,000 agreements with a cash commitment of $1.3 billion, a third of this amount coming from industry. In 1994, the number of CRADAs in the Department of Energy's laboratories alone passed the 1,000 mark, one year before the Agency's target for enhancing cooperation with industry. However, a backlash appeared in the form of a government commission that recommended that the labs "attend to their knitting" of mission-oriented research and development. The future role of the labs and their participation in CRADA is still in flux. Nevertheless, the CRADA process is institutionalized. Even if some government labs are not seeking out industry partners as actively as before, every government lab is open to offers of cooperation from industry. Around 900 new CRADAs are now established every year in the federal labs.

Private firms have benefited from using advanced facilities and collaborating with highly skilled scientists and engineers. Success stories tell of many new advanced products and technologies. A common outcome is a licensing agreement, where the firm gets exclusive or nonexclusive rights to the research and development result. Cooperative research projects are also beneficial to the federal laboratories, helping them keep their capabilities at a high quality level and reducing the costs of their mission research and development. In addition, industry money enables them to maintain their activity levels in times of budget cuts and other changes. The general point is that an agreement must imply a "win–win" situation and benefit both parties. Both save money by doing the research together rather than separately, and they gain from access to each other's knowledge and facilities.

In the beginning, most CRADAs were formed between research and development centers and large firms, but the share of small firms has been steadily increasing. Some departments report that the small business share is now between a third and a half of all agreements. The contracting arrangements have been made easier, and the larger number of awards under other programs (STTR, ATP, and more) have probably also accounted for the increased involvement of small firms.

The Federally Funded Research and Development Centers and How to Get in Touch with Them

Most federal laboratories, or federally funded research and development centers, are found under the following departments and agencies:

1. Department of Agriculture
2. Department of Commerce
3. Department of Defense
4. Department of Energy
5. Department of Health and Human Services
6. National Aeronautics and Space Administration (who has its own version of CRADAs called Space Act Agreements)
7. National Institutes of Health

The Department of Energy (DOE) manages the largest system of research and development facilities, with an annual budget of more than $6 billion. Some of the biggest are the national laboratories Argonne, Brookhaven, Los Alamos, Oak Ridge, and Sandia, all with several thousand employees and boasting more than twenty Nobel Prize winners all together. Most of these facilities were originally created for the Manhattan Project to develop the atomic bomb during World War II. Although these labs retain considerable responsibilities for nuclear weapons stewardship and environmental cleanup purposes, they have research groups in a vast array of technical and scientific fields. One may find departments in computer science, electronics, materials, and life sciences among the largest laboratories.

Note that although there are more than 700 labs, only a few of them are major players when it comes to CRADAs. Around 70% of the agreements are made with 19 of the labs and 100 labs make virtually all such contracts. A large and active technology transfer office is a good indication of a lab that is interested in forming CRADAs.

When entering into partnerships, DOE follows five simple principles, that are representative for the other agencies as well.

1. Partnerships must directly support departmental missions.
2. They should have the potential to provide economic and other benefits to the nation.
3. They must be formed in a fair and open manner.
4. Best business practices must be used.
5. The results must be measurable.

A good place to start to get an overview of laboratories and the different types of agreements available in a given agency is to identify the subunit with overall responsibility for external agreements. In the DOE, such a starting point is the Technology Partnerships Office. This office provides information on CRADAs and the different laboratories managed by the DOE. Much information is also available on the World Wide Web (see the section "CRADAs on the Web" at the end of this chapter).

Another possibility is naturally to contact the federal laboratory directly. The larger ones have offices for partnerships (e.g., technology transfer offices, industrial technical development centers, offices of research and technology application) that will be able to provide more concrete information about the scientific and technical areas covered at the laboratory. Available licenses and technologies ripe for commercialization are other types of information that could best be received from the research and development centers directly.

If this looks a bit confusing, it is because every lab has its own way of doing external agreements. This was one of the main factors behind the success of CRADAs in the first place. Every research and development center was allowed to enter into agreements using this general format, but could customize the agreements to meet its special needs and those of its industrial partners.

It is important to note that the larger laboratories in most cases also have a good overview of sources of funding (for instance, on their Web pages) and may thus be a good gateway to programs such as the SBIR and ATP. They also often have information on more local funding programs. An example is Argonne National Laboratory that provides facts and advice on special programs in the state of Illinois.

This works the other way around as well. Manufacturing Extension Partnership (MEP) Centers usually are knowledgeable about the competencies of federal labs in their region. The same applies to technical points of contact for the SBIR and STTR programs. Their technical network could very well extend into some of the labs so that they can advise you on where to go to find information or facilities that you need.

How the Agreements Work

The most important step in the process is for the private company and the federal laboratory to come to a common understanding of a research and development project and problem worth undertaking. Ideally, this should be something that contributes to the laboratory attaining its mission, in addition to being useful to the company. Because of budget cuts or changed missions (e.g., nuclear weapons treaties), it is to be expected that the federal research and development centers will be more receptive to external ideas. It is important to be aware that the laboratories do not compete with private industry. They will not take on projects that an industrial firm (or private consultants) would be likely to carry out.

After agreement has been reached on the nature and content of the joint venture, the formal contract should be completed. For most small firms, the shorter version of the standard CRADA contract will apply. Both the short and full form standard contracts are available on the World Wide Web.

The formal legal language might seem like a barrier at first, but the contract is an important document. Especially important are the parts on intellectual property rights and disclosure of information. Small firms especially should be aware that if their attorneys are general practitioners with no special expertise in intellectual property rights, they might advise their clients not to enter into a CRADA. If you feel that the collaboration with a government laboratory is important to your firm, you have two choices. Ideally you will consult an attorney with the requisite special expertise. However, if you cannot afford this option, you may decide after carefully reading the proposed agreement to sign the document and go forward.

Usually, the laboratories will agree not to disclose information for a period of up to five years (e.g., postpone possible scientific publication) until after the project is completed. Often the private firm must agree as well to keep confidential information secret. For many of the research and development centers, special nondisclosure agreements will have to be completed.

The CRADA agreement will spell out the nature of the intellectual property rights determining the disposition of the ownership of the results from the research and development project. Because CRADAs are cost-shared, both parties basically own the results. A common arrangement is a license agreement, where all the revenue that is generated by the research and development results goes to the firm, who in turn pay a fee to the laboratory. An exclusive license means that the laboratory cannot sell the results to anybody else (at least not for the same kind of use), while a nonexclusive deal makes that possible.

Another use of the CRADA mechanism is to commercialize technology developed in federal laboratories. Firms have the opportunity to license technology that has already been developed in federal research and development centers, through both exclusive and nonexclusive deals. Indeed, all larger labs and many smaller ones maintain technology transfer offices to assist companies in making these arrangements. An additional possibility is to arrange to further develop such a technology through a CRADA.

The practical work arrangements, or the *statement of work,* will have to be agreed upon for each project. It is common in CRADAs that some of the firm's employees work at the facilities of the federal research and development center. The opposite is also possible—to have scientists and engineers from the laboratory come and work in the facilities of the firm. In general, one should see to it that the relevant expertise, personnel, and facilities are shared to the benefit of both parties. This could be problematic for the smallest firms that have recently started up, and that do not have much in the way of facilities or equipment. On the other hand, start-up companies may have key people with unique expertise to contribute to a CRADA project.

Finally, there are many other different kinds of possible relationships with the federal laboratories. Acquiring licenses of technology already developed has been mentioned. It is also possible to buy research and development services from the laboratories without entering into a partnership, but the private firms then have to pay all the costs of the research and development project. However, the company may then take full title to the inventions created. Some laboratories, furthermore, offer opportunities of personnel exchange—industry researchers can work at their site, or vice versa, on research of mutual interest but without signing a CRADA.

Last but not least, several federal research and development centers provide short-term technical assistance to companies with technical problems requiring unique expertise. An example is Argonne National Laboratory that provides up to five days of assistance at no cost to the company if a problem is accepted.

Types of Projects—Choose the Right One and Increase the Chances of Success

As mentioned, there are many types of CRADAs available. A typology of the content of agreements could look like this:

1. A window on new technology and an opportunity to be plugged into the scientific and technical network is provided. Some large firms have entered CRADAs to keep in touch with what is happening in

scientific and technical fields that are important to them without necessarily having concrete goals in mind.

2. To solve a large problem: Several of the most well known CRADAs concern a number of labs, large firms, and small firms and involve many technical fields with an aim. For example, to "build a clean car."

3. To solve a concrete problem: This is the common aim of many small firms approaching the labs; they need to get a short-term technical problem solved. Most often CRADAs will not be the best way to do this. Some labs instead offer other types of short-term advice and assistance.

4. To develop a product/technology: This is another common aim of small firms, but these CRADAs can be more difficult to bring to fruition. Some laboratories, such as Sandia, are making a special effort in this direction by establishing incubator facilities and encouraging employees to take leaves of absence to work with a start-up or found a new firm themselves. However, it should be kept in mind that product development is not the strength of most of the labs, but many are willing to make an effort.

5. To validate or test a product or technology: Large proportions of successful small business CRADAs have had such aims. The small firm has developed a technology that does not always behave predictably or that needs to be tested in a certain context. The advanced equipment of many labs, and the expertise in testing, validation, simulation, and so on may make them the right place to go with an already developed technology that has to be improved or better documented before taking it further.

This typology is based on the experience of firms, lab officials, and government officials who have had CRADA responsibility. The message is clear: If you are a small firm, a CRADA agreement concerning product development or solving short-term technical problems is probably not going to work out very well. That is, unless you feel certain that you are on the same technical wavelength as the lab people and that you understand each other completely. Most of the successful agreements with small firms have aimed to test and validate a technology.

Communication is the key to good CRADAs. A number of them fail simply because the firm is not able to state the problem they have in a way that the lab personnel understand, or the technical people in the two parties do not speak the same language. It is best to formulate your problem well before approaching a lab that you think could have the solutions you need.

CRADAs on the Web

There is no "one stop shop" to find information on the national labs. However, some of the addresses below might be helpful to get you started.

http://www.federallabs.org

This is the server of an organization called the Federal Lab Consortium. It contains information on the organization, a "lab locator" where you can find labs in different scientific and technological areas, and a list of technologies available for licensing. Points of contact are listed and there is a page of links to individual labs. To find a lab working in a specific field, submit your areas of interest and then the consortium personnel will advise you further.

http://www.nttc.edu

The National Technology Transfer Center (NTTC), which was established by Congress in 1989, is oriented to match licensable technologies developed in labs and universities with federal funding to the needs of firms. There is a list of technology transfer links and documents (including a description of CRADAs), as well as a number of products and services offered by the organization. Part of the Web site is organized by different technologies (e.g., environmental, manufacturing). You can also find links to other relevant programs such as SBIR solicitations.

http://www.mep.nist.gov

On the Web pages of the Manufacturing Extension Partnership (MEP), there is a list (with links) of MEP centers in each state. These centers should also have knowledge of federal labs in their state or region.

http://www.sba.gov

For a general overview of both federal and state resources oriented at private firms and small business in particular, the Web pages of the Small Business Administration can be a good starting point.

http://www.business.gov

This is the Web site of the U.S. Business Advisor. Its purpose is to provide business with access to federal government information, services, and transactions.

The Small Business Administration

The Small Business Administration (SBA) is the federal agency founded in 1953 to assist small business. It is now responsible for administrating the SBIR and STTR programs in the participating federal agencies. Although SBA is a federal agency, through its local units it can also be regarded as a source of help and a guide to funding sources at the state level. SBA has a central organization, but it provides valuable assistance to small businesses through offices or centers in each state and district. SBA is oriented toward helping small firms with funding and advice.

In this next section, the following will be presented:

1. The Small Business Administration in brief
2. SBA at the local and regional level
3. Main SBA financial programs
4. Centers and other programs
5. SBA and other similar small business resources on the Web

The Small Business Administration in Brief

There are Small Business Administration offices and program offices in all states, as well as the District of Columbia, the Virgin Islands, and Puerto Rico. Congress created SBA in 1953 to help America's entrepreneurs form successful small enterprises. Its main functions are to improve small firms' access to financing through banks and to make advice, information, and training available to small firms at the local level. To get help from the SBA, the firm must be independently owned and operated, not dominant within its field, and fall within certain size standards. The size standards vary according to the type of business. 500 employees are a common limit but in some businesses, firms can have up to 1,000 employees and still be eligible for support from the SBA. In other industries, such as agriculture, limits are based on revenue, which can vary from $500,000 to $5 million.

It is important to be aware that you will not get "free" money in the form of start-up or expansion grants. The SBA provides financial assistance in the form of loan guarantees rather than direct loans. In 1995, the SBA had a portfolio guaranteeing over $27 billion in loans to 185,000 small businesses. In that year alone, the Small Business Administration guaranteed over 60,000 loans totaling $9.9 billion. In the same year, management and technical assistance were provided to nearly 1,000,000 small businesses through Small Business Development Centers and the Service Corps of Retired Executives volunteers.

SBA at the Local and Regional Level

In addition to the central administration in Washington, there are both regional and district offices. The regional offices also have mainly administrative responsibilities, plus some educational and networking tasks. The SBA district offices, on the other hand, are the points of delivery for most SBA programs and services.

Bear in mind, though, that many of the SBA programs are offered through distinct organizations. Small Business Development Centers and the Service Corps of Retired Executives have already been mentioned. There are also centers oriented toward businesses owned by women, companies run by native Americans, socially and economically disadvantaged businesses, and more. The closest field office of the SBA should be able to lead you in the right direction.

Almost all the different centers are found locally in states and cities. There are more than 900 Small Business Development Centers. For the firms, the federal level of the SBA will function mainly as a gateway to more locally available information and service.

Main SBA Financial Programs

As mentioned above, one of the most important functions of the SBA is to guarantee loans to small businesses that cannot obtain financing on reasonable terms through normal lending channels. In general, the basic guarantee program is used to fund varied long-term needs of small firms. Loans are available for many business purposes, such as real estate, expansion, equipment, working capital, or inventory. For loans of $100,000 or less, the SBA can guarantee 80% of the loan amount. When the loan is larger, the guarantee rate is 75% for up to $750,000. The interest rate is not to exceed 2.75 over the prime lending rate. For working capital, maturities are up to 10 years, and up to 25 years for fixed assets.

Another interesting loan program is called low documentation loans, where the purpose is to reduce the paperwork involved in loan requests of $150,000 or less. Here, the SBA uses a one page application and relies on the strength of the individual applicant's character and credit history. However, the applicant must first satisfy all of the lender's requirements. For start-ups or firms about to expand, a pilot program called Microloan can furnish the company with short-term loans of up to $25,000 for the purchase of machinery and equipment, furniture and fixtures, inventory, supplies, and working capital. The amount cannot be used to pay existing debts, and the loans are made through SBA-approved nonprofit groups who also provide counseling and educational assistance.

Yet another general loan program is oriented toward short-term, cyclical working-capital needs. There are also several programs that in different ways encourage and give incentives to selected banks or venture capital institutions across the nation to make more loans to the small business community. Under some of these programs, lending institutions are licensed to work with the SBA. These are called Small Business Investment Companies (SBICs), of which there are almost 300. Your nearest SBA district office or Small Business Development Center will be able to provide more information.

Furthermore, there are two prequalification loan programs, oriented toward women-owned and minority-owned small businesses. In these programs, the SBA can prequalify a guarantee for loan applications of

$250,000 or less before the applicant goes to a bank. This means that the applicant's reliability, credit, experience, and such are in focus rather than assets. Note, however, that these two programs are not available everywhere; again, the district office will be the information source. The rest of the loan programs are oriented toward small, defense-oriented firms that have been adversely affected by defense cuts, and small, export-ready businesses. The SBA also provides disaster assistance if the firm is affected by a natural (nonagricultural) disaster.

Centers and Other Programs

Small Business Development Centers (SBDC) are a cooperative effort of the private sector, the educational community, and federal, state, and local governments, but the SBDC program is administered by the SBA. The centers provide management and, in some cases, technical assistance to current and prospective small business owners, as well as a wide variety of information and guidance. There are currently more than 950 service locations nationwide, with 57 lead SBDCs, which are a good source of information on SBA programs in general.

The SBDCs are mainly administered at the state level and have different services that are often targeted toward the type of firms found locally. Some centers give technical advice, others focus on business plans and funding, and some on both. They also offer courses, for instance, in writing business plans which will be required if you are applying for a loan in a bank and will use an SBA loan guarantee. All the advice and services offered are free, although a few of the centers charge a small fee for some of their courses. The centers are found on campuses of colleges and universities, and they will often have good ties to both the local technical and financial community.

Another type of center is the Business Information Center, described as SBA's technology toolbox where the latest in high-tech hardware, software, and telecommunications is provided for the help of small businesses. There are around 40 such centers in operation. The Service Corps of Retired Executives (SCORE), which is a program that matches volunteers with small businesses that need expert advice, provide counseling and training in the centers. SCORE is sponsored by SBA, and management and technical advice are shared free of charge with present and prospective owners and managers of small firms. In 1995, there were 388 local SCORE chapters with nearly 13,000 members also servicing 800 other locations.

There are special SBA programs that support centers, providing advice and information. These are especially oriented toward businesses owned and operated by women through 58 women's business centers, veterans (most through the Department of Veteran Affairs), Native Americans through several reservation-based Tribal Information Centers, and socially and economically disadvantaged businesses and communities (important here are the so-called one-stop capital shops).

Although these are not necessarily directly oriented toward small firms in general, the SBA runs several federal procurement programs. A common purpose of these is to make it easier for small businesses to participate in competitions for government contracts. Many activities are directed toward federal agencies, urging them to break out of historically sole-source contracts typically given out to large firms and informing them about the small business community. Small firms that have been denied government contracts for perceived lack of ability, may find interest in a program that can provide them with a certificate of competency. A computerized, national database of small businesses that are interested in federal procurement opportunities is also maintained by the SBA program.

Finally, there are some nationwide information programs. In 1983, the Answer Desk was established, a semiautomatic telephone service where callers are helped with questions about starting and running businesses. Counselors are available Monday through Friday, 9:00 a.m. through 5:00 p.m., Eastern Time. The service is open to the general public, and the toll free telephone number is (800) U-ASK-SBA. Furthermore, a library of business management publications, videos, and computer programs is also produced and maintained by the SBA. The library items are available by mail for a small fee. Publications that cover the different SBA programs and services are sent free of charge. Last, but not least—considerable information is available on-line. The SBA has its own electronic bulletin board and an extensive World Wide Web site. Relevant addresses are listed at the end of the section. Of interest here is also the U.S. Business Advisor, a Web site that functions as a single link to all the business information and services that the government provides.

In addition to the above, the SBA administers the SBIR and STTR programs, which are covered in Chapter 5 of this book. These programs have been initiated to make sure that small firms receive a fair share of federal research and development funding.

SBA and Other Similar Small Business Resources on the Web

The SBA Web site, http://www.sba.gov, is comprehensive with much information and many links. Help for small firms is organized under the headings "starting," "funding," and "expanding" in addition to other links to disaster assistance and the SBIR/STTR programs. An on-line library with SBA publications and files is found on the site.

There are links to all SBA regional and district offices shown on a U.S. map. On their Web pages you will find information on local activities, such as conferences, courses, and the Service Corps of Retired Executives in your area. Many of the local and regional resources have their own Web pages, and the links to them can be found on the SBA's local resource pages.

SBA has made its own small business start-up kit. In the kit which is available on-line you will find information concerning several topics. The index, with links, can be found on the CD-ROM accompanying this volume.

1. Is entrepreneurship for you?
2. Getting started (e.g., types of businesses)
3. Finding funding
4. Regulations (e.g., as related to intellectual property rights)
5. SBA assistance
6. Local sources of assistance

On the page http://www.sba.gov/inv, you will find lists of all SBA approved Small Business Investment Companies (SBICs) by state, with contact information (text file with no links). At http://www.sba.gov/sbdc you can find out more about the Small Business Development Centers (SBDCs). There is a list of centers in all states with information about getting in touch with them.

Another interesting Web page is the U.S. Business Advisor, found at the URL http://www.business.gov. This is a gateway to all information and resources provided by the government.

The home page of the Service Corps of Retired Executives (SCORE) is http://www.score.org. Apart from information about SCORE, the page is a starting point for getting "e-mail counseling." There is also information about workshops, success stories, and a list of frequently asked questions (FAQs). You have the opportunity to find the SCORE chapter closest to you by entering your zip code. A map with the closest SCORE chapter plotted onto it is returned. This site is also comprehensive and a good starting point for finding small business resources on the Web. Since SCORE is a nonprofit organization, it might be a better place to start than many of the small business sites run by consulting companies and others that primarily offer specific products.

Manufacturing-Oriented Programs

There are two central programs oriented toward improvements in manufacturing and technologies: the Manufacturing Extension Partnership (MEP) and the Department of Defense's Manufacturing Technology Program (ManTech). Like the Small Business Administration, MEP is neither purely federal nor does it belong only at the state level. It has federal support and a central organization, providing assistance to firms through regional and local centers. MEP is a program that has been started to make it easier for small manufacturers to upgrade to modern methods and technologies in production and management. ManTech is focused upon improvements (i.e., costs, time, quality, etc.) in the manufacturing of weapon systems in a few broad technological areas. While most of the MEP services will have to be paid for, ManTech funding can in some cases be received as pure grants, without cost to the firm.

In this section, the following will be presented:

1. A brief presentation of MEP
2. Federal and local levels working together
3. MEP centers at the state level
4. Services offered by MEP centers
5. The Manufacturing Extension Partnership on the Web
6. The ManTech program in brief
7. Major thrusts and technologies of ManTech
8. ManTech funding and industry cost-sharing
9. ManTech on the Web

A Brief Presentation of MEP

The Manufacturing Extension Partnership is oriented toward small and medium-sized manufacturers. In short, MEP is a national system of community and state-based nonprofit organizations and related services that provides small manufacturers with access to resources, information, and expertise, both public and private, to increase their use of modern manufacturing practices, technologies, and techniques.

Apart from two national centers, all services in the MEP are locally driven. The partnership program does receive federal support, however, although mostly for outreach activities. MEP's headquarters can be found in the Department of Commerce's National Institute of Standards and Technology (NIST) in Gaithersburg, Maryland, near Washington, DC. State and federal support for MEP totaled $70 million in 1992. More than 60,000 firms have been helped by MEP since it was started at the end of the 1980s.

Improving national competitiveness is the mission behind MEP. The background of the program is that many small manufacturers have been slow in modernizing their activities. MEP's purpose is thus to provide new and cutting-edge technology, production techniques, and business practices, giving small firms the opportunity to network with others in the same situation and gain benchmarking insights. It is also asserted that consultants are mainly targeting larger firms, making it more difficult for the smaller ones to get high-quality, unbiased advice and assistance. Increased cooperation between states and between local organizations is also a desirable outcome for the federal government.

As with the SBA programs, MEP does not hand out money. Although the MEP centers receive federal and often state and local support, all services must be paid for. The advantage is that small manufacturers are able to adopt the newest technologies and practices that are developed nationwide. Preliminary evaluations indicate that MEP is succeeding in making small manufacturers more competitive.

Federal and Local Levels Working Together

Many MEP activities were initiated at the state level after officials realized the importance to local economic development of growing your own firms rather than relying on attracting firms to relocate by providing subsidies. States had for many years sought information, coordination, and support for manufacturing extension from federal government. There was also a growing awareness at the federal level of support provided by governments of global competitors (e.g., the Fraunhofer system in Germany and the Kohsetsushi centers in Japan). There was also national interest in keeping small manufacturers as a vital portion of the U.S. economy. Thus, the federal government provided funds and assistance to help states develop plans for manufacturing extension services.

In 1988, Congress directed NIST to begin helping the nation's smaller manufacturers adopt and apply performance-improving technologies as needed to meet intensifying domestic and global competition in manufacturing. NIST was selected because of its expertise in manufacturing engineering and its long-standing tradition of productive partnerships forged with public and private organizations at the national, state, and local levels.

A variety of regional, national, and program development activities are conducted. Regionally, MEP works with the states or local organizations to establish manufacturing extension centers or expand existing services that assist smaller manufacturers. Future centers are cultivated through MEP's State Technology Extension Program, which enables states to research, plan, and begin building the organizational relationships needed to deliver manufacturing extension services. All states now participate in the program. At the national level, MEP is developing a uniform system to help centers evaluate and continuously improve the services they offer.

To increase the breadth and depth of capabilities at each center and of the entire network, MEP and the individual centers have developed relationships with nearly 700 different organizations. Among these partners are nonprofit technology or business assistance centers, nonprofit economic development organizations, community colleges and technical schools, private consultants, universities and four-year colleges, and federal agencies. A national example is that, together with the U.S. Environmental Protection Agency, MEP recently launched a program aimed at helping smaller manufacturers solve environmental concerns in the most cost-effective manner—before they become problems requiring regulatory or compliance action.

The partnering organizations are also increasingly seeing the MEP network as a means of delivering other critical services to the small and medium-sized manufacturers that previously have been hard to reach. Linking the centers also gives the opportunity to achieve economies of scale, share best practices, and learn new techniques. In other words, national technology and information resources come to the state and local level, and the local technology and resources are being made available nationwide.

MEP Centers at the State Level

MEP-affiliated centers and their regional outreach offices are located in all 50 states and Puerto Rico. There are approximately 300 regional offices delivering services to manufacturers nationwide, and 78 extension centers. The number of centers has been steadily growing, after merit-based competition. All new extension systems compete for MEP funding, and proposals are judged on industry need, market awareness, and service commitment and delivery.

In total, around 2,000 field engineers and other specialists, with hands-on manufacturing experience, work at the centers and their outreach offices. The centers are led by industry boards, and all have state organizations as partners. Furthermore, all receive federal support, but federal funds cannot be used to pay for the services provided. Centers can use the funds to bring down the cost of change, to perform research, or to conduct worker training. The centers charge fees for these services or for the use of other resources. Federal support primarily covers outreach activities. Still, all centers are nonprofit organizations, often found on university and college campuses.

Services Offered by MEP Centers

Centers provide direct services to smaller manufacturers in areas such as production techniques, technology applications, and business practices. Solutions are offered through a combination of direct assistance from center staff and outside consultants. Because of the large difference between states and regions in the country, each center has tailored its services to meet the needs dictated by its location and manufacturing client base. Still, some common services are offered by most extension centers. These include helping manufacturers assess their current technology and business needs, define avenues for change, and implement improvements.

All centers will also encourage clients to establish continuous improvement programs instead of using the MEP services to solve one particular problem. MEP centers do not force companies to work with them. Companies that are interested in modernization must show that they have the commitment and willingness to invest the resources necessary to initiate and implement improvements.

The typical first project that a center undertakes would be an assessment to analyze the company's current operations and identify opportunities for improvement. Subsequent projects might be in the area of quality assurance, business information systems, production process improvements, plant layout, market development, computer-aided design, computer integrated manufacturing, waste reduction, environmental services, material engineering, workforce development, rapid prototyping, or other manufacturing priorities.

Some of the MEP-affiliated centers also offer other services, similar to those of the Small Business Administration's SBDCs. For example, some MEP centers offer support to small businesses related to finding funding for innovative activities. The centers could be a good source of information on various local programs that, although they often are small, could be important steps for winning the larger SBIR and ATP grants.

The Manufacturing Extension Partnership on the Web

The URL of MEP is http://www.mep.nist.gov. It is a brief introduction to the program and the services that are offered. There are a number of success stories available on-line, as well as links to other manufacturing resources on the Web.

Probably the most useful page on the Web site is a list of all MEP centers, accessible both through a clickable U.S. map and a text listing. Each center also has its own information page with data on the particular services offered, its location, and how to get in touch with that center. Most of the local centers have also set up their own Web pages now, which can be accessed through the central information pages. The clickable text list of centers is also found on the accompanying CD-ROM, along with some short files presenting the MEP and what it can do for you.

The ManTech Program in Brief

The Department of Defense's Manufacturing Technology Program (ManTech) is a large military program with an annual budget of almost $150 million. The main focus is on new manufacturing technologies that can reduce costs, improve quality, and otherwise make the production of weapon systems more efficient. Although it focuses on affordable, low-risk development and production of weapon systems, many of the previous ManTech projects have been dual use—the technologies have had both military and civilian applications.

Pure research and development of prototype projects are normally not considered by this program. ManTech starts with a manufacturing technology that has proven its feasibility at the laboratory level, but has not yet been taken a step further. Since a working prototype is often the result of an SBIR Phase II grant, ManTech could be a good source of funding after a military SBIR grant has been successfully used.

The program has three objectives. First, in the weapon system design phase, the objective is to assure design for so-called six-sigma manufacturing (low variability). Second, in the production phase, the objective is to emphasize low cost, high quality manufacturing, efficient factory operations, and supplier interactions, and the decoupling of unit cost from production volume. Third, in the support and maintenance phase, the objective is to concentrate on efficient repair processes, rapid, low-cost spare and replacement parts acquisition, and efficient maintenance and repair operations. The prime rationale for the program is that there is a large potential for reducing non-value-added costs in typical defense companies compared to top performing, world class manufacturing companies. Projects are selected based on their opportunities for cost reductions and their possibilities of accelerating progress toward commercial viability.

ManTech has a broader target than MEP. ManTech projects are executed with all types of organizations such as prime contractors, subcontractors, suppliers, hardware and software vendors, industrial consortia, centers of excellence, universities, and research institutes. Still, the ManTech program managers work closely with and deliver information and services to the Manufacturing Extension Centers of the MEP.

There is also frequent collaboration with the DARPA, NASA, the Department of Commerce, the Department of Energy, and the National Science Foundation. In other words, if you have SBIR grants from nonmilitary sources like NASA, DOC, DOE, and NSF, ManTech could still be a relevant source of Phase III funding. In some cases, award winners have also managed to receive additional funding from other federal sources in connection with a ManTech project (e.g., from acquisition programs in the DOC and DOE).

There are four players in the ManTech budget: the Defense Logistics Agency (DLA), the Army, the Navy, and the Air Force. The two latter are the big ones, contributing more than 80% of the program's funding. The funding for the ManTech program has been decreasing since the mid 1990s, but now seems to have stabilized between $130 million and $140 million annually. The president's budget request for fiscal year 1999 plans to keep the funding at this level until 2003.

Major Thrusts and Technologies of ManTech

The program is structured around three major thrusts:

1. Manufacturing and engineering systems, which is concerned with techniques to model and improve the manufacturing enterprise;
2. Processing and fabrication, which involves improvements to manufacturing processes on the shop floor with an emphasis on process maturation in the areas of composites, electronics, and metals; and

3. Advanced industrial practices, concerned with the implementation of world-class, best practices to create major improvements in cost, cycle time, and quality.

There are six main technology areas:

1. *Metals Processing and Fabrication*   Focuses on manufacturing science and technology related to performing accurate and repeatable processing of metals and other materials that use the same processes.

2. *Composites Processing and Fabrication*   Coordinates all manufacturing technology development efforts for all types of composite materials and structures (polymer matrix composites, ceramic matrix composites, metal matrix composites, and carbon matrix composites).

3. *Electronics Processing and Fabrication*   Concerned with manufacturing and processing technology for electronic materials, devices, integrated circuits, subassemblies, and subsystems.

4. *Advanced Manufacturing Enterprise*   Addresses benchmarking, advanced manufacturing management, supply base management and technology, and manufacturing and engineering systems with a view toward advancing the defense industrial enterprise toward full integration with world-class engineering systems and industrial practices.

5. *Sustainment and Readiness*   Addresses critical repair processes, systems, and related manufacturing issues for Department of Defense weapon systems.

6. *Energetics and Munitions*   Focuses on developing safe, environmentally acceptable, and affordable manufacturing technologies for energetic materials and munitions.

You can find contact information within a number of specific technological areas on ManTech's Web pages. It could also be rewarding to get in touch with military acquisition and logistics program managers because they are the main customers of ManTech.

For each of these areas, a Defense Technical Area Plan is made by relevant personnel. The plan also contains concrete objectives as to what the ManTech program should aim to achieve in the upcoming five-year period. Because there is no central solicitation or invitation to compete for awards in ManTech, the technical areas will be your gateway to more information about how to apply for funding from the program.

ManTech Funding and Industry Cost Share

The program does not normally fund feasibility studies at the laboratory level. The costs of capital equipment and facilities necessary to implement the technology, above an incidental level, are not allowed as ManTech costs. ManTech provides seed funding to encourage the expenditure of industry funds to bring new technology to the manufacturing enterprise and, generally, this funding represents a minor portion of the total cost.

Awards are made on the basis of competition. In general, all awards require cost-sharing in which the ratio of recipient cost to Government cost is two to one. However, there are two important exceptions to this rule: If the technology (1) is not likely to have any immediate and direct commercial application (it is not dual use, or at least not in the near future) or (2) is sufficiently high risk to discourage cost sharing by non-federal government sources, the requirements for cost-sharing could be lowered. Another potential exclusion to the cost sharing requirement is if the project will be carried out by an institution of higher education.

This means that the extent of cost-sharing is directly proportional to the near-term benefits companies receive and inversely proportional to the level of business risk. The objective is to ensure that ManTech fully funds only those things that are defense-essential and beyond the normal risk of industry. In other words, ManTech funding can, in some cases, be awarded as grants with no requirements for funding from other sources.

Of course, many of the ManTech projects have been dual use, and hence, have required the recipient to come up with some funding of its own. Several projects have concerned the production of advanced parts for military equipment on commercial manufacturing lines. However, if your technology is at this stage of development with both military and civilian applications, you may be able to get the interest of the private venture capital community as well.

ManTech on the Web

The ManTech Web site can be found at http://mantech.iitri.org. It is quite comprehensive, well structured, and frequently updated. The common features of federal technology programs' Web sites are here. An overview of the program, links to other programs, information on points of contact, and a number of success stories can be found.

There are several documents describing the technology thrust areas in more detail, including clear and concrete technological and manufacturing objectives for the next five years and levels of funding. These files are included on the CD-ROM that accompanies this book. A comprehensive list of publications can be found, which is also included on the CD-ROM, such as the program's plan for the next five years.

The Army Advanced Concepts & Technology II Program

Another military program relevant to entrepreneurs and innovative firms, is the Advanced Concepts & Technology II Program, referred to as ACT II.

The purpose of this initiative is to "push mature technologies" out of the laboratory and into military applications. On the average between 25 and 30 projects have been selected annually for awards of up to $1.5 million. Although the awards can be large, it is an extremely competitive process.

In this section, the following will be presented:

1. A brief look at the ACT II program
2. How and when to apply
3. ACT II on the Web

A Brief Look at the ACT II Program

The program was started in fiscal year 1994, and to date (spring 1999), 125 projects have received funding. ACT II is described as a partnership between different Army organizations such as the U.S. Army Training and Doctrine Command (TRADOC), battle labs, and the Army's research, development, and acquisition community.

The only common denominators of technologies that have received support are that they in one way or another have been of interest to the Army to improve defense capabilities. Previous awards have been made in fuel cell technology, laser radar technology, and hands-free wireless communications technology, as well as in decision support systems and training systems.

The program provides funding to demonstrate the technical feasibility of such technologies that, if successful, may

1. Shape TRADOC requirements
2. Be integrated into existing Army research and development programs
3. Be selected for the Army Rapid Acquisition Program
4. Transition directly to an existing end item

The maximum award size is $1.5 million and the planned period of performance is not to exceed one year. This means that ACT II targets technology at a different stage of development than, for instance, the SBIR program, where the award size is half of ACT II but the project time is twice as long. Funded projects are targeted to specific battle lab demonstrations to determine their war-fighting contributions. ACT II projects are frequently cost-shared or leveraged efforts, partly supported by others.

How and When to Apply

Like most other programs of this type, awards are made on a competitive basis. Each year a Broad Agency Announcement (BAA) is released, usually in May. In the BAA, the specific technical topics that are in focus that fiscal year are described. The technical topics are developed by personnel in different laboratories and other organizations. On the ACT II Web site there is information about whom to contact in various battle labs. ACT II is a mission-oriented program, and it is unlikely that projects will get funded if they do not contribute to Army goals and technological aims.

The BAA for fiscal year 2000 opened in late April 1999. However, one month earlier, it was released in draft form. In other words, the topics are available earlier than in the BAA. The closing date of the announcement and the deadline for proposals is early June.

ACT II has an application process that differs from most other programs described in this book. The ACT II process has two phases.

In the first phase, potential applicants are asked to submit two-page concept papers in response to that year's technical topics. The deadline is a month after the release of the BAA. The concept papers are evaluated for technical merit and war-fighting contribution.

This results in an invitation to the most promising proposers to submit full proposals, with a deadline in July (or a month after the concept paper deadline). Such proposals are similar to those of many other programs; they are limited to 25 pages plus a cost estimate. A final evaluation results in a small selection of proposals to fund. The entire process takes around four months. In other words, the process is relatively quick and not very time-consuming to begin with.

However, the success rates are low, comparable to the SBIR program or even lower. In fiscal year 1999, 420 concept papers were received. After the first evaluation, approximately 100 applicants were asked to submit full proposals. Of these, 17 projects received funding in the end. Thus, the success rate is about 17% if we only count the full proposals, and much lower if you count the concept papers of the first phase. Annual program funding has varied from $10 million to $40 million in earlier years, so it is difficult to know how hard the competition is going to be until the final budgets are settled.

ACT II on the Web

The program's Web site is found on http://www.aro.ncren.net/arowash/rt/actii.htm. It does not contain much information apart from the broad agency announcement, which also includes the relevant forms for submitting a proposal. As with many other programs of this kind, the success examples and program accomplishments take up a large part of the total Web space. In brief, the ACT II Web site contains the following:

1. Program description
2. Success stories (program accomplishments)
3. Some publications
4. The broad agency announcement

5. Information about the program in previous years with listing of awards to date

6. Points of contact

Conclusion

The above programs represent a "patchwork quilt" that has grown up since World War II. Nevertheless, these programs have several common elements: a focus on small firms as central to technology development, economic growth, and job creation; a mechanism for collaborative projects among small and large firms; and a presence among firms, universities, national laboratories, and not-for-profit organizations. Although many of these programs began with the idea of applying science to the development of technology, programs have also been created starting from specific technological needs, initially in the military but now increasingly in civilian areas.

There is an underlying common theme to all these programs that technology development is central both to national defense and economic and social development. Moreover, over time, national security and economic and social development are increasingly related. Indeed, several new programs have recently been created to increase these interconnections.

These ideas to promote innovation and entrepreneurship may seem commonplace and accepted wisdom at present. However, the idea that government should play a role in association with industry and academia in fostering the introduction of new technology, especially into civilian industry, is still controversial to many.

Indeed, in the discussions within the committee that produced *Science: The Endless Frontier* (Bush Report) in 1944, just before the close of World War II, the potential role of government in developing small technology-based firms was discussed. The committee was split. Some felt that the government could play a useful role, others not. In hindsight, we can see that the United States has developed both a role for government in the sponsorship of basic research in academia and in technology development in industry and links between these two efforts that has made the U.S. economy the world's most dynamic.

PART III
THE EVOLUTION OF PUBLIC VENTURE CAPITAL

Congressional pressure on the National Science Foundation (NSF), the U.S.'s basic research funding agency founded in 1952, arose in the 1970s to make research funds more available to small businesses. In response, Roland Tibbets, a program officer at NSF, and his colleagues, invented the prototype for the Small Business Innovation Research Program (SBIR). This new program synthesized NSF's classic peer review procedures with the nurturing culture of the early venture capital industry.

Through a highly competitive process, the SBIR funds high-tech start-ups and other innovative small firms to move their research toward the market, solve government technical problems, or combine both tasks. Why does the federal government support entrepreneurs and innovative small businesses? How has this traditionally been accomplished? Why have SBIR, ATP, CRADAs, and Dual Use become the main mechanisms for support of innovation? What is the story behind the evolution of public entrepreneurship?

Public entrepreneurship would appear to be a contradiction in terms. Is not the entrepreneur the classic private sector personality who takes risks against great odds to realize an innovation? Is not the bureaucrat the classic public sector personality who administers the minutia of existing rules and regulations?

Nevertheless, just as bureaucrats can be found in business, entrepreneurs can be found in government. For example, in the late 1960s and early 1970s, government patent counsels, Norman Latker at NIH and Jesse Lasken at NSF, devised an administrative process to turn over ownership of intellectual property rights to universities that established technology transfer and patent licensing offices.

The reluctance of companies to utilize the practical outcomes of government-funded academic research was overcome by giving them a place to go to obtain a clear right to commercialize. When Secretary of Health, Education, and Welfare, Joseph Califano, halted the process on the grounds that it was contrary to the principle of free dissemination of knowledge, the two patent counsels informally called upon the legislative process. They advised members of a network of universities and small businesses, passing the Bayh-Dole Act of 1980, a charter for university technology transfer that made their earlier administrative innovation into law. Jesse Lasken, who drafted the bill, later said, "It is probably the most important thing I have done in my 30 years in government."[1]

Since the passage of the Bayh-Dole Act, government agencies have continued to make strides in the realm of public venture capital. In 1999, the CIA announced the establishment of a non-profit subsidiary company, "In Q-It," that will provide funds to develop new companies in information technology fields of interest to the agency ("CIA Makes Foray Into Venture Capital," *New York Times*, Wednesday, September 29, 1999, p. 1). Through the formation of this new venture capital company by a government agency, a formerly indirect process has become open and direct. Nevertheless, the $28 million that In-Q-It has available for investment, by itself and in cooperation with partners, is a small amount in comparison to the several billions of dollars collectively available from other government agencies.

Overview

To understand the evolution of public venture capital, it is necessary to answer several questions:

- Why did the federal government decide to support industrial innovation?
- How did this become a government task?
- Why were the programs described in this book established?

The following chapters undertake to answer these questions:

Chapter 8: The Origins of Federal Responsibility for Innovation—Describes the role of the government as given by the Constitution, the roles of university and military research as they evolved, and the diffusion of technology over time.

Chapter 9: The U.S. Government Research and Development Funding System—Describes the various models that have developed in the U.S. to support science and technology.

Chapter 10: Modes of Government Intervention—Describes the three main modes of science and technology policy: linear model; hidden or indirect industrial policy; and recent experiments in direct intervention.

Chapter 11: Conclusion: Science Policy as Industrial Policy—Discusses the government's rationale for its role in industrial policy.

Notes

1. Etzkowitz, Henry (1998), "Tech Transfer Cornerstone: The Pre-History of the Bayh–Dole Act I," *Technology Access Report*, June (11: 6, pp. 12, 13); "Tech Transfer Cornerstone: Passing the Bayh-Dole Act II" *Technology Access Report*, November (11:11, p. 10) and December (11:12, p. 11).

CHAPTER 8 · THE ORIGINS OF FEDERAL RESPONSIBILITY FOR INNOVATION

CONTENTS

THE ORIGINS OF FEDERAL RESPONSIBILITY FOR INNOVATION

Introduction

There is no official U.S. innovation policy. However, there is a U.S. innovation system, which has evolved from a number of historical occurrences, including:

1. The patent clause in the Constitution and later initiatives to promote inventions
2. Exploration of natural resources after new lands were acquired
3. Farmers' need to improve crops
4. Universities' role in assisting agriculture
5. Depression-inspired programs—"electrification," housing, and household appliances
6. World War II military needs
7. Postwar initiatives

The Patent Clause in the Constitution

With the exception of the Office of Scientific Research and Development, which formed as a result of World War II, the United States has not had a government agency with overarching responsibility for research and development. Nevertheless, an industrial policy is outlined in the Constitution in the form of a patent system to encourage invention and protect inventors rights.[1] The Constitution states that: "The Congress shall have the power to promote the progress of science and useful arts by securing for limited times to authors and inventors the exclusive rights to their respective rights and discoveries." With no recorded debate, paragraph 8, section 8 of article 1 was included late in the deliberations of the constitutional convention, perhaps inspired by inventor John Fitch's demonstration of a steamboat to members of the convention on August 22, 1787.

In an early instance of patent harmonization, a single format was mandated "...to provide patents as wide as the nation to support markets as large as the nation," according to a recent observer.[2] Individual states had previously granted monopolies to inventors of new technology and developers of existing technology through specific laws, but these were, of course, not valid outside their boundaries.

Even without providing funds, the usual indicator of a government policy, government encouraged innovation by establishing the rules of the game. George Washington, for example, supported importation of inventions and encouragement of invention at home in a section of his 1790 State of the Union address that we would now call "technology transfer and innovation policy." Congress then implemented the constitutional clause, passing a patent statute with procedures giving individual inventors state sanction to reap the benefits of their intellectual property. However, this right was later partially taken away by the creation of corporate laboratories that required employees to sign over their rights.

The use of intellectual property rights, both as a regulatory mechanism and as an incentive system, is a significant theme of industrial policy to this day. The patent system encouraged exchange of information, through disclosure and litigation, drawing together "the inventors in one part of the country with the local innovators in another."[3] Abraham Lincoln, the only President to be awarded a patent, believed that patenting added "...the fuel of interest to the fire of genius."[4] Indeed, the Bayh–Dole Act of 1980, discussed below, renewed the original intention of the Constitution by guaranteeing a share of the reward from invention to individual academic inventors and their employers.

Exploration of Natural Resources

Early 19th-century presidents and congressional leaders promulgated a series of earth sciences initiatives, reflecting the fact that one of the most important issues the country faced was to identify its natural resources. Even though it was purchased for a nominal fee, the land was essentially taken from its previous inhabitants and systematically explored and used. This required scientific investigation, such as the Lewis and Clark expedition to survey the Northwest. President Jefferson sent Lewis to Philadelphia to meet with scientific leaders and train in the different fields of science that would be needed to collect useful information.[5] Research in the earth sciences was also supported through the foundation of the Coast and Geodetic Survey to map coastal waters for shipping and commerce.

Meeting Farmers' Needs

U.S. industrial policy was also propelled by social movements. For example, farmers in the early 19th century who were interested in using science to improve farming methods established "test plots" on their farms. However, when they realized that as individual farmers they could not do systematic research, they pressed their state legislators to find ways to organize research on their behalf. In 1816, Connecticut established the first Agricultural Experiment Station as a result of this pressure from below.[6]

However, as in most cases of successful pressure for state intervention, the activity was not undertaken directly by the federal government. Rather than establishing institutes for agricultural research, the federal government contributed, along with the states, to the establishment of agricultural research units at universities in each state. This is a model of decentralized centralization typical of U.S. government intervention, not only in the economy but in social policy and other areas as well.[7]

The Role of the University

Even though the United States lacked a national university system, research universities, both public and private, became performers of federal government sponsored-research, undertaking other public tasks as well. Institutions of higher education were adapted to disseminate research findings as well as older knowledge. The initial colonial colleges were oriented toward classical learning with Latin, Greek, and mathematics emphasized, to prepare ministers and other professionals. The classical academic format was adapted in new institutions to teach practical knowledge in agriculture and related scientific disciplines. The first state university to teach agriculture was established in Connecticut, and then, since resources were limited, it was decided to link the experiment station to the university and have the same people who were responsible for investigation also engage in teaching.

A dissemination model was created that connects research to users, not only through the teaching of students, but also through a system of agents mediating between farmers and researchers. Extension agents sought out problems that the farmers faced, brought them back to the university for investigation, and then assisted farmers in introducing research findings into practice. In effect, at that time they invented the feedback loops in innovation between researchers and users that we are still trying to rediscover at this point in connection with industrial innovation.

In undertaking government tasks, universities also influenced the direction of government policy by interpreting their mission broadly. Thus, some applied research programs took on basic attributes once funds were provided. Although the emphasis continued to be on solving local problems, academic researchers were able to set their own research direction to a large degree. Taking off on their own ideas, they expressed their interest in fundamental research rather than sticking to the narrow definition under which they were funded. Thus, researchers justified their involvement in genetics research on the grounds of eventual contribution to agriculture, a claim that was eventually borne out with the development of hybrid corn.

Depression-Era Initiatives

Social policy was carried out through technology diffusion by the Roosevelt administration during the 1930s. A major objective of the New Deal was to speed the spread of existing technology such as refrigerators, heating and cooking technologies, radios, and other electrical appliances to a broad range of the population. By inducing suppliers of electricity and manufacturers of appliances to lower their costs, a broader market was created. As a result, production of devices increased and thus social policy also became industrial policy.

The goal of government policy was to raise the standard of living through electrical modernization. Good housing and access to electrical appliances were the prerequisite of a relatively small proportion of the population during the prosperity of the 1920s. These benefits were spread to broader segments of the population through federal housing and mortgage programs that set national standards for construction and installation of electricity in dwellings during the 1930s depression. Programs such as the FHA (Federal Housing Authority) subsidized loans for persons who would never have previously met banking requirements for home ownership. Although people still dealt with their local banks, the standards by which these financial institutions operated and the composition of their clientele were transformed by government initiatives.

The Role of Military Research

The next major federal science and technology (S&T) initiative came from an academically elite group, scientists and engineers who had worked for the military during World War I, but who were convinced by the experience that their subsidiary role impeded innovation. Just before the U.S. entry into World War II, they convinced President Roosevelt that the armed forces needed assistance in weapons development. Therefore, the Office of Scientific Research and Development (OSRD) was placed under the direction of academics such as Vannevar Bush, the director of the Carnegie Institute of Washington and former dean at MIT, and James Conant, the president of Harvard University, rather than government officials or industrialists.[8] OSRD, which was organized just before World

War II, had broad responsibilities for research and development in the early stages of production across the military services.[9] At that time, large scale laboratories were mostly in industry with a few notable exceptions such as the Berkeley cyclotron and the Cal Tech wind tunnel.[10] The OSRD had to draw together researchers from universities across the country to a few sites to establish similar capabilities.

Under wartime emergency conditions, cooperation between universities, industry, and government temporarily superseded academic norms of disciplinary isolation and business *laissez-faire* antipathy to government. Formats were established for all of these parties to openly communicate and work together. For example, scientists from the Massachusetts Institute of Technology (MIT) "Rad Lab" went into the battlefields as observers on airplanes with the radar sets to see how the crews were using them and fed their experience back into the designs before the radar sets went into mass production.[11] Similarly, engineers from manufacturing companies came to the research site at MIT to start designing production lines before the designs were finalized. A "seamless web" of technology transfer and feedback loops from research and development to production could be maintained under the impetus of the war effort.

Postwar Initiatives

The wartime innovation system could not serve as a model for civilian innovation at the time. The conservative Vannevar Bush, who had worked for President Roosevelt, disagreed in principle with the president's interventionist economic polices of the "New Deal" that were put in to rescue capitalism from the 1930s depression. Bush was responsible for the report "The Endless Frontier" which can be described as a strategic plan for the U.S. postwar science and technology effort. The plan related especially to translating the lessons learned in improving U.S. military strength and medical technology through research in universities and national laboratories during World War II, as well as civilian issues such as housing and transportation. The final published draft of the "Endless Frontier" proposed to place disbursement of funds under control of scientific colleagues operating through the neutral criteria of "best science" peer review. The prestige attained by scientists, especially physicists, as a result of their wartime accomplishments, was sufficient to give them control of a basic research funding agency, the National Science Foundation (NSF). Even so, NSF was not founded until several years later in 1952 after a series of disputes over its scale, scope, and mode of operation were resolved.[12]

For a brief period during and just after World War II, the military research and development system was organized according to an ad hoc spiral model with numerous feedback loops among research, development, and production. Academic and industry collaboration was the norm in important efforts such as the "Rad Lab" (for radar), the Manhattan Project (for the atomic bomb), and the Distant Early Warning Line, or DEW (for early aircraft detection).

OSRD was disbanded immediately after the war and replaced by individual service research and development (Offices of Naval, Army, and Air Force Research) in the Department of Defense, established in 1947. A political struggle between advocates of military versus civilian control of atomic energy resulted in the Manhattan Project laboratories being moved from the control of the Army to a new agency, the Atomic Energy Commission, that eventually became the Department of Energy. The system of multiple research and development agencies in the Department of Defense and Department of Energy, which were laboratories with similar missions, encouraged competition but also resulted in duplication of effort and increased costs. The result was a loose confederation of the military services, with only limited controls available to coordinate them. The considerable responsibility that had been given to OSRD was returned to the individual military services after the war.

Despite the ideological conflict, a system of federal funding for research and development was continued after the war, both for military and basic research. The social sciences and humanities were also funded, with area studies and communications research created as World War II and Cold War aids.[13] The splintering of the OSRD, the closest the United States has come to a Department of Science, gave rise to a multiplicity of separate agencies within the armed forces, the nominally civilian Atomic Energy Commission, and the NSF. A loose decentralized system was created, with each interest group having its own agency. The creation of a variety of research funding agencies operating according to distinctly different principles is the source of contemporary contrasting approaches. This contrast can be seen within the SBIR program: the NSF/NIH (National Institutes of Health) basic research model, driven by the investigators, and the DOD model, in which the program officer exercises considerable discretion and initiative.

Summary: Roots of innovation/industrial policy can be found in:

1. The patent system proposed in the Constitution and later initiatives to promote inventions;
2. Exploring U.S. natural resources and social movements (e.g., farmers);
3. The early mission of universities related to supporting agriculture through "experiment stations" and other R&D and outreach/user-involving activities;
4. Social policy orientation (e.g., "electrification"); and
5. Development of "Centers of Excellence" at universities and national laboratories with practical missions (often improved military strength).

Notes

1. Mayer, David (1994), *The Constitutional Thought of Thomas Jefferson.* Charlottsville, VA: University of Virginia Press, p. 354, n.23.

2. Dobyns, Kenneth (1997), *The Patent Office Pony: A History of the Early Patent Office.* Fredericksburg, VA: Sergeant Kirkland's, p. 16.

3. McGraw, Judith, ed. (1994), *Early American Technology: Making and Doing Things from the Colonial Era to 1850.* Chapel Hill: University of North Carolina Press, p. 327.

4. Dobyns, Kenneth (1997), *The Patent Office Pony: A History of the Early Patent Office.* Fredericksburg, VA: Sergeant Kirkland's, p. 101.

5. Ambrose, Stephen (1996), *Undaunted Courage: Meriwether Lewis, Thomas Jefferson and the Opening of the American West.* New York: Simon and Schuster.

6. Rossiter, Margaret (1976), *The Emergence of Agricultural Science.* New Haven, CT: Yale University Press.

7. Bensel, Richard (1990), *Yankee Leviathan: The Origins of Central State Authority in America, 1859-1877.* Cambridge, MA: Cambridge University Press; Osborne, David (1990), *Laboratories of Democracy.* Boston: Harvard Business School Press.

8. Pursell, Caroll (1979), "Science Agencies in World War II: The OSRD and Its Challengers." In Nathan Reingold, ed., *The Sciences In the Amercan Context.* Washington, DC: Smithsonian Institution Press.

9. Etzkowitz, Henry (2000), *The Second Academic Revolution: MIT and the Rise of Entrepreneurial Science.* London: Gordon and Breach.

10. Hanle, Paul (1982), *Bringing Aerodynamics to America.* Cambridge, MA: MIT Press.

11. Buderi, Robert (1996), *The Invention That Changed The World.* New York: Simon and Schuster.

12. England, J. Merton (1982), *A Patron for Pure Science: The National Science Foundation's Formative Years.* Washington, DC: National Science Foundation.

13. Simpson, Christopher (1994), *Science of Coercion: Communication Research and Psychological Warfare, 1945–1960.* New York: Oxford University Press.

CHAPTER 9 • THE U.S. GOVERNMENT RESEARCH AND DEVELOPMENT FUNDING SYSTEM

CONTENTS

THE U.S. GOVERNMENT RESEARCH AND DEVELOPMENT FUNDING SYSTEM

Introduction

After World War II, the United States created a system for research and development support with two starting points that came from opposite directions. One source was government agency needs for research while the other was scientists' ideas for fundamental investigation. This "dual linear" model presumes a one-way flow from basic to applied research, in one direction, and from mission requirements to scientific and technological capabilities, in the other.

These two contrasting approaches influence the organization and operation of government-supported research programs, including the SBIR. One is a contract process, originating with the funder's choice of specific topics, while the other is a grant process, beginning with the proposer's ideas. Although the contract mode is more focused and the grant method less specific, the parameters, whether narrow or broad, are set by the funding agency.

In response to the Soviet Union's success in putting a satellite (Sputnik) into space in 1957, the United States created a third model. In the DARPA (Defense Advanced Research Projects Agency) model, one could begin in the middle as well as at either end to address and expedite solutions to technology problems with defense implications.

In this chapter, we will take a closer look at he following:

- The Contract Model
- The Grant Model
- The DARPA Model
- The Product Development Model

The Contract Model and the "Proof-of-Concept" Approach

Contracts are used by both civilian and military agencies. The contract model typically begins with a problem identified by an agency. The agency seeks a solution to the problem through research and development (R&D). An explicit arrangement is made that includes a specified result, the "deliverable," at the end of the project. Both parties should feel comfortable in advance that they can specify the outcome and commit to a timetable for the production and delivery of the result. This usually happens more at the applied end of the research spectrum. Federal support has been oriented toward achieving major cost reductions, for example, in energy technologies and improvements in their environmental performance.

While the contract model is predominate within the armed forces, the military is also a significant funder of basic research. Similarly, while the NSF and NIH fund basic research through grants, other civilian agencies such as the National Aeronautics and Space Administration (NASA) operate primarily through contracts.

The United States has furthermore adopted the so-called *proof-of-concept* approach in many research and development programs. This procedure insures that enough is learned to establish the technical viability and basic engineering feasibility of a concept, and to forecast its expected economic and environmental performance standards. This also permits industry to make decisions concerning whether the concept merits further development. Industry action beyond this phase is crucial if anything is to happen.

In the armed forces, mission requirements originate within military strategic planning and are then translated into desired technical capabilities. Subsequent research and development then predominantly takes place in the specialized industrial subsection, consisting of firms that are tied to the military and that primarily build weapons systems.[1] Sometimes the requirements come from the government and the firms then conduct research and development to realize the military's specifications. The firms also put forth their own ideas for new weapons systems and then get seed funding to develop a concept or build a prototype. The DOD SBIR programs basically follow this model with technical personnel within the armed forces defining specific topics and issuing requests for proposals to meet its requirements.

In theory, the DOD defines its external research and development needs and finds contractors to meet them. In practice, defense contractors play an important role in initiating research and development projects that can eventually translate into development contracts for these same firms if sufficient support is built up within the DOD and Congress. The firm that performs the original research and development is quite likely to be the recipient of an award to build the systems. This might occur despite formal requirements that all research and development results are turned over to the DOD to allow an open competition for the next stage in the event it is warranted.

Large firms have been major players in the defense research and development system, mostly because contractual arrangements have been extremely complicated. This has made it difficult for small businesses to enter the process, even though their ideas might be excellent. Some have argued that because of this, the system has not been innovative enough (a reason often used to promote the SBIR and Dual Use programs where contractual arrangements are simpler).

The Grant Model

The grant model typically begins with a government agency establishing general topics for which investigators are invited to compete for funds. A grant is more open-ended than a contract in terms of what is expected. Without being sure of what the end result may be, it would be difficult to promise or expect a particular outcome.

Certainly the differences are not absolute. A contract may fail to produce the promised "deliverable" but may come up with interesting results nevertheless and be considered a success. A grant for a basic research topic may unexpectedly result in a useful device or a theoretical discovery on a different topic. On the downside, a contract may woefully underestimate costs and fall far short of achieving the promised result. A grant may wander off the topic without achieving significant results elsewhere or may produce a disparate collection of uninteresting findings on the specified topic.

The government grant model developed out of the experience of the Office of Naval Research (ONR) in the early postwar period. The ONR was the predecessor of the National Science Foundation (NSF), which was founded in 1952. The experience of the ONR demonstrated that it was possible for a government agency to support academic research on terms that were acceptable to the academic community.

The NSF approach delegates primary decision making authority to the research community. This approach incorporates a two-step process that is coordinated by the program manager. The initial step is the solicitation of written reviews of the proposal by experts in the field. Some are selected from a group recommended by the applicant while others are chosen solely by the program manager. The next step is a meeting of the program "panel," a self-perpetuating group whose members choose their successors with the advice and consent of the program manager. These representatives of the discipline recommend proposals to be funded. The formal decisions are made higher up in the organization, but panel recommendations are rarely overturned. In this model, the program manager provides administrative support for a research funding process in which decision making authority lies with the research community and is exercised through its representatives.

NSF program managers influence the funding decision in various ways (e.g., through the selection of reviewers). On the surface, this is a purely administrative decision. In actuality, choice of persons to conduct a review can influence the results of the review through their theoretical and methodological preferences. Similarly, the program manager can influence meetings of the review panels by guiding discussion and offering interpretations of the reviews. The manager is the most knowledgeable person about the proposals since the panelists appear in Washington for a few days only twice a year; the manager, even if short-term, is the expert.

The NSF concentrates on the funding decision. Although final reports on the results are required, there is little, if any, monitoring of the research process itself. This approach is based on the assumption of a self-organized research community with the funding agent acting as a representative of the community rather than as an organizer.

The Defense Advanced Research Projects Agency (DARPA) and the DARPA Model

The military agency DARPA (formerly known as ARPA) was created in the DOD in 1958, the aftermath of the crisis brought about by the Soviet Sputnik space achievement. Its responsibilities were to pursue a wide range of far reaching projects spanning the research and development spectrum. Its mandate was to create broader, longer range technology development and research infrastructure projects, filling the gaps between the Navy, Army, and Air Force research and development programs. DARPA funding at universities helped create new interdisciplinary fields such as materials science and computer science. In the course of fulfilling its mandate, the agency also served as a venture capitalist to firms like Silicon Graphics and SUN Microsystems.

DARPA was given broad authority to identify and support leading-edge technology with potential military relevance. Its goals are to pursue highly imaginative and innovative research ideas and concepts offering significant military utility. It is also to support and manage projects assigned by the Secretary of Defense and marshal advanced research through a demonstration of its feasibility for military application. DARPA's role in basic research is to develop new ideas (usually high-risk and high-payoff) from conception to hardware prototype for transfer to service development agencies. DARPA does not conduct in-house research but does rely on military departments and other government agencies for technical and administrative support. Programs are conducted through contracts with industrial, university, and nonprofit organizations and with selected Army, Navy, and Air Force laboratories.

The agency's programs traditionally focus on technology development and proof-of-concept demonstrations, as well as on scientific investigation into advanced basic technologies of the future. It has previously been mandated to support only those initiatives that promise significant advancement in United States national security interests, while lowering costs through technological advances or preparing for further technological progress. DARPA's branches include Aerospace and Strategic Technology, Defense Sciences, Information Science and Technology, Nuclear Monitoring, Tactical Technology, and Defense Manufacturing.

DARPA has been considered to be a success due to its strategy of focusing considerable resources, over a period of years, on strategic targets with long-term payoffs for defense goals. For example, DARPA was instrumental in developing the academic discipline of computer science in the United States by providing research and infrastructure support for a few key departments at MIT, Stanford, Carnegie–Mellon, and the University of California at Berkeley during the 1960s and 1970s. These departments became models for other universities who later established degree programs in the new discipline. Although computer science certainly would have eventually emerged as an independent discipline, DARPA support arguably sped up the process and gave the United States a lead in this field.

Precursor to the Internet

One of DARPA's greatest achievements was a by-product of an effort to facilitate the research process among the computer scientists that the agency was supporting in universities across the country. Computer scientists had realized quite early that data could be transferred among machines though telephone lines. Messages could also accompany the data, making available instructions and advice on its use. In principle and practice, messages could also be transferred among linked computers on any other topic as well. Thus was born electronic mail (e-mail) and computer networks (the ARPANET). From the 1960s, DARPA supported links among its major research sites in academia, industry, and government. Projects were funded at the University of California at Los Angeles and in Cambridge, Massachusetts, at the firm of Bolt, Beranek, and Newman, among others, to develop protocols and systems to make this network reliable and expandable.

In the late 1980s, the ARPANET was transferred to the NSF where it became the Internet, with NSF given lead responsibility to develop the system into the so-called information highway. As the Internet grew from a few thousand to more than 15 million users by the mid-1990s, with extensive commercialization taking place, the Internet's origins as a government project was often forgotten. Indeed, as President Clinton noted in his 1999 State of the Union address, the development of the Internet has called attention to government's role in fostering technological innovation.

A Seamless Web of Innovation

In the DARPA model, an agency program may fund a university research group, center, or collaboration of academic researchers to produce a prototype of a technology. If the academic group is successful, they may take the next step and independently arrange financing and undertake organizing of a firm. As a firm, they may then apply for and receive funds from the same agency, typically from DARPA itself. The firm, then, continues research and development on the technology for which its academic predecessors, now typically principals of the firm, produced the prototype.

The SUN Microsystems workstation, for example, emerged as a commercial product though this process. SUN, in fact, stands for Stanford University Network. Silicon Graphics similarly emerged from a DARPA supported research project at the Stanford Computer Science Department. Both of these companies became billion dollar corporations within a decade of their founding. The process of directly contracting for a university research unit to produce a prototype, rather than it emerging as a by-product of research, is largely peculiar to this agency. Extending university research and development into prototyping has proven to be an effective means of industrial policy, whether or not the technology is eventually taken up by the military.

Civilian Interpretation of DARPA—ATP

The gap that opened up between research and the introduction of new technology was addressed in the military in the late 1950s through the founding of DARPA. It was then addressed in civilian research and development in the late 1980s through the establishment of the Advanced Technology Program (ATP), following the DARPA model.

A civilian version was established that reflected both the culture of the agency into which it was inserted, the National Institute of Standards and Technology (NIST), and DARPA, from which the original leadership came. Ideas and practices successfully utilized in DARPA were transferred, resulting in ATP's concept of focused programs, a portfolio of related research and development consortia and projects.

The Product Development Model

The federal government has periodically become involved in product development, typically under pressure of national emergency or international competition. Examples of responses to national emergencies include the formation of the Manhattan Project, the purpose of which was to develop the atomic bomb during World War II, and the effort to develop synthetic fuels during the oil crises of the 1970s. Examples of responses to international competition include the Apollo Missions, the driving purpose of which was to land a man on the moon ahead of the Soviet Union; and SEMATECH, the government-funded R&D consortia created to help the semiconductor industry save its markets from loss to Japanese competitors.

SEMATECH is recognized as having made a significant contribution to the U.S. semiconductor industry's efforts in regaining international leadership in the field. The consortia became so successful that eventually it was able to dispense with government funding. On the other hand, the Synthetic Fuels Corporation (SFC), an initiative of the Carter administration, is viewed as less successful.

The SFC was an initiative of the Carter administration and was largely dismantled by the Reagan administration. The SFC did not provide contracts or grants but rather operated much as an investment bank during its brief period of active life. Through the competitive award of loan guarantees, price guarantees, purchase agreements, and direct loans, the SFC could reduce the financial risk to industry associated with constructing and operating first-of-a-kind commercial size plants. Not surprisingly, these very features made it suspect to the Reagan administration. They viewed each of these measures as interference with the operation of the market. The SFC was also authorized to participate as a joint venture sponsor in projects and to initiate up to three corporation-owned facilities.

The Energy Security Act divided the corporation's activities into two distinct phases. The corporation was supposed to solicit, evaluate, and assist synthetic fuel projects that fell within the technological and resource diversity requirements of the act during the initial phase. The SFC, drawing upon experience gained during this phase, was mandated to prepare and submit to Congress a comprehensive strategy for national synthetic fuel production. Although a few projects were started, none were seen through to completion.[2]

The SFC is regarded as too dependent on the technology developed by a single company with government playing too great a role.[3] More recent models, such as SEMATECH, emphasize drawing upon the resources of several companies, universities, and government laboratories to develop new technology. The active life of the SFC was too short to determine whether it could have made a significant contribution to commercialization of energy research and development. Nevertheless, for the United States it was, to this date, a highly unusual instance of an active role for government in civilian industrial policy.

Summary: Main models in the U.S. research and development funding system.

Contracts

1. Based on government agency needs
2. Activities are likely to be pulled in an applied direction

3. Common in the Department of Defense and most other government agencies with specific missions
4. Proposal review often internal and there is an agreement on "deliverables"

Grants

1. Based on scientists' ideas for fundamental investigation
2. Found mainly in the National Science Foundation (NSF) and the National Institutes of Health (NIH), as well as in military and energy research
3. The basis of the grant model is linear–fundamental research leads to applied work and development and finally to commercial products
4. Most often external review (especially in the NSF and NIH)

The DARPA model

1. Projects often draw on resources in government, industry, and academia, bringing them together in defining new important technological areas and in carrying out the specific projects, resulting in a nonlinear R&D process
2. Model found in the Defense Advanced Research Projects Agency and in the Advanced Technology Program

The Product Development model

1. Government gets directly involved in product development under conditions of national emergency or intense international competition in critical technology areas.

Notes

1. Melman, Seymour (1970), *Pentagon Capitalism*. New York: McGraw Hill.
2. Vietor, Richard (1984), *Energy Policy in America Since 1945: A Study in Business-Government Relations*. Cambridge, MA: Cambridge University Press, pp. 330–331.
3. Hafner, Katie. 1993. "Does Industrial Policy Work? Lessons from Sematech." *New York Times*, Sunday, November 7, p. F5.

CHAPTER 10 · MODES OF GOVERNMENT INTERVENTION

CONTENTS

MODES OF GOVERNMENT INTERVENTION

Postwar Period—Science Funding Policy

There are currently three modes of government intervention for the purpose using science and technology (S & T) for social and economic development. These modes evolved over time and can be considered the United States S &T policy. They will be described further below:

1. Postwar period—Science funding policy based on the linear model
2. Late 1970s through the early 1980s—Hidden or indirect industrial policy in which government deputizes agents on its behalf
3. Late 1980s to the present—Experiments in direct industrial policy

Science policy is industrial policy in the United States even though the latter is a forbidden term in the American political lexicon. U.S. scientific policy is typically oriented toward practical goals, even when stated as long-term objectives as in the 1945 *Endless Frontier* report that laid the groundwork for government funding of academic research in the postwar era. Science is seldom publicly justified as an element of culture to be pursued solely for its intrinsic worth. Fundamental scientific research is the avowed responsibility of the National Science Foundation (NSF), but even NSF has significant practical responsibilities for engineering, science education, and, most recently, the Internet.

The Linear Model

Successful wartime experience made government research support acceptable to academic scientists. In the postwar era, federal government funding of research was, in the long term, expected to lead to new technologies and new products, a more leisurely version of the wartime, forced-draft invention and production of new weapons. Putting funds into a research process at one end and obtaining practical outcomes, after some or much time, at the other end is called the *linear model*.

Despite its successes, the linear model has come under questioning as an adequate explanation of how innovation, the translation of research into new products and services, actually takes place. In addition to breakthroughs derived from research findings, incremental innovation occurs by enhancement of production processes as well as through improvements called forth by customer requirements and suggestions. Thus, "pure" research based on scientific curiosity, emphasized by the linear model, is only one among several drivers of innovation. Not surprisingly, the linear model still retains great appeal among the academic science community.

Emphasizing the key role of basic research, academics benefit from the linear model's justification for disbursement of government research funds to them. Indeed, given sufficient time, useful results are produced.

Output of Science: Products, Technologies, and Spin-offs

In an increasing number of scientific fields, the gap between basic research and application is closing. Several studies have shown that many new industrial products and new technologies have been based on government-sponsored basic research. Technological developments have long been an important argument for support of research, but specific cases have been difficult to document due to the inevitability of multiple discovery.[1]

Should the invention of the transistor be credited to wartime research on diodes at Purdue University or to the postwar Bell Laboratory initiative in semiconductor physics for the purpose of simplifying telephone switching systems? Should the digital computer be credited to Professor Atanasoff, a researcher at Iowa State University in the 1930s, or to the Army-sponsored program that enabled Eckert and Mauchly to build the ENIAC, an electronic digital computer, at the University of Pennsylvania during World War II?

In the 1960s, the relationship between military and space research and the civilian economy was formulated in terms of "spin-off" of technologies, an unintended but useful side effect of such research and development.[2] The expectation was that advanced weapons and space research could be translated into an extra boost for the civilian economy. This was not seen to be a major purpose of the research but rather as a by-product and an additional justification for it.

Many doubts have been raised concerning the effectiveness of this spin-off activity.[3] Indeed, some supposedly advanced space technologies translated into civilian use, such as the Teflon nonstick coating for pots and pans, actually had civilian antecedents before they were incorporated into the space program. Nevertheless, technology transfer, originally used to provide an additional justification for an agency's mission, has become a continuing government objective.

The creation of spin-off firms from government sponsored technology projects has been accepted as a positive indicator of useful side effects of research and development funding. Defense procurement, and research and development sponsorship, has indirectly encouraged academic and industry cooperation in the electronics industry through the spin-off process. The availability of research and development funding and contracts for components encouraged a high volume of new firm formation from universities as well as industry.[4]

The need of the Department of Defense (DOD) for advanced electronics led it to play the role of "virtual" venture capitalist to many new firms in this industry. In Massachusetts, for example, the spin-off process from MIT faculty and students has had a measurable positive impact on the Massachusetts economy, creating a significant percentage of that state's economic growth.

Late 1970s through the Early 1980s—
Indirect Industrial Policy

The gap between research and product development had been temporarily reduced under wartime pressure in the 1940s. Lacking these pressures, an innovation gap opened up again in the early postwar era, but this was not recognized at the time given the preeminence of U.S. industry. A slow moving technological pace was acceptable, even favored, by companies in the forefront of their industries who could prosper by meeting wartime induced shortages with existing product lines. Large companies could afford to maintain central laboratories separated from their production sites, taking only limited advantage of their capabilities.

This innovation gap did not come into public view until the 1970s when U.S. manufacturers began to fall behind Japanese competitors in the consumer electronics and automobile industries. However, the ability of government to assist industry, and even industry's ability to assist itself, was limited at the time by the strength of the belief that government involvement was inappropriate and that maintaining competition precluded cooperation among firms.

Although it was more difficult to justify government intervention in response to international competition than for wartime initiatives, action was eventually attempted. In the late 1970s, responding to international competition and the decline of major industries, the Carter administration proposed a reindustrialization policy with programs to assist industry. However, the policy was blocked by adherents of the prevailing *laissez-faire* ideology. In the mid-1980s, the government helped establish the SEMATECH R&D consortia in response to the Japanese challenge to U.S. dominance in semiconductor chips. This action was held to represent nothing more than an exceptional response to a particular problem.

The unwillingness of the United States to subsidize the development of civilian technology, which was commonplace in Europe, coincided with pressure from universities to clarify the status of intellectual property arising from federally sponsored research. This confluence of circumstances led to the creation of a "hidden industrial policy" that went from the government, through the universities, and reached firms indirectly. A series of policies and programs evolved in a piecemeal manner, connecting universities and national laboratories to industry. A variety of measures were put in place, including an enhanced role for academic research in the national innovation system.

Expediting Technology Transfer

Both proponents and opponents of industrial policy could agree that the enormous amount of potential intellectual property that had accumulated in the universities, arising from federal research grants, should be privatized. Research results with potential commercial utility were in an uncertain legal status—who really owned them? Officially, of course, the federal government owned these rights. Given the strength of anti-industrial policy sentiment, the federal government was hardly going to engage in commercialization activities. Nor were private firms willing to undertake these tasks in the absence of a clear title. If they did produce something successful, other firms could try to claim the technology, stating that they had an equal right to it as taxpayers and citizens. For this reason, such government-owned intellectual property tended not to be utilized.

A 1968 study identified few instances of federally funded and patented research being put to use. Well in advance of public recognition of an innovation gap, a few patent attorneys in U.S. research agencies became concerned about the perceived difficulties in translating research into economic activity.

Largely at their own initiative, patent lawyers at government-funded NIH and NSF established administrative procedures to allow universities to acquire patent rights to federally funded research. This was done on the condition that universities create professional in-house technology transfer capacities to arrange patenting and licensing. For universities not wishing to make such an extensive commitment, procedures were created for case by case exceptions.

Still, patenting federally funded academic research was questioned by many legislators and members of the executive branch. They believed that it was poor public policy, and even immoral, for research paid for by the taxpayers to be put up for sale to private industry. They believed such research should be freely published and disseminated through traditional academic procedures. In response, it was argued that lack of patenting created an insurmountable obstacle to commercialization. Such an obstacle might cause a company interested in developing technology from academic research to think twice. After all, if they were successful but they were not entitled to intellectual property protection, another company could lay claim to the same research.

The Bayh–Dole Act

Individual negotiations between federal research agencies and universities, establishing the terms of access to patent rights arising from federally sponsored research, were eventually generalized by law in the Bayh–Dole Act. The law gave ownership of intellectual property, arising from federally funded research, to the universities. In 1862, the Morill Act assigned government-owned land to a special class of universities to support the development of agriculture. In 1980, the Bayh–Dole Act turned over intellectual property rights emanating from federally funded research to all universities as a "virtual" equivalent of a land grant.

Under the law, universities were obligated to make an effort to commercialize these rights. Universities lacking a technology transfer office soon established one. They typically hired an industrial scientist in a field in which the university had potentially commercial research or they gave the responsibility to an attorney on staff.

The One-Third Rule

Some professors who were already working with industry argued that placing an administrative office between themselves and their corporate sponsors would impede industrial relations. The issues were resolved by dividing the financial results of research among the investigator, the investigator's department, and the university as a whole.

A one-third rule, which took into account the general interest of the university and the particular interests of entrepreneurial faculty, was acceptable to both faculty groups and was widely adopted. The positive academic response to Bayh–Dole sped the diffusion of mechanisms for transfer of technology from a few universities, such as MIT, Stanford, and the University of Wisconsin, that had specialized in this task to a broader array of schools. Academia helped supply industry with improved technology as a result of this low-key, indirect, federal innovation strategy that, with no appropriation of funds, changed the rules of the game.

Outcomes of Hidden Industrial Policy

Schools such as MIT and Stanford, which had been anomalies within the U.S. academic system, now became the models for other universities to emulate. The university technology transfer office would focus on areas of research with commercial possibilities, identifying potential intellectual property for patenting, licensing, and making sales contacts to industry.

Soon, professional groups appeared and organized regular meetings and conferences to bring university technology transfer offices together with industry scouts to facilitate the transfer process. Within 15 years, technology transfer activities became a significant money-maker for a few universities that originated significant technologies. Others are still gearing up their offices or waiting for technologies to receive health and safety approvals so that the royalty flow to the university and its faculty can begin.

The relationship between government sponsored research and development and economic development, through the intermediary of universities and firms, is complicated and controversial. Hard numbers are difficult to obtain and should be used cautiously. According to one, estimate the contribution to the U.S. economy by academic technology transfer is likely to be approximately 50,000 jobs, $9 billion in product sales, and $1.5 billion in tax revenues in 1992. These figures are said to be growing at a rate of 25% to 30% per year.[5]

Some members of Congress have called for the federal government to take back some of the intellectual property rights that it gave away in 1980. The feeling has been expressed by some members of Congress that the universities were earning too much money. Proposals were made for the government to retain some of the intellectual property rights emanating from federally funded research at universities. By the time this threat to university technology transfer had developed, the academic technology transfer profession had grown significantly. It developed its own professional association, the Association of University Technology Managers (AUTM), with a regular schedule of national and regional conference and training programs for prospective technology transfer officers as well as specialized media.

In response to the growing controversy, AUTM organized a Congressional hearing through its own supporters in Congress, demonstrating that the original intent of the legislation in establishing academic technology transfer was to gain national benefit from the long-term outcomes of technology transfer. AUTM argued that these processes of technology transfer in the universities should be left alone. The return to government would come from increased taxes in the future and government should not try to interfere and possibly short-circuit the process.

Thus, the outcome of the late 1970s debate over whether to have a federal civilian industrial policy was that nothing was done directly. Nevertheless, hidden industrial policy and programs to carry it out were set in motion indirectly. The Bayh–Dole Act was passed to clarify the ambiguities in federal intellectual property rights by turning them over to the universities—but with a condition. The proviso was that universities had to take steps to commercialize this intellectual property.

From 1980, academic institutions managing significant federal research grants started administrative offices and began to experiment with various models of technology transfer and relations with industry. Most of these formats for academic–industry relations had been developed earlier in the century at MIT and then were taken up at Stanford after World War II. Since 1980, these practices have been generalized throughout the research university system.

The Late 1980s to the Present—Experiments in Direct Industrial Policy

Until the Clinton Administration, only a hidden industrial policy was politically acceptable at the national level. Ideological prohibitions against breaching *laissez-faire* walls between government and industry required elaborate subterfuge to make intervention possible.

Segregation of research and production was reinforced as a consequence of the *laissez-faire* policies of the Reagan administration. During this era, the validity of government support for basic research at universities was accepted, but there was a strong aversion to support of research in companies. Thus, government supported cooperative research and development projects among companies—or academia and industry were avoided—because the Reagan and Bush administrations thought of industry as an improper partner for government. A few exceptions were made, under pressure from industry, as the result of a strongly felt need to meet Japanese competition in semiconductors and microelectronics. However, even as the technology gap widened due to the passivity of the executive branch, Congress attempted to bridge it. Legislative initiatives to encourage closer linkages between universities and companies partially closed the technology gap, at least in principle.

The U.S. industry was criticized for focusing on short-term results and reducing its commitment to long-term research and development. Suffering pressures on profits, many firms that had maintained central research laboratories shut them down or downsized them. This created long-term as well as short-term industrial research and development gaps in many U.S. industries in the headlong rush to catch up to the Japanese in incremental, production-based innovation. In comparison to the United States, Japanese and European governmental agencies assisted firms in their countries with long-term projects.

Founding the ATP

Congress, toward the end of the Bush administration, defined this gap in the United States as a "market failure" when concerns about Japanese competition in high technology were at their height. Congress authorized the Advanced Technology Program (ATP), a government supported technology program, to spur industrial innovation in order to counter the threat.

Several modest programs, most notably the ATP and the Technology Reinvestment Project (TRP), received dramatically increased funding with the advent of the Clinton administration. The ATP is directly oriented at industry, with universities allowed to participate only as junior partners in consortia. Nevertheless, university researchers often play a key part since it is their research that is being commercialized through awards to companies in quite a few cases.

Although many in Congress would still like to eliminate the ATP on the grounds that it interferes with the market, the likelihood is that it will persist at a more modest funding level. The ATP has shifted its granting strategy from large to small companies, thereby making the program more politically viable. Although the ATP also distributed funds to small firms, most of its early funds and publicity were focused on consortia of large companies. One example was the program involving the three major U.S. auto companies to build a "clean car."

As a result of the publicity about funding to large companies, the ATP was attacked by many Democrats and Republicans as an example of "corporate welfare." Rather than viewing the funds as a necessary supplement to induce companies to engage in long-term research and development, the focus was on the undeniable fact that these firms clearly could afford to fund the project, if only they had the collective will to do it.

Founding the SBIR

The Small Business Innovation Research (SBIR) program was established to provide government research funds to small companies. Companies with fewer than 500 employees are eligible to participate in a highly competitive award process to receive these funds which are awarded as grants, not loans, with no direct payback expected by government. SBIR funds are given out as grants to small companies to develop new technology. In effect, the SBIR program has become a public venture capital program, supplying seed funding to establish new high-tech firms.

The SBIR is the largest and least controversial of the federal government technology programs, in part because it is directed at small business which is generally accepted as a good thing by people of various political persuasions. Although officially targeted at existing firms, SBIR has become a means for academic and corporate scientists, experienced in grant writing, to gain the seed funds to start their own technology venture. Founded to improve small business access to federal research funds, SBIR has taken on a new dimension; it has become a firm formation and job creation mechanism in a number of high-technology fields where the federal government supports research.

The SBIR Program began as a small-scale initiative in NSF, combining small business support with funding for high-quality research and technology. Roland Tibbetts, the founding director of SBIR said, "The starting point was that we saw a potential for economic development in cutting-edge research, but that there were no venture capital firms or others that were willing to take the risk of supporting activities with a very uncertain outcome. We were also interested in focusing on tomorrow's jobs, creating firms in tomorrow's businesses with international competitiveness."[6] SBIR thus reflects the growing awareness of technology as an important factor in economic growth. Another important goal was to increase the return on investment of federal research and development dollars. To SBIR's founders, ". . . hi-tech small firms seemed to be the best vehicle for doing that."[7]

When it was suggested that the experimental SBIR program in NSF should be extended to additional agencies, many academic researchers objected, fearing that it would take money away from their research and development support. Proponents of the SBIR recalled that "because of the large opposition against the program, we had to choose our words very carefully, which contributed to making the program very good and bullet-proof."

By describing a phase model of the entrepreneurship process and the role of the federal government in each phase, the SBIR created a neutral language for direct government intervention in the economy. The strong focus on scientific and technical criteria fit well with basic research criteria previously accepted by the government. An advocate of SBIR and similar initiatives said, "We definitely see the programs as a de facto industrial policy, but we cannot use that term, so we usually call it research and development policy and things like that instead; but it [the SBIR] is a federal program that has created a whole lot of new industrial activity."[8]

There are now ten federal agency SBIR participants who are required to set aside 2.5% of their total research budgets for the program. Currently, more than $1.1 billion is awarded annually, and more than 40,000 grants have been made since the early 1980s. Many highly successful firms have started out with SBIR grants. In interviews, program managers point to the most successful cases as a justification in its own right for continuing the program.

The Origins of Dual Use

By the late 1980s, (1) the rising cost of defense technologies and (2) the realization that civilian technological advance had often outpaced military technological advance gave rise to programs to couple military and civilian technological development. Despite these justifications, such "dual use" programs became controversial because of objections to government becoming involved in civilian technology development. The result has been that high-profile programs have been disbanded, but "dual use" lives on in low-key initiatives.

The TRP was started at about the same time as ATP. TRP's mission was to identify technologies that had been developed in defense companies and to bring them into civilian use. Although TRP was short lived, out of its ashes have emerged various "dual use" programs in the Army, Navy, and Air Force.

A proponent of the TRP in the Department of Defense recalled, "The opponents had a number of fundamental problems. They would say that this was government meddling in the economy, this was government trying to pick winners and losers, and that these were defense dollars that were being misused subsidizing nondefense purposes." After the controversy died down, the concept of dual use was accepted.

The SBIR, ATP, and dual use programs represent something new in U.S. industrial policy. These programs fill gaps in the innovation system where opportunities for funding and collaboration traditionally have been weak. In addition, or as a result, they fit nicely into a sequence. It is not uncommon for a company to start out with one or more SBIR grants, and then proceed to obtain ATP or dual use awards when the technology has reached a more mature stage in its development. Government programs encourage technology entrepreneurs to move from one phase of their career in a company, university, or government laboratory to starting a series of new firms in the course of an entrepreneurial career. Government thus plays an important role, not just in funding the research and development system, but also as a public entrepreneur, seeing that research results are put to use generating jobs and wealth.

Summary: Modes of Public Entrepreneurship

The linear model

1. Premise: the research process is seen as linear from basic research through applied research to development
2. Implication: government should spend money on basic research, and practical results will follow "at the other end" of the process
3. Results: many spin-offs (products, technologies, firms, etc.) from basic research
4. Problems: model does not seem to reflect well the process that most innovations go through; mission-oriented R&D (especially military and energy) does not seem to be an effective way of creating spin-offs

Indirect industrial policy

1. Premise: a need to commercialize results from federally funded R&D and to keep up with international competition (especially Japanese), combined with strong ideological opposition toward "industrial policy"
2. Implication: change legislation to carry out support of industrial innovation indirectly through universities and other agents
3. Results: increase in patenting and licensing
4. Problems: still gaps in the innovation system; not all results can be patented or protected in similar ways

Direct industrial policy

1. Premise: there are gaps between science and innovation systems that need to be targeted through special programs and efforts; a "valley of death" where neither the private sector nor the existing scientific institutions will venture

2. Implication: establish federal programs that target the technological and economic areas that others do not touch
3. Results: many successful cases (projects and firms) from the programs
4. Problems: could the successes have been paid for by the private sector; how do you draw the boundaries?

Notes

1. Merton, Robert K. (1963), "Resistance to the Systemic Study of Multiple Discoveries in Science," *European Journal of Sociology*, 4:237–49.

2. Sapolsky, Harvey [undated], "Military Support for Academic Research in the United States."

3. See, for instance, Nelson, Richard, Merton Peck, and Richard Kalachek (1967), *Technology, Economic Growth and Public Policy*. Washington, DC: The Brookings Institution.

4. Utterback, James, and Albert Murray (1977), *The Influence of Defense Procurement and Sponsorship of Research and Development on the Development of the Civilian Electronics Industry*. Cambridge, MA: MIT Center for Policy Alternatives.

5. Stevens, Ashley (1993), Personal communication to Henry Etzkowitz, October 14, Ashley Stevens, then Director of the Office of Technology Transfer (OTT) at Dana–Farber Cancer Institute, Harvard University Medical School.

6. Gulbrandsen, Magnus (1997), Interview with Roland Tibbets, Founding Director of SBIR at NSF, November, Washington, DC.

7. Ibid.

8. Ibid.

CHAPTER 11 • CONCLUSION: SCIENCE POLICY AS INDUSTRIAL POLICY

CONTENTS

CONCLUSION: SCIENCE POLICY AS INDUSTRIAL POLICY

Introduction

The previous chapter of Part III have shown the historical roots of federal science and technology programs and their consequences, both intended and unintended. Based upon this discussion, consider this question: Does the United States have an industrial policy, a specific role for the federal government in creating and developing industries and jobs, beyond general measures to encourage economic health such as regulating the supply of money and credit?

The United States is generally believed not to engage in industrial policy, with the exception of national emergencies.[1] During World War II, the federal government expanded the aircraft and steel industries and created an entirely new industry to construct the atomic bomb. Lesser crises, such as increased international competition for American manufacturers during the 1970s, have also called forth a federal response. Since much U.S. industrial policy takes place through indirect means, it does not rise to visibility as part of a general schema.

However, if viewed more broadly, a comprehensive U.S. industrial policy can be discerned from more than 200 years of actions supporting invention, development, and diffusion of technology. Indeed, the combination of indirect as well as direct interventions suggests that the United States has the world's strongest industrial policy, despite a reputation to the contrary. A portfolio of federal programs addresses needs of firms that are:

1. At different stages of development (from start-up to maturity)
2. Of varying size (micro, small, large)
3. Of varying levels of technology (high, low, midtech)

Industrial policies operate at three levels in the United States—first, as science or research funding policy; second, as hidden industrial policy in which government deputizes agents on its behalf; and third, in the form of explicit public actions. U.S. industrial policy, whether officially intended as such or not, can be recognized in its entirety as a comprehensive, if not fully integrated, portfolio of policies and programs.

In most countries, industrial policy takes place primarily through direct assistance to industrial sectors and their member firms. Due to ideological resistance, the United States often pursues industrial policy by indirect means, encouraging other institutions to carry out public purposes. For example, by giving over intellectual property rights generated from federally funded research to the universities, it was expected that academic institutions could more easily interface with industry, without causing the controversy that was expected to be generated by a direct government/ industry relationship.

The driving forces of current U.S. science policy are (1) the contraction of the military R&D and (2) the need to make government supported research contribute more fully to the civilian economy in order to meet increased international economic competition. The United States has had a dual economy since World War II, civilian (market-based) and military (government-controlled). Ideological prohibitions against breaching *laissez-faire* walls between government and industry have required elaborate subterfuges to make direct intervention possible.

During the Cold War, national security was invoked to support measures in such diverse areas as education and transportation policy. State governments maintained their industrial policies on the grounds of traditional responsibilities for supporting local economies. The federal government, however, was expected to refrain from such activities save for the exemptions granted by all-out war. It was only military and space competition with the former Soviet Union that provided exceptions to this ideology.

Given the resistance to a role for government, when intervention is decided upon, it is typically carried out indirectly. The university was the institution of choice in three key instances: agriculture (mid-nineteenth century), the military (World War II), and industry (1970s). Although industrial policy is still an unacceptable term to many who believe that the strength of the economy resides solely with business, the dependence of business on technology and the role of government as a supporter of technology development for various purposes continues to grow. Thus, controversies also grow as the issue of government intervention affects an increasing number of topics.

In a host of advanced technical fields, from semiconductors to high-definition TV, there are disputes over the proper role of government. The ideological issue has been clearly put aside only for defense, on national security grounds; health, on humanitarian and political grounds; and agriculture, on the basis of political pressure from farmers during the 19th century. In every other industrial area, either at the point of decline or promise of growth, the ideological barrier stemming from adherence to *laissez-faire, laissez-passer* ideas must be overcome.

A variety of means have been put in place to further reduce the ever closing gap between science and utilization, between market needs and those not yet foreseen, and among existing suppliers of new technology, and new firms that are yet a gleam in their future founder's eye.

In this chapter we will discuss:

1. The emergence of a government role in technology development for civilian industry.
2. The rationales that have been offered for government playing a more active role in the support of science, technology, and industry.

The Emergence of a Government Role in Technology Development for Civilian Industry

Government can only set general outlines in civilian innovation policy for fear that it will be accused of attempting to "pick winners." Ideologically, government is often perceived as naturally and inevitably incompetent, despite manifest success in military, health, and agricultural innovation, exemplified by the Manhattan Project, the Internet, and hybrid corn. Thus, in response to political realities, the topics that the civilian federal technology programs deal with are not rigidly set from above. These programs draw for general themes upon critical technologies lists or the interests of program managers. However, the agencies also call meetings on technology themes in different parts of the country.

"Bottom-Up" Planning

Once a program like the ATP agrees that a proposed technology is deserving of special attention, a conference call is issued. The conference brings together program managers with representatives from companies that are interested in working on the technology. Academics also attend; they cannot always initiate a proposal but can participate in these programs as members of company-led consortia.

The meetings are held in workshop settings in which the discussion focuses on the area of blockage that needs to be addressed to move the particular technology forward. Once a consensus is reached, the next step is that the program conducts a competition for the funds in which both technical and business reviews are carried out. In the ATP and dual use programs, companies also have to commit matching funds. Through this process, government involves itself directly in support of civilian research and development.

These brainstorming sessions, attended by government, industry, and academic representatives, constitute an informal planning system. Planning is done jointly by the government side and the industry side, with both large and small companies participating as well as academics. Out of these discussions, the requests for proposals are made much more specific. Instead of being directed toward a general critical technology that is typically too broad a category for targeting innovation, the planning process reduces the general category to a particular point where the people who are closest to the technology agree that a blockage exists.

Through this format, instead of a "top-down" planning hierarchy (as existed in the former Soviet Union), a "bottom-up" planning process is being created in the United States. Out of the discussions among people from government, industry, and university, the direction of government technology programs is shaped and the funds are then given out. This planning process is typical of the newer efforts like ATP and dual use programs in the Department of Defense. SBIR is still, to a large extent, based on the older models of contracts and grants, although conferences and workshop discussions are common in this program as well.

Rationales for Government Support of Science, Technology, and Industry

The conflicting visions between an active federal government and "the government that governs least, governs best" are as old as the United States itself. The pendulum seems to have swung over to the "active government" side in the last two decades. Justifications for public intervention have become more widely accepted, and aiding small business is generally accepted today.

Risk analysis, both technical and business, is now the basis for decision-making by these programs. Successful innovation requires "the running of two gauntlets: the commercial and the technological."[2] Therefore, programs to foster innovation should strive to reduce business or technical risk (or both).

Justifications for public sector involvement in industrial development vary according to the role one initially accepts for government. A scale can be described, ranging from a basic view that government intervention should be kept to a minimum, to the view that government intervention is obvious in all domains of society. At the minimum end of the scale (i.e., where the strongest justifications are needed), one finds market failure. As the only acceptable framework within neoclassical economics, market failure is the single most important argument for government intervention.[3]

Basic research is a well-known case of public subsidy because of market failure. Government funding of basic research is accepted in countries all over the world.[4] The analytical justifications, based on neoclassical economics, state that private firms are likely to under-invest in basic research because:

1. Results are highly uncertain;
2. The innovating firm might not be the one reaping the benefits; and
3. Most private firms have a short-term focus (on profits today); investment in most basic research requires a long-term focus (postponing profits).

Spill-Over Effects

In the United States, the concept of "spill-over" is often utilized to justify government intervention. Although specific interventions are typically motivated politically on grounds of maintaining national industrial competitiveness, they are difficult to justify on these grounds alone in the United States.

In neoclassical economic theory, the government intervention that produces the most widespread benefits or spill-overs to firms not directly involved is the most acceptable warrant for the expenditure of public funds.[5] Of course, too broad a spill-over flowing across national boundaries might defeat the very purpose of the intervention. Thus, in practice, what is desired is an acceptable justification for limited spill-overs that leave the initiators with special advantages and lead time but not so complete a grasp of the benefits of the innovation that it cannot, in a reasonable time and at a moderate royalty rate, be utilized by other firms to advance the industry as a whole.[6]

Precompetitive R&D

The idea behind precompetitive R&D is that government should support research and development that is not directly linked to the market, even though the funding is not confined to basic research. A pragmatic definition is often assumed, where precompetitive R&D is the research and development that competing firms will collaborate on. In practice, this frequently means focusing on generic technologies like biotechnology, materials, and information technology. The concept is controversial.

At the other end of the scale, where the role of government in industrial development is taken for granted, analytical justifications are hardly needed at all. It is sufficient that there is good reason to believe that the undertakings will make social goals more attainable. However, under *laissez-faire* conditions, government cannot afford to be perceived as taking the leading role, lest it draw unwanted political attack. Thus, the strength of anti-interventionist ideology has the unintended consequence of drawing the diverse institutional spheres (i.e., university, industry, and government) together in new partnerships. As government takes a more active role in innovation policy, whether through initiatives directed toward universities or industry, these institutional spheres are typically drawn into the decision making process since government is constrained from making a decision on its own.

If It Walks Like a Duck and Talks Like a Duck . . .

The growing realization that science and technology, driven by the disbursement of federal research funds, has become a major driver of economic growth has led some of the most conservative regions of the country to press for a more geographically equitable distribution of these funds. They have even pressed for an increase in funding. The Texas congressional delegation has, for example, taken the lead in calling for a doubling of the NIH budget. Their belief is that expansion of funding will make it possible for their state's universities to capture a larger amount of funding in the short term, spurring economic growth in Texas in the long term. Thus, the research funding "have nots" have joined with the "haves" who are suffering from increased competition to demand an increase in research funding budgets.

Another science and technology funding mechanism has been constructed through the regular congressional appropriation process. It works the same way as appropriations for roads and bridges or any local improvement that a senator or a member of Congress wishes. This is accomplished by adding an attachment to a bill for something else. In the most recent list, the number of roads and bridges are relatively few in contrast to the past. Instead, much of the special funds are directed at research centers to be established at local universities on topics of interest and import to the local areas. This is another form of science policy, again through political pressures from below, this time from the universities themselves who have been outside of the federal research funding system but who want to build up and increase their capabilities.

Research funding has also expanded, driven "bottom-up" by social movements concerned with curing various diseases. These pressures have played a significant role in postwar science policy. Medical research was also supported to meet military needs during World War II, but the major impetus to the development of medical and biological research at universities in the past several decades has come from social movements and lobbying groups directed toward the cure of diseases. The social movements to cure diseases, from cancer to heart disease to Alzheimer's, support voluntary associations that fund research. These associations typically feel they are not able to raise sufficient funds to accomplish their goal. They exert political pressure to expand the federal role in health research.

This has been accomplished by expanding the National Institutes of Health and by supporting funding of health research at the universities. NIH existed from the mid-nineteenth century but on a very small scale. The institutes grew during the postwar period and multiplied through the efforts of social movements interested in curing diseases, using research to solve health problems. Research at NIH was greatly expanded and an extramural research program was established that has become the mainstay of research support for (1) academic research in biology and related fields in universities and (2) clinical research in the medical schools. An unintended side effect of this public investment was the creation of the biotechnology industry.

The innovation environment currently being created in the United States combines elements of a "bottom-up" planning system at the federal level. It also includes the various state programs that grew up during the 1980s when the federal government removed itself from supporting near market technological development. The federal government currently supplies funds to the states to expand their outreach programs to improve manufacturing in firms. At the local level, innovation systems are emerging based upon strategic alliances connecting companies and the national laboratories, drawing upon industry, state, and federal funds for joint projects.

Notes

1. Nester, William R. (1997), *American Industrial Policy: Free or Managed Markets?* New York: St. Martin's Press.

2. Kline, S., and N. Rosenberg (1986), "An Overview of Innovation." In R. Landau and N. Rosenberg (eds.), *The Positive Sum Strategy: Harnessing Technology for Economic Growth.* Washington DC: National Academy Press, p. 275.

3. Cowen, T. (ed.) (1992), *Public goods and Market Failures. A Critical Examination.* New Brunswick, NJ: Transaction Publishers; Griliches, Z. (1998), "Issues in Assessing the Contribution of R&D to Productivity Growth," *Bell Journal of Economics*, 10:92–116.

4. Nelson, Richard (1959), "The Simple Economics of Basic Scientific Research," *Journal of Political Economy*, 67:297–306; Arrow, K.J. (1962), "Economic Welfare and the Allocation of Resources for Invention." In R. Nelson (ed.), *The Rate and Direction of Inventive Activity.* Princeton, NJ: Princeton University Press, pp. 609–625. Reprinted in N. Rosenberg (ed.), *The Economics of Technical Change.* Harmondsworth (UK): Pelican, pp. 164–181.

5. Jaffee, A. (1986), "Technological Opportunities and Spillovers of R&D: Evidence from Firms/ Patents, Profits and Market Value," *American Economic Review*, 76(4): 984–1001.

6. Etzkowitz, Henry, Christiane Gebhardt, Susan Giesecke, and Karen Baird (1998), Science Policy Institute Report: *The Health Informatics Initiative (HII): A Qualitative Evaluation of an ATP Focused Program.* Purchase, NY: State University of New York.

PART IV
QUICK REFERENCE GUIDE TO CURRENT GOVERNMENT PROGRAMS

In this chapter, we provide contact information, data on deadlines, size of awards, and other useful information. Changes can be significant from year to year. There may be adjustments of deadlines, minimum and maximum amounts, people to contact, and so on. Before preparing and submitting a proposal, you should, therefore, check for current information on the program's Web site.

The information provided in this section was obtained primarily from the Web and previous solicitations and awards, and supplemented by materials from an e-mail questionnaire sent to some of the program managers. For future volumes, we intend to rely more heavily on data gathered directly from the programs, entered into a database, and updated periodically.

The following information will be presented, as available, for the various programs:

1. Name
2. Agency/organization (for the Small Business Innovation Research program, where the subprograms are large and locally managed)
3. Address
4. Phone and fax numbers
5. General e-mail (when applicable)
6. Web Page
7. Program officer (with contact information when other than above)
8. Type of program (public seed capital, research funds, development funds, proof of concept funds, etc.)
9. Technology preferences
10. Type of financing (grants, loans, technology transfer, matching funds, etc.)
11. Minimum/maximum amounts (and maximum project duration)
12. Special considerations (e.g., women, minorities)
13. Deadlines (release dates for invitations to submit proposals, proposal deadlines)
14. Additional information

Name

Advanced Technology Program, National Institute for Standards and Technology

Address

Advanced Technology Program
A430 Administration Building
National Institute of Standards and Technology
Gaithersburg, MD 20899-0001

Phone

(800) ATP-FUND [(800) 287-3863]

Fax

(301) 926-9524 or (301) 590-3053

E-mail

atp@nist.gov

Web Page

http://www.atp.nist.gov

Type of Program

Public R&D funds are oriented at the "middle ground" between basic research and product development (neither of which is supported in pure form). Proposals are evaluated for their scientific and technological merit, and for their potential for broad-based economic benefits, with both parts weighed equally.

Technology Preferences

Project proposals within all technological areas are welcome. Peers chosen to evaluate the proposals are selected by "technology area boards" in electronics, information technology, biotechnology, materials and chemicals, and manufacturing.

Current focused programs and technological areas that are under development for future ATP support include (with points of contact for future areas)

1. Adaptive Learning Systems
2. Catalysis & Biocatalysis Technologies
3. Component-Based Software
4. Digital Data Storage
5. Digital Video in Information Networks
6. Information Infrastructure for Healthcare
7. Manufacturing Composite Structures

8. Materials Processing for Heavy Manufacturing

9. Microelectronics Manufacturing Infrastructure

10. Motor Vehicle Manufacturing Technology

11. Photonics Manufacturing

12. Premium Power

13. Selective-Membrane Platforms

14. Technologies for the Integration of Manufacturing Applications

15. Tissue Engineering

16. Tools for DNA Diagnostics

17. Vapor Compression Refrigeration Technology.

18. Combinatorial Chemistry and Materials Research—John Hewes (john.hewes@nist.gov)

19. Composites in Civil Applications—Felix Wu (felix.wu@nist.gov)

20. Condition-Based Maintenance—Richard (Chuck) Bartholomew (richard.bartholowmew@nist.gov)

21. Genetic Manipulation in Animals: Advanced Transgenesis and Cloning—Rosemarie Hunziker (rosemarie.hunziker@nist.gov)

22. Initiatives in Healthcare Informatics—Bettijoyce Lide (bettijoyce.lide@nist.gov) and Jayne Orthwein (jayne.orthwein@nist.gov)

23. Intelligent and Distributed Engineering Design—Mary Mitchell (mary.mitchell@nist.gov) and Simon Szykman (simon.szykman@nist.gov)

24. Intelligent Control—Mary Mitchell (mary.mitchell@nist.gov) and Richard Bartholomew (richard.bartholomew@nist.gov)

25. Interoperable Infrastructures for Distributed Electronic Commerce—Shirley Hurwitz (shirley.hurwitz@nist.gov) and Mary Mitchell (mary.mitchell@nist.gov)

26. Microsystems and Nanosystems Technology—Jack Boudreaux (jack.boudreaux@nist.gov)

27. Motor Vehicle Manufacturing Technology—Jack Boudreaux (jack.boudreaux@nist.gov)

28. Nano and MEMS Technologies for Chemical Biosensors—Howard Weetall (howard.weetall@nist.gov)

29. Organic Electronics Technology—Michael Schen (michael.schen@nist.gov)

30. Semiconductor Lithography—Purabi Mazumdar (purabi.mazumdar@nist.gov)

31. Tissue Engineering—Rosemarie Hunziker (rosemarie.hunziker@nist.gov)

32. Tools for Engineered Surfaces—Clare M. Allocca
(clare.allocca@nist.gov)

33. Wireless Communications—Elissa Sobolewski
(elissa.sobolewski@nist.gov)

Type of Financing/Maximum Amount

Grants/cost sharing. The single-applicant requirement for cost sharing is that the company covers its indirect costs. Direct costs of single applicants are 100% reimbursable up to $2 million. Costs of subcontracting are regarded as directs costs, that is, a firm, university, federal lab, and such, if subcontracting to a single applicant can recover both direct and indirect costs from the ATP.

Special Considerations

None. Although the ATP was earlier viewed as oriented toward large firms, more than half of its awards have gone to small firms. In recent years in response to criticism of the amount of funding that was made available to large firms, ATP has increasingly focused on the role of start-ups and small firms in the advancement and diffusion of technology.

Deadlines

In fiscal year 1999, there was one competition with a final deadline in mid-April. This is likely to continue.

Additional Information

Much weight is put on business criteria, especially compared to the SBIR program. There is the possibility of getting feedback on preproposals. The applicants who receive the most positive evaluations on their proposals enter the "semifinalist round" consisting of interviews by a panel of experts at the ATP headquarters.

Name
Army Advanced Concepts & Technology II (ACT II) Program

Address
Army Material Command

Phone **Fax**
(703) 617-8260 (703) 617-8261

Web Page
http://www.aro.ncren.net/arowash/rt/actii.htm

Contact—Army Material Command
Maj. John Lemondes (phone numbers above)

E-mail
jlemondes@hqamc.army.mil

Contact—Procurement/Broad Agency Announcement
Kathryn C. Terry

Phone **Fax**
(919) 549-4337 (919) 549-4310

E-mail
terry@aro-emh1.army.mil

Contact—TRADOC Battle Lab
Maj. Reba Lyons

Phone
(757) 728-5984

E-mail
lyonsr@monroe.army.mil

Type of Program
Technology push—developing military applications from mature technologies

Technology Preferences
None in particular beyond the criteria that it be relevant to the armed forces. Moreover, the technology has to have been proved feasible in the laboratory. As in other programs, previous solicitations (invitations to compete for funding) can yield considerable useful information about what the program personnel considers important technical areas.

Type of Financing
Contracts. However, it is common for projects to be cost-shared or leveraged by others.

Maximum Amounts
$1.5 million for a project lasting a maximum of one year

Special Considerations
None in particular

Deadlines
The Broad Agency Announcement is released in May (and prereleased in draft form a month earlier). Two-page concept papers are due in June. The most promising papers result in an invitation to submit a full proposal (with a short deadline of approximately a month). These are evaluated in August and September, and contracts should be signed by December.

Additional Information
Of the full proposals, 17% received funding in fiscal year 1999. If concept papers are counted, the rate of success is approximately 4%.

Name
Dual Use Science & Technology Program (DU S&T)

Address
Office of the Secretary of Defense, S&T
5203 Leesburg Pike, Ste. 1401
Falls Church, VA 22041

Phone
(703) 681-9312

General E-mail
dus&t@acq.osd.mil

Web Page
http://www.dtic.mil/dust/

Program Officer—Office of the Secretary of Defense
Dan Petonito

Phone   **Fax**
(703) 681-5451   (703) 681-3722

E-mail
petonidh@acq.osd.mil

Program Officer—Navy
Cathy Nodgaard

Address
Office of Naval Research
Code 36
800 N. Quincy St.
Arlington, VA 22217-5660

Phone   **Fax**
(703) 696-0289   (703) 696-4884

E-mail
nodgaac@onr.navy.mil

Program Officer—Air Force
Dr. Joan Fuller

Address
SAF/AQRT
1060 Air Force Pentagon
Washington, DC 20330-1060

Phone
(703) 588-7867

Fax
(703) 588-0588

E-mail
fullerjo@af.pentagon.mil

Program Officer—Army
Dr. Robert S. Rohde

Address
SARDA-TR
Assistant Secretary of the Army, Research, Development and Acquisition
2511 Jefferson Davis Highway
Arlington, VA 22202-3911

Phone
(703) 601-1515

Fax
(703) 607-5962

E-mail
rohder@sarda.army.mil

Type of Program
Development funds

Technology Preferences
In general, all projects must involve a "dual use" technology with both military utility and a sufficient commercial potential to support a viable industrial base. In fiscal year 1999, the technical topic headlines were:

1. Affordable Sensors
2. Advanced Propulsion, Power, and Fuel Efficiency
3. Information and Communications Systems
4. Medical and Bioengineering
5. Weapons Systems Sustainment
6. Distributed Mission Training
7. Advanced Materials and Manufacturing
8. Environmental Technologies

Type of Financing
Matching funds (the general rule is one to one private funding to government funding). The DU S&T program pays 25% of the costs, and the relevant military service another 25%. A higher level and/or higher "quality" (more money in practice, not other types of costs that can be attributed to the project) are very beneficial in the proposal evaluation process.

Minimum/Maximum Amounts

No specifications. Mean awards size the last years has been slightly above $1 million (half from DU S&T and another half from the Army, Navy or Air Force).

Special Considerations

No special considerations (but as in all programs, minority institutions, small businesses, and historically black colleges and institutions are encouraged to participate).

Deadlines

The Broad Agency Announcement (or joint solicitation), which is the "call for white papers and proposals," is released in August. "White papers"—which are a synopsis of the planned proposal, including a rough cost estimate—are due at the end of September. Full proposals are due in mid-December.

Additional Information

The future of the DU S&T program is under review. Some expect it to continue at the same scale as today ($30 million–$60 million annual program budget), others believe that dual use will be completely transferred to the individual military services, and that the development and support of dual use technologies will become the normal state of affairs in the whole Department of Defense. In any case, there might be more opportunities for dual use funding than what is available through the DU S&T program. Program Officers in the individual military services (see above) can be a good place to start for more information.

Note that DU S&T contracts are not subject to ordinary Federal Acquisition Regulations. Special contractual arrangements have been developed that offer possibilities for negotiating intellectual property rights.

Name

Commercial Operations and Support Savings Initiative (COSSI)

Web Page

http://www.acq.osd.mil/es/dut/

Program Officers—Office of the Secretary of Defense

Rich Mirsky and Diane Larriva

Phone

(703) 681-5452 and (703) 681-5457

E-mail

mirskyra@acq.osd.mil and larrivd@acq.osd.mil

Program Officers—Navy

Charles Borsch and Tom McDonald

Phone

(703) 601-1682 and (703) 9180 x112

E-mail

borsch.charles@hq.navy.mil and mcdonaldtw@navsea.navy.mil

Program Officers—Air Force

Capt. Terry Dannenbrink and Maj. Scott Pearl

Phone

(937) 255-7210 x3905 and (703) 588-7819

E-mail

dannentl@ntnotes2.wpafb.af.mil and pearlsm@pentagon.af.mil

Program Officers—Army

Juan Millan and Carol Gardinier

Phone

(703) 617-5192 and (703) 617-4389

E-mail

jmillan@hqamc.army.mil and cgardinier@alexandria-emh1.army.mil

Type of Program

Proof of concept funds; insertion of developed commercial products/technologies ("items") into military systems.

Technology Preferences

These will be described in the solicitation. In general, it is a good strategy to discuss your ideas with program managers well in advance of submitting a proposal to get a sense of the relevance of your technology to the military.

Ideally, in advance of making an application, need of a potential military customer would already have been identified, assuring a good transition of the technology, a close partnership, and perhaps an additional source of funding.

Type of Financing

Matching funds. In general, at least 25% of the project costs must come from private sources. A higher level (or "quality") of cost-share is highly beneficial in the proposal review process.

Minimum/Maximum Amounts

No specifications

Special Considerations

None in particular

Deadlines

There was no award competition in fiscal year 1999. The program is expected to receive around $90 million for fiscal year 2000. Check with the Web site for more information. Previous proposal deadlines have been in the summer (the solicitation has been released in the spring).

Additional Information

Proposals must include written support from a "military customer" defined as the organization with the authority to modify the system and purchase the kits.

Name
DARPA—Defense Advanced Research Projects Agency

Address
N/A

E-mail
webmaster@darpa.mil (who will take you further)

Phone
(703) 696-0104 (general DARPA help line)

Web Page
http://www.darpa.mil

Type of Program
Advanced research and development, mainly in state-of-the-art technologies. Scientific/technical quality and relevance to program goals and DARPA mission are the criteria by which proposals are selected.

Technology Preferences
High-risk advanced technologies. One-fifth of DARPA's $2 million annual R&D budget goes to new programs/projects. One source of information on technical interests is the DARPA SBIR topics. DARPA has technical offices in the following fields, which also indicates some of the areas of interest:

1. Defense Sciences Office
2. Electronics Technology Office
3. Information Systems Offices
4. Information Technology Office
5. Sensor Technology Office
6. Tactical Technology Office
7. Discoverer II

Type of Financing
Grants, contracts, special arrangements, and cost-sharing

Maximum Amounts
None. DARPA projects range in size from less than a million to several hundred million dollars, and subcontracts can vary just as much.

Deadlines
A number of different solicitations released at different times every year. The best time to influence new project ideas is in the Spring.

Special Considerations
None in particular.

Additional Information
Historically, one out of three preproposals get funded.

Name
Manufacturing Technology Program (ManTech)

Address
Office of the Director, Defense Research & Engineering
(Laboratory Management/Technology Transition)
Skyline 2, Suite 1403
5203 Leesburg Pike
Falls Church, VA 22041-3466

Phone
(703) 681-9339

Fax
(703) 681-4669

E-mail
dcundiff@acq.osd.mil

Program Officers
T. Daniel Cundiff, ManTech Staff Specialist

Web Page
http://mantech.iitri.org

Type of Program
Proof of concept funds (feasibility at the laboratory level must be established in advance)

Technology Preferences
In general, all projects must be oriented toward improving the manufacture of weapon systems and their parts. Weapon systems is broadly defined (a military submarine is considered a weapon system). The program's technical thrust areas are:

1. Metals Processing and Fabrication

2. Composites Processing and Fabrication

3. Electronics Processing and Fabrication

4. Advanced Manufacturing Enterprise (benchmarking, advanced manufacturing management, supply base management and technology, and manufacturing and engineering systems)

5. Sustainment/Readiness (repair processes, systems, and related manufacturing issues)

6. Energetics/Munitions

Type of Financing
Matching funds (general rule two to one private funding to government funding) or grants if the technology has high business risk and is sufficiently long-term

Minimum/Maximum Amounts
No specifications

Special Considerations
No special considerations

Deadlines
No mentioned deadline

Name
Manufacturing Extension Partnership (MEP)

Address
Building 301, Rm C121
National Institute of Standards and Technology
Gaithersburg, MD 20899-0001

Toll Free Phone
1-800 MEP-4MFG (to locate your closest MEP center or to connect to headquarters)

Phone
(301) 975-5020

Fax
(301) 963-6556

Web Page
http://www.mep.nist.gov/

Type of Program
Various services oriented at small and medium-sized manufacturers, everything from process improvement to market development and solving Year 2000 (Y2K) problems

Technology Preferences
None in particular, although the local MEP centers will often be tailored to the clusters of businesses in their region

Type of Financing
The firm has to pay for all services offered, but the centers are nonprofit and often linked to colleges and universities, so the services are probably relatively inexpensive compared to private consultants

Minimum/Maximum Amounts
No specifications

Special Considerations
Oriented to small and medium-sized manufacturing firms

Deadlines
No deadlines

Additional Information
There are MEP centers and regional outreach offices at more than 300 locations in all states and Puerto Rico.

Name
Small Business Innovation Research Program (SBIR)

Agency/Organization
United States Department of Agriculture (USDA)

Address
Cooperative State Research, Education & Extension Services
United States Department of Agriculture
Stop 2243
1400 Independence Avenue SW
Washington, DC 20250-2243

Phone   **Fax**
(202) 401-4002   (202) 401-6070

Web Page
http://www.reeusda.gov/sbir/

General Contact
Dr. Charles F. Cleland, Division Director, SBIR Program

E-mail
ccleland@reeusda.gov

Additional Contact
Ruth Lange, Assistant Program Director, SBIR Program

E-mail
rlange@reesuda.gov

Type of Program
R&D funds (technical and commercial criteria are considered). The program is based on a three-phase process:

1. Phase I—the start-up phase; typically exploration of the technical merit or feasibility of an idea or technology

2. Phase II—the work phase; typically prototype development, evaluation of commercial potential

3. Phase III—the commercialization phase; no SBIR funds available for this purpose (although SBIR program managers can be useful contacts)

Technology Preferences
Topic headlines from the 1999 solicitation, which are to continue in fiscal year 2000:

1. Forests and Related Resources
2. Plant Production and Protection
3. Animal Production and Protection
4. Air, Water, and Soils
5. Food Science and Nutrition
6. Rural and Community Development
7. Aquaculture
8. Industrial Applications
9. Marketing and Trade

Type of Financing
Grants

Maximum amounts
$65,000 for Phase I projects (lasting maximum six months); $250,000 for Phase II projects

Special Considerations
Oriented to small firms (fewer than 500 employees)

Deadlines
A solicitation (invitation to compete for funding in certain technological areas) is released once every year, usually at the beginning of June. The closing date is usually around three months after the release of the solicitation.

Additional Information
The USDA is the sixth largest SBIR participant.

Name
Small Business Innovation Research Program (SBIR)

Agency/Organization
Department of Health and Human Services [incl. National Institutes of Health (NIH)]

Address
PHS SBIR/STTR Solicitation Office
13685 Baltimore Avenue
Laurel, MD 20707-5096

Phone   **Fax**
(301) 206-9385   (301) 206-9722

E-mail
a2y@cu.nih.gov

Web Page
http://www.nih.gov/grants/funding/sbir.htm

Program Officers
A number of people work on the SBIR program or in connection with it. See solicitation for information on points of contact at each National Center or laboratory. For general information use the contact data above. For specific contact information, see below:

Type of Program
R&D funds (technical and commercial criteria are considered). The program is based on a three-phase process:

1. Phase I—the start-up phase; typically exploration of the technical merit or feasibility of an idea or technology
2. Phase II—the work phase; typically prototype development, evaluation of commercial potential
3. Phase III—the commercialization phase; no SBIR funds available for this purpose (although SBIR program managers can be useful contacts)

Technology Preferences
The DHHS SBIR program supports all types of projects that are health-related. In general, the NIH carries out and sponsors basic and applied scientific inquiries related to the causes, diagnosis, prevention, treatment, and rehabilitation of human diseases and disabilities; the fundamental biological processes of growth, development and aging, and the biological effects of the environment. Concrete topics change from year to year. They are developed by:

1. National Institutes of Health (NIH): National Institute on Aging, National Institute on Alcohol Abuse and Alcoholism, National Institute of Allergy and Infectious Diseases, National Institute of Arthritis and Musculoskeletal and Skin Diseases, National Cancer Institute, National Institute of Child Health and Human Development, National Institute on Drug Abuse, National Institute on Deafness and Other Communication Disorders, National Institute of Dental and Craniofacial Research, National Institute of Diabetes and Digestive and Kidney Diseases, National Institute of Environmental Health Sciences, National Eye Institute, National Institute of General Medical Sciences, National Heart, Lung, and Blood Institute, National Human Genome Research Institute, National Institute of Mental Health, National Institute of Neurological Disorders and Stroke, National Institute of Nursing Research, National Center for Research Resources, National Complementary and Alternative Medicine, National Library of Medicine

2. Trans-NIH Research Programs

3. Centers for Disease Control and Prevention (CDC): National Institute for Occupational Safety and Health, National Center for Injury Prevention and Control, National Center for Infectious Diseases, National Center for Chronic Disease Prevention and Health Promotion National Immunization Program, National Center for HIV, STD, and TB Prevention

4. Food and Drug Administration (FDA)

Type of Financing start here
Grants and contracts

Maximum amounts
$100,000 for Phase I projects (lasting six months). $750,000 for Phase II projects (lasting two years). There are possibilities of proposing longer periods of time and greater amounts of funds if it is necessary for completion of the project but normally projects are tailored to the general limits.

Special Considerations
Oriented to small firms (fewer than 500 employees). NIH suggests that grants can add value to an academic institution's intellectual property, provided that a small firm has been started by some of the scientists that are employed by the institution. Place on application face page to indicate "women-owned" and/or "socially and economically disadvantaged"

Deadlines
A solicitation (invitation to compete for funding in certain technological areas) is released three times every year. The applications are normally due in mid-April, mid-August, and mid-December. STTR Grant Applications: April 1, August 1, December 1; SBIR contract proposals: first week of

November. Because of a thorough peer review process, the earliest possible delay between submission of application and award is seven months.

Additional Information

DHHS is the second largest SBIR participant, and with the increased support for biomedical R&D, this SBIR program is likely to grow in the coming years (as it has the last part of the 1990s).

There is a salary cap of $125,000 for the primary investigator.

If the project involves living persons or samples from living persons, or live vertebrate animals, the proposed use must be approved by an institutional review board before funding. There are also guidelines concerning the inclusion of children, women, and minorities in the subject population. Such requirements should be well known for scientists, doctors, and engineers with previous experience with NIH funding.

Mean success rate the last seven years:

- 23.1 for Phase I (highest of all SBIR programs)
- 51 for Phase II (also among the highest)

The two most common criteria for not scoring a Phase I application are lack of innovative ideas and an unfocused, diffused, or superficial research plan. A model application has been developed and is available online on the NIH SBIR Web pages, as well as on the CD-ROM accompanying this volume.

A Fast-Track review option is possible—the Phase I and Phase II applications are submitted and evaluated simultaneously, reducing (or removing) the funding gap between phases. Some special eligibility criteria apply (e.g., measurable milestones and a product development plan).

Applicants are encouraged to pay close attention to specific receipt dates for special announcements listed on the Small Business Funding Opportunities Web site as these may differ from the receipt dates under the general SBIR or STTR Omnibus Grant Solicitation.

SBIR/STTR Grant Applications are submitted to the Center for Scientific Review, National Institutes of Health, 6701 Rockledge Drive, Rm 1040-MSC 7710, Bethesda, MD 20892-7710.

Name
Small Business Innovation Research Program (SBIR)

Laboratory/Organization/Agency
National Institute of Aging (National Institutes of Health, Department of Health and Human Services)

Program Officer
Dr. Miriam F. Kelty

Phone   **Fax**
(301) 496-9322   (301) 402-2945

E-mail
mk46u@nih.gov

Name
Small Business Innovation Research Program (SBIR)

Laboratory/Organization/Agency
National Institute on Alcohol Abuse and Alcoholism (National Institutes of Health, Department of Health and Human Services)

Program Officer
Dr. Michael Eckardt

Phone   **Fax**
(301) 443-6107   (301) 443-6077

E-mail
me25t@nih.gov

Name

Small Business Innovation Research Program (SBIR)

Laboratory/Organization/Agency

National Institute of Allergy and Infectious Diseases (National Institutes of Health, Department of Health and Human Services)

Program Officer

Allan Czarra

Phone	**Fax**
(301) 496-7291	(301) 402-0369

E-mail

ac20a@nih.gov

Name
Small Business Innovation Research Program (SBIR)

Laboratory/Organization/Agency
National Institute of Arthritis and Musculoskeletal and Skin Diseases (National Institutes of Health, Department of Health and Human Services)

Research Topic
Rheumatic diseases

Program Officer
Dr. Susana Serrate-Sztein

Phone	**Fax**
(301) 594-5032	(301) 480-4543

E-mail
ss86e@nih.gov

Research Topic
Cartilage and Connective Tissue

Address
45 Center Drive, Rm 5AS-37J
Bethesda, MD 20892-6500

Phone	**Fax**
(301) 594-5032	(301) 480-4543

Program Officer
Dr. Bernadette Tyree

E-mail
bt16w@nih.gov

Research Topic
Muscle Biology

Program Officer
Dr. Richard Lynn

Phone	**Fax**
(301) 594-5128	(301) 480-4543

E-mail
rl28b@nih.gov

Research Topic
Skin Diseases

Program Officer
Dr. Alan N. Moshell

Phone   **Fax**
(301) 594-5017   (301) 480-4543

E-mail
am40j@nih.gov

Research Topic
Orthopaedics

Program Officer
Dr. James Panagis

Phone   **Fax**
(301) 594-5055   (301) 480-4543

E-mail
jp149d@nih.gov

Research Topic
Bone biology

Program Officer
Dr. William Sharrock

Phone   **Fax**
(301) 594-5055   (301) 480-4543

E-mail
ws19h@nih.gov

Research Topic
Bone diseases (program officer also responsible for bone imaging, osteoporosis intervention, prevention, and diagnosis)

Address
Natcher Building, 5AS-43E
Bethesda, MD 20892-6500

Phone   **Fax**
(301) 594-5055   (301) 480-4543

Web page
http://www.nih.gov/grants/funding/sbir/htm

Program Officer
Dr. Joan McGowan
Director, Cartilage and Connective—NIAMS/NIH

E-mail
jm106v@nih.gov

Name
Small Business Innovation Research Program (SBIR)

Laboratory/Organization/Agency
National Cancer Institute (National Institutes of Health, Department of Health and Human Services)

Research Division
Division of Cancer Biology

Address
6701 Rockledge Drive
Rockledge II Building, Rm 6186
Bethesda, MD 20892-7910

Phone   **Fax**
(301) 435-2688   (301) 480-0146

Supplemental Information Available
Advice and Information on SBIR/STTR Programs at NIH may be found at http://deainfo.nci.nih.gov/awards/sbir_sttr/sbir_nih.htm

Program Officer
Jo Anne Goodnight
NIH SBIR/STTR Program Coordinator

E-mail
jg128w@nih.gov

Research Division
Division of Cancer Control and Population Sciences, topic: Cancer Epidemiology and Genetics

Program Officer
Burdette W. Erickson, Jr.

Phone   **Fax**
(301) 496-9600   (301) 402-4279

E-mail
be13u@nih.gov

Research Division
Division of Cancer Control and Population Sciences, topic: Multimedia Technology and Health Communication in Cancer Control. This includes, for instance, computer applications, advanced telephone technologies, videos, cable and broadcast television, radio, animation, digital imaging, smart cards, the Internet, or the Web.

Address
6130 Executive Blvd. EPN-232
Bethesda, MD 20892-7330

Phone   **Fax**
(301) 496-8520   (301) 480-6637

Web Page
http://dccps.nci.nih.gov

Program Officer
Connie Dresser

E-mail
cd34b@nih.gov

Research Division
Division of Cancer Treatment and Diagnosis, Technology Development Branch

Program Officer
Dr. Jennifer Couch

Phone   **Fax**
(301) 402-4185   (301) 402-7819

E-mail
jc332a@nih.gov

Research Division
Division of Cancer Treatment and Diagnosis, Biochemistry and Pharmacology

Address
Executive Plaza North, Rm 841, National Cancer Institute
Bethesda, MD 20892

Phone   **Fax**
(301) 496-8783   (301) 402-5200

Web Page
http://dtp.nci.nih.gov

Program Officer
Dr. George S. Johnson

E-mail
gj16m@nih.gov

Research Division
Division of Cancer Treatment and Diagnosis, Diagnostic Imaging Program—accepting topics related to diagnostic messages in all modalities including image guided treatment

Address
6130 Executive Boulevard
Rockville, MD 20852

Phone   **Fax**
(301) 496-0735   (301) 480-5785

Program Officer
Dr. Manuel J. Torres-Anjel

E-mail
mt71d@nih.gov

Research Division
Division of Cancer Treatment and Diagnosis, Radiation Research Program

Program Officer
Dr. Helen B. Stone

Phone   **Fax**
(301) 496-9360   (301) 480-5785

E-mail
hs50d@nih.gov

Research Division
Division of Cancer Treatment and Diagnosis, Biological Response Modifiers

Program Officer
Dr. Craig Reynolds

Phone   **Fax**
(301) 846-1098   (301) 846-5429

E-mail
cr45u@nih.gov

Research Division
Division of Cancer Prevention

Program Officer
Dr. Barry Portnoy

Phone   **Fax**
(301) 496-9569   (301) 496-9931

E-mail
bp22z@nih.gov

Name
Small Business Innovation Research Program (SBIR)

Laboratory/Organization/Agency
National Institute of Child Health and Human Development (National Institutes of Health, Department of Health and Human Services)

Address
6100 Executive Blvd, Rm 2A03
Rockville, MD 20852

Phone   **Fax**
(301) 402-4221   (301) 402-0832

Web Page
http://www.nichd.nih.gov/

Program Officer
Dr. Louis A. Quatrano

E-mail
lq2n@nih.gov

Name

Small Business Innovation Research Program (SBIR)

Laboratory/Organization/Agency

National Institute on Drug Abuse (National Institutes of Health, Department of Health and Human Services)

Address

6001 Executive Blvd, Rm 5230 MSC9591
Bethesda, MD 20892-9591

Phone	**Fax**
(301) 443-6071	(301) 443-6277

Web Page

www.nida.nih.gov/Funding/SBIR_STTR.html

Program Officer

Cathrine A. Sasek, Ph.D.

E-mail

csasek@nih.gov

Name

Small Business Innovation Research Program (SBIR)

Laboratory/Organization/Agency

National Institute on Deafness and Other Communication Disorders (National Institutes of Health, Department of Health and Human Services).

Address

6120 Executive Blvd, 400-C, MSC 7180
Bethesda, MD 20892-7180

Phone   **Fax:**

(301) 402-3458   (301) 402-6251

Program Officer

Dr. Lynn E. Huerta

E-mail

lh99s@nih.gov

Technology Preferences

Generally related to devices to aid research, prevention, and therapeutics for hearing, balance, speech, voice, language, smell, and taste disorders.

Name
Small Business Innovation Research Program (SBIR)

Laboratory/Organization/Agency
National Institute of Dental and Craniofacial Research (National Institutes of Health, Department of Health and Human Services)

Program Officer
Dr. Joyce A. Reese

Phone   **Fax**
(301) 594-2088   (301) 480-8318

E-mail
jr55r@nih.gov

Name
Small Business Innovation Research Program (SBIR)

Laboratory/Organization/Agency
National Institute of Diabetes and Digestive and Kidney Diseases (National Institutes of Health, Department of Health and Human Services)

Research Topic
Diabetes, Endocrinology, and Metabolic Diseases

Program Officer
Dr. Barbara Linder

Phone   Fax
(301) 594-0021   (301) 480-3503

E-mail
bl99n@nih.gov

Research Topic
Digestive Diseases and Nutrition

Program Officer
Dr. Judith Podskalny

Phone   **Fax**
(301) 594-8876   (301) 480-8300

E-mail
jp53s@nih.gov

Research Topic
Kidney, Urologic, and Hematologic Diseases

Program Officer
Dr. Charles H. Rodgers

Phone   **Fax**
(301) 594-7717   (301) 480-3510

E-mail
cr36d@nih.gov

Name

Small Business Innovation Research Program (SBIR)

Laboratory/Organization/Agency

National Institute of Environmental Health Sciences (National Institutes of Health, Department of Health and Human Services)

Program Officer

Dr. Michael J. Galvin, Jr.

Phone　　　　**Fax**

(919) 541-7825　　(919) 541-5064

E-mail

mg63c@nih.gov

Name
Small Business Innovation Research Program (SBIR)

Laboratory/Organization/Agency
National Eye Institute (National Institutes of Health, Department of Health and Human Services), whose technical preferences are related to devices and drugs for visual disorders.

Address
6120 Executive Blvd., Suite 350
Bethesda, MD 20892-7164

Phone	**Fax**
(301) 496-5301	(301) 402-0528

Web Page
http://www.nei.nih.gov

Program Officer
Dr. Ralph Helmsen

E-mail
rh27v@nih.gov (or rjh@nei.nih.gov)

Name
Small Business Innovation Research Program (SBIR)

Laboratory/Organization/Agency
National Institute of General Medical Sciences (National Institutes of Health, Department of Health and Human Services)

Research Topic
Cell Biology and Biophysics

Program Officer
Dr. Jean Chin

Phone   **Fax**
(301) 594-2485   (301) 480-2004

E-mail
jc99s@nih.gov

Research Topic
Genetics and Developmental Biology

Program Officer
Dr. Paul Wolfe

Phone   **Fax**
(301) 594-0943   (301) 480-2228

E-mail
pw1w@nih.gov

Research Topic
Pharmacology, Physiology, and Biorelated Chemistry. This is a very general area, and previous applications have been related to broadly applicable biomedical research and research tool development.

Program Officer
Dr. Peter Preusch

Phone   **Fax**
(301) 594-1832   (301) 480-2802

E-mail
pp27g@nih.gov

Name
Small Business Innovation Research Program (SBIR)

Laboratory/Organization/Agency
National Heart, Lung, and Blood Institute (National Institutes of Health, Department of Health and Human Services)

Research Topic
Heart and Vascular Diseases

Program Officer
Dr. Rosalie Dunn

Phone	**Fax**
(301) 435-0505	(301) 480-1454

E-mail
rd39w@nih.gov

Research Topic
Lung Diseases

Program Officer
Dr. Robert Musson

Phone	**Fax**
(301) 435-0222	(301) 480-3557

E-mail
rm65o@nih.gov

Research Topic
Lung Diseases (additional contact)

Program Officer
Ann Rothgeb

Phone	**Fax**
(301) 435-0202	(301) 480-3557

E-mail
ar31t@nih.gov

Research Topic
Blood Diseases and Resources

Program Officer
Susan E. Pucie

Phone	**Fax**
(301) 435-0079	(301) 480-0867

E-mail
sp34j@nih.gov

Research Topic
Epidemiology and Clinical Applications

Program Officer
Dr. Thomas Blaszkowski

Phone   **Fax**
(301) 496-1841   (301) 496-0075

E-mail
tb33i@nih.gov

Name
Small Business Innovation Research Program (SBIR)

Laboratory/Organization/Agency
National Human Genome Research Institute (National Institutes of Health, Department of Health and Human Services)

Research Topic
Ethical, Legal, and Social Implications (ELSI) of Genomics and Genetics Research

Program Officer
Elizabeth Thomson

Phone   **Fax**
(301) 402-4997   (301) 402-1950

E-mail
et22s@nih.gov

Research Topic
All other research topics under this institute

Program Officer
Dr. Bettie J. Graham

Phone   **Fax**
(301) 496-7531   (301) 480-2770

E-mail
bg30t@nih.gov

Name
Small Business Innovation Research Program (SBIR)

Laboratory/Organization/Agency
National Institute of Mental Health (National Institutes of Health, Department of Health and Human Services)

Institute Web Page
http://www.nimh.nih.gov

Research Topic
Basic and Clinical Neuroscience Research

Program Officer
Dr. Michael F. Huerta

Phone	**Fax**
(301) 443-3563	(301) 443-1731

E-mail
mh38f@nih.gov

Research Topic
Mental Disorders, Behavior, and AIDS

Address
6001 Executive Blvd., Rm 6-201
Rockville, MD 20852

Phone	**Fax**
(301) 443-6100	(301) 443-9719

Program Officer
Dr. Louis Steinberg

E-mail
ls24d@nih.gov

Research Topic
Services and Intervention Research

Program Officer
Dr. Kenneth G. Lutterman

Phone	**Fax**
(301) 443-3373	(301) 443-4045

E-mail
kl121o@nih.gov

Name
Small Business Innovation Research Program (SBIR)

Laboratory/Organization/Agency
National Institute of Neurological Disorders and Stroke (National Institutes of Health, Department of Health and Human Services)

Research Topic
Convulsive, Infectious, and Immune Disorders

Program Officer
Dr. F. J. Brinley, Jr.

Phone   **Fax**
(301) 496-6541   (301) 402-0303

E-mail
fb18u@nih.gov

Research Topic
Fundamental Neuroscience and Developmental Disorders

Program Officer
Dr. Deborah Hirtz

Phone   **Fax**
(301) 496-5821   (301) 402-1501

E-mail
dh83f@nih.gov

Research Topic
Stroke, Trauma, and Neurodegenerative Disorders

Program Officer
Dr. William Heetderks

Phone   **Fax**
(301) 496-1447   (301) 480-1080

E-mail
wh7q@nih.gov

Name

Small Business Innovation Research Program (SBIR)

Laboratory/Organization/Agency

National Institute of Nursing Research (National Institutes of Health, Department of Health and Human Services).

Address

45 Center Drive
Bethesda, MD 20892-6300

Phone	**Fax**
(301) 594-5970	(301) 480-8260

Web Page

http://www.nih.gov/ninr

Program Officer

Dr. Hilary Sigmon

E-mail

hs38k@nih.gov

Technology Preferences

No special technological/scientific preferences, although focus naturally should be on health and have some kind of connection to nursing research.

Name
Small Business Innovation Research Program (SBIR)

Laboratory/Organization/Agency
National Center for Research Resources (National Institutes of Health, Department of Health and Human Services)

Research Topic
Biomedical Technology: Bioengineering and Biomedical Computing

Program Officer
Dr. Richard Dubois

Phone
(301) 435-0755

E-mail
rd42p@nih.gov

Research Topic
Biomedical Technology: Imaging, Molecular Structure, and Function

Program Officer
Dr. Abraham Levy

Phone
(301) 435-0755

E-mail
al26y@nih.gov

Research Topic
Biomedical Technology: Electron Microscopy, Mass Spectrometry

Program Officer
Dr. Mary Ann Markwell

Phone
(301) 435-0755

E-mail
mm4i@nih.gov

Research Topic
Biomedical Technology: All other topics in this general area

Program Officer
Dr. Karl Koehler

Phone
(301) 435-0755

E-mail
kk129z@nih.gov

Research Topic
Research and Development in Comparative Medicine (with special focus on R&D related to laboratory animals)

Address
One Rockledge Center, Rm 6030
6705 Rockledge Drive, NIH
Bethesda, MD 20892-7965

Phone   **Fax**
(301) 435-0744   (301) 480-3819

Program Officer
Dr. Leo Whitehair

E-mail
lw29k@nih.gov

Research Topic
Clinical Technology Applications

Program Officer
Dr. David Wilde

Phone   **Fax**
(301) 435-0790   (301) 480-3661

E-mail
dw171w@nih.gov

Research Topic
Development of Discovery-Oriented Software for Science Education

Program Officer
Dr. Fred W. Taylor

Phone   **Fax**
(301) 435-0788   (301) 480-3770

E-mail
ft24j@nih.gov

Research Topic
All other research topics within the mission of the center

Program Officer
Dr. Louise Ramm

Phone   **Fax**
(301) 435-0879   (301) 480-3658

E-mail
lr34m@nih.gov

Name

Small Business Innovation Research Program (SBIR)

Laboratory/Organization/Agency

National Center for Complementary and Alternative Medicine (National Institutes of Health, Department of Health and Human Services)

Address

31 Center Drive, Building 31, Rm 5B-37
Bethesda, MD 20892

Phone   **Fax**

(301) 594-2013   (301) 594-6757

Web Page

http://altmed.od.nih.gov

Program Officer

Dr. Geoffrey Cheung

E-mail

gc38f@nih.gov

Name
Small Business Innovation Research Program (SBIR)

Laboratory/Organization/Agency
National Library of Medicine (National Institutes of Health, Department of Health and Human Services)

Program Officer
Peter Clepper

Phone   **Fax**
(301) 496-3113   (301) 402-2952

E-mail
pc49n@nih.gov

Name
Small Business Innovation Research Program (SBIR)

Laboratory/Organization/Agency
Trans-NIH Research Programs (National Institutes of Health, Department of Health and Human Services)

Research Topic
Replacement or Reduction of Animals Used in Research

Program Officer
Dr. Louise Ramm

Phone   **Fax**
(301) 435-0879   (301) 480-3658

E-mail
lr34m@nih.gov

Research Topic
Development of Synthetic and Natural Biomaterial Reference Materials

Program Officer
No name listed; Head, Biomaterials and Tissue Engineering Program, Bioengineering Research Group, National Heart, Lung, and Blood Institute

Phone   **Fax**
(301) 435-0513   (301) 480-1336

Research Topic
Sleep Disorders Research

Address
NCSDR/NHLBI/NIH
6701 Rockledge Dr., Rm 10038
Bethesda, MD 20892-7920

Phone   **Fax**
(301) 435-0199   (301) 480-3451

Web Page
http://www.nhlbi.nih.gov/nhlbi/nhlbi.htm

Program Officer
Dr. James Kiley

E-mail
kileyj@nih.gov

Name
Small Business Innovation Research Program (SBIR)

Laboratory/Organization/Agency
National Institute for Occupational Safety and Health (Centers for Disease Control and Prevention, Department of Health and Human Services

Address
1600 Clifton Road, NE
Atlanta, GA 30333

Phone   **Fax**
(404) 639-3343   (404) 639-4616

Web Page
http://www.nih.gov/grants/funding/sbir1/sbir.htm#niosh

Program Officer
Dr. Roy Fleming

E-mail
rmf2@niood1.em.cdc.gov

Technology Preferences
The main focus is devices, instruments, and equipment that can be used to evaluate, measure, or control occupational hazards.

Name

Small Business Innovation Research Program (SBIR)

Laboratory/Organization/Agency

National Center for Injury Prevention and Control (Centers for Disease Control and Prevention, Department of Health and Human Services)

Program Officer

Ted Jones

Phone   **Fax**

(770) 488-4824   (770) 488-1662

E-mail

tmj1@cdc.gov

Name
Small Business Innovation Research Program (SBIR)

Laboratory/Organization/Agency
National Center for Infectious Diseases (Centers for Disease Control and Prevention, Department of Health and Human Services)

Program Officer
Ken Fortune

Phone   **Fax**
(404) 639-0890   (404) 639-4195

E-mail
kef2@cidod1.em.cdc.gov

Name

Small Business Innovation Research Program (SBIR)

Laboratory/Organization/Agency

National Center for Chronic Disease Prevention and Health Promotion (Centers for Disease Control and Prevention, Department of Health and Human Services)

Program Officer

Dr. Janet Fulton

Phone   **Fax**

(770) 488-5430   (770) 488-5473

E-mail

jkf2@cdc.gov

Name
Small Business Innovation Research Program (SBIR)

Laboratory/Organization/Agency
National Immunization Program (Centers for Disease Control and Prevention, Department of Health and Human Services)

Program Officer
Bruce G. Weniger

Phone   **Fax**
(404) 639-8779   (404) 639-8834

E-mail
bgw2@cdc.gov

Name
Small Business Innovation Research Program (SBIR)

Laboratory/Organization/Agency
National Center for HIV, STP, and TB Prevention (Centers for Disease Control and Prevention, Department of Health and Human Services)

Program Officer
Alfred Harry

Phone   **Fax**
(404) 639-8186   (404) 639-8610

E-mail
ah@cdc.gov

Name
Small Business Innovation Research Program (SBIR)

Laboratory/Organization/Agency
Food and Drug Administration (Department of Health and Human Services)

Program Officer
Robert L. Robins

Phone   **Fax**
(301) 827-7185   (301) 827-7106

E-mail
rrobins@bangate.fda.gov

Name
Small Business Innovation Research Program (SBIR)

Agency/Organization
Department of Defense

Address
OSD/SADBU
U.S. Department of Defense
3061 Defense Pentagon, Rm 2A338
Washington, DC 20301-3061

Phone   **Fax**
(800) 382-4634   (800) 462-4128

E-mail
SBIRHELP@teltech.com

Web Page
http://www.acq.osd.mil/sadbu/sbir/

Program Officers
Jon Baron, SBIR Program Manager

E-mail
Baronj@acq.osd.mil

Type of Program
R&D funds (technical and commercial criteria are considered). The program is based on a three-phase process:

1. Phase I—the start-up phase; typically exploration of the technical merit or feasibility of an idea or technology

2. Phase II—the work phase; typically prototype development, evaluation of commercial potential

3. Phase III—the commercialization phase; no SBIR funds available for this purpose (although SBIR program managers can be useful contacts)

Technology Preferences
The Department of Defense SBIR program sponsors projects in almost all technical areas, so it is necessary to check the solicitations to see which areas are of special interest. A small number of reviewers are chosen for each technical topic, most often coming from defense laboratories. In general, all projects must serve a DOD need and have commercial applications in private and/or military markets, and they must be early-stage R&D projects. See also references under the individual military participants.

Type of Financing
Contracts

Maximum amounts
Between $60,000 and $100,000 for Phase I projects (in general lasting up to six months).
Between $500,000 and $750,000 for Phase II projects (generally lasting two years).

Special Considerations
Oriented to small firms (fewer than 500 employees).

Deadlines
A solicitation (invitation to compete for funding in certain technological areas) is released two times every year (but not all defense organizations participate in both). The first one is released in October, accepting proposals from December, and closing in January. The second solicitation is released in May, accepting proposals from July, and closing in August. A presolicitation announcement is made public before the ordinary solicitation. This is the first indication of what scientific and technological areas will be open for proposals in the upcoming award competitions. During and before the presolicitation scientists and engineers who have come up with scientific and technological focus areas are available for questioning.

Potential applicants also have the opportunity to use the DOD online interactive topic information system to get (anonymous) answers to technical questions.

Additional Information
DOD is the largest SBIR participant, providing around half the total SBIR budget. In 1997, more than 1,500 Phase I and 639 Phase II awards were made. The main defense participants are, starting at the largest (these are described in separate documents):

1. Air Force
2. Navy
3. Army
4. Ballistic Missile Defense Organization
5. Defense Advanced Research Projects Agency
6. Office of the Secretary of Defense
7. Defense Threat Reduction Agency
8. Special Operations Command

The three last ones are comparatively small. For more details on these programs, contact the DOD central SBIR office described above.

A Fast Track process has been established to reduce the funding gap between the two phases. If the project qualifies for the Fast Track (separate application needed, along with follow-on funding commitment from an outside investor), the Phase II proposal is evaluated quickly and the company can receive between $30,000 and $50,000 in interim funding. Note that the Fast Track Phase II success rate is exceptionally high—93% of proposals have been selected.

Mean success rate of all Defense SBIR projects has been 15% for Phase I proposals and 40% for Phase II. However, the rate varies much between the different defense participants (see separate entries for details).

Name
Small Business Innovation Research Program (SBIR)

Agency/Organization
Air Force (Department of Defense)

Address
Department of the Air Force
HQ/AFMC/STXB
4375 Chidlaw Road, Suite 6
Wright-Patterson AFB, OH 45433-5006

Phone	**Fax**
(800) 222-0336	(937) 476-1086

Web Page
http://www.afrl.af.mil/sbir/index.htm

Program Officer
Jill Dickman, Air Force SBIR/STTR Program Executive

E-mail
dickmar%20@afrl.af.mil

Type of Program
R&D funds (technical and commercial criteria are considered). The program is based on a three-phase process:

1. Phase I—the start-up phase; typically exploration of the technical merit or feasibility of an idea or technology
2. Phase II—the work phase; typically prototype development, evaluation of commercial potential
3. Phase III—the commercialization phase; no SBIR funds available for this purpose (although SBIR program managers can be useful contacts)

Technology Preferences
The Air Force SBIR program sponsors projects in almost all technical areas, so it is necessary to check the solicitations to see which areas are in focus. In the last solicitations, between 200 and 300 different topics have been developed. Note that although improved military strength is the general goal, projects are often found in areas that might not be directly connected to military purposes. Environmental issues are a good example—although the Environmental Protection Agency (EPA) has its own SBIR program, the Air Force SBIR set aside for environmental issues is more than twice the total EPA SBIR budget.

Research topics in the Air Force come from a number of Directorates and Centers, located at different Air Force bases/laboratories around the country. For SBIR contacts in each Directorate, see separate entries in this reference guide.

Type of Financing
Contracts

Maximum amounts
$100,000 for Phase I projects (in general lasting nine months).
$750,000 for Phase II projects (two years).

Special Considerations
Oriented to small firms (fewer than 500 employees).

Deadlines
The Air Force participates in the first annual Department of Defense solicitation (invitation to compete for funding in certain technological areas). It is released in October, accepting proposals from December, and closing in January. In the period after release but before proposals are accepted, all "topic authors" (scientists and engineers who have come up with scientific and technological focus areas) are available for questioning. After that, potential applicants have the opportunity of using the DOD online interactive topic information system to get (anonymous) answers to technical questions. The Air Force issues its own "presolicitation" announcement (check with their Web site or the *Commerce Business Daily*).

Additional Information
Nearly 50% of Phase I contract recipients make it successfully to Phase II. This is one of the highest Phase II success rates of all SBIR programs.

The Air Force is the largest Department of Defense SBIR participant, with an annual budget of more than $200 million.

Name
Small Business Innovation Research Program (SBIR)

Laboratory/Agency/Organization
Air Force Office of Scientific Research (AFOSR) (Air Force, Department of Defense)

SBIR Contact
Chris Hughes

Phone
(202) 767-6962

E-mail
chris.hughes@afosr.af.mil

Topic Comment
AFOSR directs the Air Force's basic research program, for example in disciplines like physics, electronics, materials, chemistry, math, and computers, as well as biological environmental sciences and all engineering disciplines associated with aerospace issues.

Name
Small Business Innovation Research Program (SBIR)

Laboratory/Agency/Organization
Air Vehicles Directorate (Wright-Patterson AFB) (Air Force, Department of Defense)

Address
2130 Eighth St., Bldg 45
Wright-Patterson AFB, OH 45433-7542

Phone   **Fax:**
(937) 255-5066   937-255-6788

Web Page
http://www.va.afrl.af.mil/

SBIR Contact
Madie Tillman

E-mail
madie.tillman@va.afrl.af.mil

Topic Comment
Air Vehicles has responsibility for the development and integration of Fixed Wing Air Vehicle Technologies. The Directorate's technological preferences are related to Aeronautical Sciences, Aerospace Structures and Flight Systems.

Name
Small Business Innovation Research Program (SBIR)

Laboratory/Agency/Organization
Propulsion Directorate (Wright Patterson AFB) (Air Force, Department of Defense)

SBIR Contact
Dottie Zobrist

Phone
(513) 255-6024

E-mail
zobrist@wf.wpafb.af.mil

Topic Comment
The Propulsion Directorate mission is to create and transition propulsion and power technology for military dominance of air and space.

Name
Small Business Innovation Research Program (SBIR)

Laboratory/Agency/Organization
Sensors Directorate (Wright Patterson AFB) (Air Force, Department of Defense)

SBIR Contact
B. Marleen Fannin

Phone
(937) 255-5285 ext. 4117

E-mail
fanninbm@sensors.wpafb.af.mil

Topic Comment
The Sensors Directorate is responsible for developing technologies to collect, measure, and interpret important military information and deny the enemy the same.

Name

Small Business Innovation Research Program (SBIR)

Laboratory/Agency/Organization

Materials & Manufacturing Directorate (Wright Patterson AFB) (Air Force, Department of Defense)

Address

Materials & Manufacturing Directorate AFRL/MLOR
2977 P Street, Rm 419, Ste. 13, Bldg 653
Wright-Patterson AFB, OH 45433-7746

Phone   **Fax:**

(937) 656-9221   (937) 656-4831

Web Page

http://www.ml.wpafb.af.mil/techxfer/sbir/sbir.htm

SBIR Contact

Sharon E. Starr

E-mail

starrse@ml.wpafb.af.mil

Topic Comment

The Materials and Manufacturing Directorate mission is to plan and execute the Air Force's program for materials and manufacturing processes in the area of basic research, exploratory development and advanced development. It also provides support to solve system-related problems and to transfer expertise in the areas of materials and manufacturing processes.

Name

Small Business Innovation Research Program (SBIR)

Laboratory/Agency/Organization

Munitions Directorate (Eglin AFB) (Air Force, Department of Defense)

SBIR Contact

Dick Bixby

Phone

(850) 882-8591 ext. 1281

E-mail

bixby@eglin.af.mil

Topic Comment

The Munitions Directorate mission is to develop, integrate, and transition science and technology for air-launched munitions for defeating ground fixed, mobile/relocatable, air, and space targets.

Name
Small Business Innovation Research Program (SBIR)

Laboratory/Agency/Organization
Human Efficiency Directorate (Brooks AFB) (Air Force, Department of Defense)

SBIR Contact
Belva Williams

Phone
(210) 536-2103

E-mail
belva.williams@brooks.af.mil

Topic Comment
The Human Effectiveness Directorate is responsible for many different topics related to human-centered science and technology

Name

Small Business Innovation Research Program (SBIR)

Laboratory/Agency/Organization

Directed Energy Directorate (Kirtland AFB) (Air Force, Department of Defense)

Address

Air Force Research Laboratory/Directed Energy Directorate (AFRL/DE)
SBIR Program Office (Robert Hancock)
3650 Aberdeen Ave., S.E. (Bldg 497, Rm 239)
Kirtland AFB, NM 87117-5776

Phone   **Fax**

(505) 846-4418   (505) 846-8058

Web Page

http://www.de.afrl.af.mil/

SBIR Contact

Bob Hancock

E-mail

hancockr@plk.af.mil

Topic Comment

The mission of the Directed Energy Directorate is to develop, integrate and transition science and technology for Directed Energy to include high-power microwaves, lasers (diode, solid-state, semiconductor, chemical), adaptive optics, imaging and effects.

Name
Small Business Innovation Research Program (SBIR)

Laboratory/Agency/Organization
Space Vehicles Directorate (Kirtland AFB) (Air Force, Department of Defense)

Address
Air Force Research Laboratory/Space Vehicles Directorate (AFRL/VS)
SBIR Program Office (Robert Hancock)
3650 Aberdeen Ave., S.E. (Bldg 497, Rm 239)
Kirtland AFB, NM 87117-5776

Phone   **Fax**
(505) 846-4418   (505) 846-8058

Web Page
http://www.vs.afrl.af.mil/

SBIR Contact
Bob Hancock

E-mail
hancockr@plk.af.mil

Topic Comment
This Directorate deals with science and technology related to space vehicles, launch vehicles, and space concepts. More specifically, the technical areas are:

1. Technologies that revolutionize space-based surveillance and space operations to include: IR focal planes, cryocoolers, imaging, satellite control/autonomy, satellite guidance and navigation, rad-hard electronics, threat warning, attack warning, and so on.

2. Innovative technologies for development, integration and demonstration of emerging space technologies in the areas of thermal management, space power/energy storage, space structures and controls, vibration isolation, and acoustic damping.

3. Innovative technologies that enable detection and understanding of threats, both natural and man-made, to space systems plus active and passive means to mitigate those threats. Areas of concern include: solar activity effects, ionospheric impacts, space hazard mitigation, radiation environment characterization, atmospheric modeling, and so forth.

Name
Small Business Innovation Research Program (SBIR)

Laboratory/Agency/Organization
Information Directorate (located in Rome, NY) (Air Force, Department of Defense)

SBIR Contact
Janis Norelli

Phone
(315) 330-3311

E-mail
sbir@rl.af.mil

Topic Comment
The mission of the Information Directorate is the advancement and application of information systems science and technology for information dominance and its transition to air, space and ground systems.

Name
Small Business Innovation Research Program (SBIR)

Laboratory/Agency/Organization
Arnold Engineering Development Center (Arnold AFS) (Air Force, Department of Defense)

SBIR Contact
Kevin Zysk

Phone
(615) 454-6507

E-mail
zysk@hap.arnold.af.mil

Topic Comment
This is the world's largest flight simulation facility.

Name
Small Business Innovation Research Program (SBIR)

Laboratory/Agency/Organization
Air Force Flight Test Center (Edwards AFB) (Air Force, Department of Defense)

Address
195 E. Popson Ave., Bldg 2750, Rm 218
Edwards AFB, CA 93524

Phone
(661) 275-9266

Fax
(661) 275-7135

SBIR Contact
Abe Atachbarian

E-mail
abraham.atachbarian@sf.edwards.af.mil

Topic Comment
This Center conducts development test and evaluation (DT&E) on manned and unmanned aerospace systems. It also conducts flight evaluation and recovery of research vehicles and DT&E of aerodynamic decelerators. Key words for the center's main technological preferences are Test, Range, Telemetry, Environmental, Instrumentation, IR, and Radar.

Name
Small Business Innovation Research Program (SBIR)

Laboratory/Agency/Organization
Air Armament Center (Eglin AFB) (Air Force, Department of Defense)

Address
AAC/XPP
101 West D Avenue, Suite 129
Eglin AFB, FL 32542-5495

Phone   **Fax**
(850) 882-8096   (850) 882-9361

Web Page
http://www.eglin.af.mil/aac/dr/sbir.htm

SBIR Contact
Dave Uhrig

E-mail
uhrig@eglin.af.mil

Topic Comment
The Air Armament Center is responsible for development, acquisition, testing, deployment, and sustainment of all air-delivered weapons. Test and evaluation of command and control systems also falls under the Center's mission.

Additional SBIR Contact
John Cao (connected to the 46th Test Group, one of the components of the Air Armament Center. The Groups, located at Holloman AFB, is involved in several types of T&E support operations)

Phone
(505) 475-1228

E-mail
jcao@mailgate.46tg.af.mil

Additional SBIR Contact
Capt. Brett Thornhill (also connected to the 46th Test Group)

Phone
(505) 475-1244

E-mail
bthornhill@mailgate.46tg.af.mil

Name

Small Business Innovation Research Program (SBIR)

Laboratory/Agency/Organization

Air Logistics Centers (ALC) (Air Force, Department of Defense)

There are five Air Logistics Centers, all of which provide engineering, manufacturing, maintenance, repair, and support services to the Air Force operational commands. Refer to solicitation or program contacts for more information about the scientific and technological areas each center focuses upon. These are the contacts for the centers:

Center

OO-ALC, Hill AFB

SBIR Contact

Bill Wassink

Phone

(801) 777-2977

Center

SM-ALC, McClellan AFB

SBIR Contact

Capt. Paul Simonich

Phone

(916) 643-2010

Center

WR-ALC, Robins AFB

SBIR Contact

Capt. Bill Braasch

Phone

(912) 926-6617

Center

SA-ALC, Kelly AFB

SBIR Contact

Dave Grubb

Phone

(512) 945-4225

Center
OC-ALC, Tinker AFB

SBIR Contact
Don Boedeker

Phone
(405) 736-5567

Name
Small Business Innovation Research Program (SBIR)

Agency/Organization
Army (Department of Defense)

Address
US Army Material Command
Attn: AMXRO-W-SBIR Rm 8N31
5001 Eisenhower Ave.
Alexandria, VA 22333

E-mail
aro-sbir@hqamc.army.mil

Phone   **Fax**
(703) 617-8392   (703) 617-8261

Web Page
http://www.aro.ncren.net/arowash/rt/sbir.htm

Program Officer
Dr. Ken Bannister, SBIR Program Coordinator

Phone
(703) 617-7425

Type of Program
R&D funds (technical and commercial criteria are considered). The program is based on a three-phase process:

1. Phase I—the start-up phase; typically exploration of the technical merit or feasibility of an idea or technology

2. Phase II—the work phase; typically prototype development, evaluation of commercial potential

3. Phase III—the commercialization phase; no SBIR funds available for this purpose (although SBIR program managers can be useful contacts)

Technology Preferences
The Army SBIR program sponsors projects in almost all technical areas, so it is necessary to check the solicitations to see which areas are of special interest.

Topics are developed by a number of different Army organizations. See separate entries in this reference guide for SBIR contacts in these organizations.

Type of Financing
Contracts

Maximum amounts
$100,000 for Phase I projects (in general lasting six months).
$750,000 for Phase II projects (two years).

Special Considerations
Oriented to small firms (fewer than 500 employees).

Deadlines
The Army participates in the second annual Department of Defense solicitation (invitation to compete for funding in certain technological areas). It is released in May, accepting proposals from July, and closing in August. In the period after release but before proposals are accepted, all "topic authors" (scientists and engineers who have come up with scientific and technological focus areas) are available for questioning. After that, potential applicants have the opportunity of using the DOD online interactive topic information system to get (anonymous) answers to technical questions.

Additional Information
In fiscal year 1999 the Army expected to fund around 200 Phase I and 100 Phase II proposals based on a SBIR budget of around $100 million.

A special feature in the Army SBIR program is their "Quality Awards." Each year, the five most exceptional Phase II projects are selected and presented awards at a formal banquet. Apart from being a great source of recognition and publicity, this might also be a good step toward more funding opportunities. There are many other programs in the Army that are relevant to innovative firms (for instance, ManTech and ACT II, described elsewhere in this book).

Name

Small Business Innovation Research Program (SBIR)

Laboratory/Agency/Organization

SMDC—Space and Missile Defense Command (Army, Department of Defense)

SBIR Contact

Terry Bauer

Phone

(205) 955-5456

E-mail

bauert@smdc.army.mil

Name
Small Business Innovation Research Program (SBIR)

Laboratory/Agency/Organization
TECOM—Test and Evaluation Command (Army, Department of Defense)

SBIR Contact
John Schnell

Phone
(410) 278-147

E-mail
jschnel@tec1.apg.army.mil

Name
Small Business Innovation Research Program (SBIR)

Laboratory/Agency/Organization
CECOM—U.S. Army Communication and Electronics Command (Army, Department of Defense)

SBIR Contact
Joyce Crisci

Phone
(732) 427-2665

E-mail
crisci@mail1.monmouth.army.mil

Additional SBIR Contact
Suzanne Weeks

Phone
(732) 427-3275

E-mail
weekss@mail1.monmouth.army.mil

Name
Small Business Innovation Research Program (SBIR)

Laboratory/Agency/Organization
AVRDEC—Aviation Research, Development and Engineering Center (Army, Department of Defense)

SBIR Contact
Brenda Haglich

Phone
(757) 878-0085

E-mail
bhaglich@eustis-aatds1.army.mil

Name
Small Business Innovation Research Program (SBIR)

Laboratory/Agency/Organization
SBCCOM—Soldier and Biological Chemical Command (Army, Department of Defense)

Address
Attn: AMSSB-RAS, 5183 Blackhawk Road, Bldg. E3330
Aberdeen Proving Ground, MD 21010-5423

Phone	**Fax**
(410) 436-2031	(410) 436-6529

Web Page
http://www.sbccom.army.mil

SBIR Contact
Ron Hinkle

E-mail
ronald.hinkle@sbccom.apgea.army.mil

Additional SBIR Contact
Marvin Hohenstein

Phone
(410) 436-2855

E-mail
marvin.hohenstein@sbccom.apgea.army.mil

Name
Small Business Innovation Research Program (SBIR)

Laboratory/Agency/Organization
ARL—Army Research Laboratory (Army, Department of Defense)

Address
2800 Powder Mill Road
Adelphi, MD 20783-1197
ATTN: AMSRL-CS-TT (HUDSON)

Phone   **Fax**
(301) 394-4808   (301) 394-5818

Web Page
www.arl.mil

SBIR Contact
Dean Hudson

E-mail
dhudson@arl.mil

Technical Preferences
These are the main areas of ARL:

1. Weapons and Materials

2. Human Research and Engineering

3. Sensors and Electron Devices

4. Survivability/Lethality Analysis

5. Information and Science Technology

6. Vehicle Technology

7. Corporate Information and Computing

Name
Small Business Innovation Research Program (SBIR)

Laboratory/Agency/Organization
ARO—Army Research Office (Army, Department of Defense)

SBIR Contact
LTC Ken Jones

Phone
(919) 549-4200

E-mail
jones@aro-emh-1.army.mil

Name

Small Business Innovation Research Program (SBIR)

Laboratory/Agency/Organization

ARI—Army Research Institute for the Behavioral and Social Sciences (Army, Department of Defense)

SBIR Contact

Dr. Jonathan Kaplan

Phone

(703) 617-8828

E-mail

kaplan@ari.army.mil

Name
Small Business Innovation Research Program (SBIR)

Laboratory/Agency/Organization
STRICOM—Simulation, Training, and Instrumentation Command (Army, Department of Defense)

SBIR Contact
Mark McAuliffe

Phone
(407) 384-3929

E-mail
mcaulifm@stricom.army.mil

Name
Small Business Innovation Research Program (SBIR)

Laboratory/Agency/Organization
CERL—Construction Engineering Research Laboratory (Army, Department of Defense)

Address
PO Box 9005
Champaign, IL 61826-9005

Web Page
http://www.cecer.army.mil

Phone   **Fax**
(217) 373-6746   (217) 373-7242

SBIR Contact
Carol Mihina

E-mail
c-mihina@cecer.army.mil

Topic Comment
The laboratory is interested in topics in civil/mechanical engineering (including HVAC, seismic, materials technologies), and environmental quality/conservation technologies.

Name
Small Business Innovation Research Program (SBIR)

Laboratory/Agency/Organization
TEC—Topographic Engineering Center (Army, Department of Defense)

SBIR Contact
Susan Nichols

Phone
(703) 428-6631

E-mail
susan.l.nichols@usace.army.mil

Name

Small Business Innovation Research Program (SBIR)

Laboratory/Agency/Organization

NCOE (Army, Department of Defense)

SBIR Contact

Gerald Raisanen

Phone

(508) 233-4223

E-mail

graisane@natick-amed02.army.mil

Name

Small Business Innovation Research Program (SBIR)

Laboratory/Agency/Organization

ARDEC—Armament Research, Development and Engineering Center (Army, Department of Defense)

SBIR Contact

John Saarmann

Phone

(973) 724-7943

E-mail

saarmann@pica.army.mil

Name

Small Business Innovation Research Program (SBIR)

Laboratory/Agency/Organization

CRREL—Cold Regions Research and Engineering Laboratory (Army, Department of Defense)

SBIR Contact

Theresa Salls

Phone

(603) 646-4651

E-mail

tsalls@crrel.usace.army.mil

Name
Small Business Innovation Research Program (SBIR)

Laboratory/Agency/Organization
TARDEC—Tank Automotive Research, Development and Engineering Center (Army, Department of Defense)

SBIR Contact
Alex Sandel

Phone
(810) 574-7545

E-mail
sandela@cc.tacom.army.mil

Name
Small Business Innovation Research Program (SBIR)

Laboratory/Agency/Organization
WES—Waterways Experiment Station (Army, Department of Defense)

SBIR Contact
Phillip Stewart

Phone
(601) 634-4113

E-mail
stewarp@ex1.wes.army.mil

Name
Small Business Innovation Research Program (SBIR)

Laboratory/Agency/Organization
MRDEC—Missile Research, Development and Engineering Center (Army, Department of Defense)

SBIR Contact
Buddy Thomas

Phone
(256) 842-9227

E-mail
thomas-oh@redstone.army.mil

Name
Small Business Innovation Research Program (SBIR)

Laboratory/Agency/Organization
MEDICAL—Medical Research and Material Command (Army, Department of Defense)

SBIR Contact
Herman Willis

Phone
(301) 619-2471

E-mail
butch.willis@det.amedd.army.mil

Name
Small Business Innovation Research Program (SBIR)

Agency/Organization
Navy (Department of Defense)

Address
Office of the Chief of Naval Research
800 N. Quincy Street
Arlington, VA 22217-5660

Phone	**Fax**
(703) 696-0342	(703) 696-4884

Web Page
http://www.onr.navy.mil/sci_tech/industrial/sbir.htm

Program Officer
Vincent D. Schaper, Navy SBIR Program Manager

Phone
(703) 696-8528

E-mail
schapev@onr.navy.mil

Additional Contact
John Williams, Deputy Navy SBIR Program Manager

Phone
(703) 696-0342

E-mail
williajr@onr.navy.mil

Type of Program
R&D funds (technical and commercial criteria are considered). The program is based on a three-phase process:

1. Phase I—the start-up phase; typically exploration of the technical merit or feasibility of an idea or technology

2. Phase II—the work phase; typically prototype development, evaluation of commercial potential

3. Phase III—the commercialization phase; no SBIR funds available for this purpose (although SBIR program managers can be useful contacts)

Technology Preferences

The Navy SBIR program sponsors projects within 33 different broad scientific and technological areas that are broadly defined ("Materials," "Chemistry," etc.). More detailed topics are developed for each solicitation and frequently changed.

Technical topics come from various Navy sub-organizations (Commands, Centers, etc.). The SBIR contacts for these sub-organizations can be found in separate entries in the quick reference directory.

Type of Financing

Contracts

Maximum amounts

$100,000 for Phase I projects (in general lasting six months).
$750,000 for Phase II projects (two years).

Special Considerations

Oriented to small firms (fewer than 500 employees).

Deadlines

The Navy participates in both annual Department of Defense solicitations (invitation to compete for funding in certain technological areas). This means that Navy proposal deadlines are in January and August In the period after release of a solicitation but before proposals are accepted, all "topic authors" (scientists and engineers who have come up with scientific and technological focus areas) are available for questioning. After that, potential applicants have the opportunity of using the DOD online interactive topic information system to get (anonymous) answers to technical questions.

Additional Information

The Navy SBIR program is almost as large as the Air Force program with a budget of close to $200 million a year.

A special feature in the Navy is that several appendices of the proposals must be submitted over the Internet through the Navy SBIR/STTR Web site. If this is not done, the proposal will not be accepted. Program officers advise applicants not to wait until the last minute to avoid traffic trouble on the Internet.

Name
Small Business Innovation Research Program (SBIR)

Laboratory/Agency/Organization
Office of Naval Research (Navy, Department of Defense)

SBIR Program Manager
Doug Harry

Phone   **Fax**
(703) 696-4286   (703) 696-4884

E-mail
harryd@onr.navy.mil

Name
Small Business Innovation Research Program (SBIR)

Laboratory/Agency/Organization
SPAWAR—Space and Naval Warfare Systems Command (Navy, Department of Defense)

SBIR Point of Contact
Linda Whittington

Phone   **Fax**
(619) 537-0146   (619) 537-0155

E-mail
whittinl@spawar.navy.mil

SBIR Point of Contact for SPAWARSYSCEN
Larry Flesner

Phone   **Fax**
(619) 553-1044   (619) 553-6924

E-mail
flesner@spawar.navy.mil

Name
Small Business Innovation Research Program (SBIR)

Laboratory/Agency/Organization
MARCOR (Navy, Department of Defense)

SBIR Point of Contact
Joe Johnson

Phone   **Fax**
(703) 784-4801   (703) 784-2764

E-mail
johnsonj2@quantico.usmc.mil

Name
Small Business Innovation Research Program (SBIR)

Laboratory/Agency/Organization
NAVAIR—Naval Air Systems Command (Navy, Department of Defense)

SBIR Point of Contact
Carol Van Wyk

Phone	**Fax**
(301) 342-0215	(301) 757-3258

E-mail
vanwykc@navair.navy.mil

Additional SBIR Point of Contact
Melody L. VanMeter

Phone	**Fax**
(301) 342-8048	(301) 757-3258

E-mail
vanmeterml@navair.navy.mil

Name
Small Business Innovation Research Program (SBIR)

Laboratory/Agency/Organization
NAVSEA—Naval Sea Systems Command (Navy, Department of Defense)

SBIR Point of Contact
Bill Degentesh

Phone   **Fax**
(703) 602-3005   (703) 602-3460

E-mail
degenteshwm@navsea.navy.mil

Name

Small Business Innovation Research Program (SBIR)

Laboratory/Agency/Organization

NAVSUP—Naval Supply Systems Command (Navy, Department of Defense)

SBIR Point of Contact

Susan Schneck

Phone	**Fax**
(717) 605-1305	(717) 605-6389

E-mail

susan_d_schneck@navsup.navy.mil

Name
Small Business Innovation Research Program (SBIR)

Laboratory/Agency/Organization
NAWCLKE, Naval Air Warfare Center Aircraft Division (Navy, Department of Defense)

SBIR Point of Contact
Pete O'Donnell

Phone   **Fax**
(732) 323-7566   (732) 323-1282

E-mail
odonnell@lakehurst.navy.mil

Name
Small Business Innovation Research Program (SBIR)

Laboratory/Agency/Organization
NAWCTRE, Naval Air Warfare Center Aircraft Division; Propulsion (Navy, Department of Defense)

SBIR Point of Contact
Curtis Snyder

Phone   **Fax**
(301) 342-7850   (301) 342-1867

E-mail
snyder_curtis%pax4a@mr.navcad.navy.mil

Name
Small Business Innovation Research Program (SBIR)

Laboratory/Agency/Organization
NAWCMUGU, Naval Air Warfare Center Weapons Division (Navy, Department of Defense)

SBIR Point of Contact
Bill Webster

Phone   **Fax**
(760) 939-1074   (760) 939-1216

E-mail
websterwp@navair.navy.mil

Name
Small Business Innovation Research Program (SBIR)

Laboratory/Agency/Organization
NAWCTSD—Naval Air Warfare Center Training Systems Division (Navy, Department of Defense)

SBIR Point of Contact
Bob Seltzer

Phone   **Fax**
(407) 380-4115   (407) 380-4829

E-mail
seltzerrm@navair.navy.mil

Name
Small Business Innovation Research Program (SBIR)

Laboratory/Agency/Organization
NAWCAD (Acoustic Technologies Branch) (Navy, Department of Defense)

SBIR Point of Contact
David Bromley

Phone   **Fax**
(301) 342-2116   (301) 342-2098

E-mail
bromleydw@navair.navy.mil

Additional SBIR Point of Contact
Dr. Mary Eileen Farrell

Phone   **Fax**
(301) 342-2114   (301) 342-2098

E-mail
farrellma@navair.navy.mil

Name
Small Business Innovation Research Program (SBIR)

Laboratory/Agency/Organization
NFESC—Naval Facilities Engineering Service Center (Navy, Department of Defense)

Address
1100 23rd Street
Port Hueneme, CA 93043

Phone   **Fax**
(805) 982-1089   (805) 982-1409

Web Page
http://www.nfesc.navy.mil

SBIR Point of Contact
Nick Olah

E-mail
nolah@nfesc.navy.mil

Technology Preferences
Civil Engineering, Environmental Quality and Energy

Name
Small Business Innovation Research Program (SBIR)

Laboratory/Agency/Organization
Naval Facilities Engineering Command (Navy, Department of Defense)

SBIR Point of Contact
Andy Del Collo

Phone   **Fax**
(202) 685-9173   (202) 685-1569

E-mail
delcolloa@hq.navfac.navy.mil

Name
Small Business Innovation Research Program (SBIR)

Laboratory/Agency/Organization
NPRDC—Navy Personnel R&D Center (Navy, Department of Defense)

SBIR Point of Contact
Janet Held

Phone   **Fax**
(619) 553-7617   (619) 553-9973

E-mail
held@nprdc.navy.mil

Name

Small Business Innovation Research Program (SBIR)

Laboratory/Agency/Organization

NRL—Navy Research Laboratory (Navy, Department of Defense)

SBIR Technical Point of Contact

Stephen Sacks

Phone	**Fax**
(202) 767-3666	(202) 767-8215

E-mail

sacks@ccf.nrl.navy.mil

SBIR Administrative Point of Contact

Lois Byrne

Phone	**Fax**
(202) 767-6263	(202) 767-5896

E-mail

byrne@contracts.nrl.navy.mil

Name
Small Business Innovation Research Program (SBIR)

Laboratory/Agency/Organization
NSWCCARD—Naval Surface Warfare Center; Carderock (Navy, Department of Defense)

SBIR Point of Contact
James Wood

Phone   **Fax**
(301) 227-2690   (301) 227-2138

E-mail
woodje@nswccd.navy.mil

Laboratory/Agency/Organization
NSWCCRN—Naval Surface Warfare Center; Crane (Navy, Department of Defense)

SBIR Point of Contact
Greg Held

Phone   **Fax**
(812) 854-1352   (812) 854-4248

E-mail
held_g@crane.navy.mil

Laboratory/Agency/Organization
NSWCCSS—Naval Surface Warfare Center; Coastal System Station (Navy, Department of Defense)

Address
6703 West highway 98
Panama City, FL 32407

Phone   **Fax**
(904) 234-4161   (904) 235-5374

Web Page
http://www.ncsc.navy.mil

SBIR Point of Contact
Ed Linsenmeyer

E-mail
linsenmeyer_ed@ccmail.ncsc.navy.mil

Topic Comment
This Center does research and development as well as system integration and fleet maintenance with specialties in the mission areas of Mine Warfare, Amphibious Warfare, Navy Special Warfare, and Diving and Salvage. Underwater acoustics and sonar, electro-optics, low magnetic field detection, signal processing, modeling and simulation, diving equipment, unmanned vehicle technology, Computational fluid dynamics are some of the areas of technical expertise.

Laboratory/Agency/Organization
NSWCDD—Naval Surface Warfare Center; Dahlgren Division (Navy, Department of Defense)

Address
Code B04, Bldg. 1470
Dahlgren, VA 22448-5100

Phone   **Fax**
(540) 653-8906   (540) 653-2687

SBIR Point of Contact
Ron Vermillion

E-mail
rvermil@nswc.navy.mil

Name
Small Business Innovation Research Program (SBIR)

Laboratory/Agency/Organization
NSWCIH—Naval Sea Systems Command (Navy, Department of Defense)

SBIR Point of Contact
Marilyn Houser

Phone   **Fax**
(301) 744-6753   (301) 744-4339

E-mail
90U@chem.ih.navy.mil

Name
Small Business Innovation Research Program (SBIR)

Laboratory/Agency/Organization
NUWC—Naval Undersea Warfare Center (Navy, Department of Defense)

SBIR Point of Contact
Jack Griffin

Phone   **Fax**
(401) 832-7283   (401) 841-1725

E-mail
griffinj@AM.Npt.NUWC.navy.mil

Name
Small Business Innovation Research Program (SBIR)

Laboratory/Agency/Organization
SSP—Strategic Systems Program (Navy, Department of Defense)

SBIR Point of Contact
Charles Marino or Francisco Munozrovira

Phone   **Fax**
(703) 607-3444   (703) 607-2233

E-mail
SP20155@spp.navy.mil

Name

Small Business Innovation Research Program (SBIR)

Agency/Organization

Ballistic Missile Defense Organization (BMDO, part of the Department of Defense)

Address

Ballistic Missile Defense Organization
Attn: TORI/SBIR (Bond), suite 809
1725 Jefferson Davis Hwy.
Arlington, VA 22202

Phone   **Fax**
(800) WIN-BMDO   (703) 693-3013

E-mail

bmdo@futron.com

Web Page

http://www.winbmdo.com

Program Officer

Thomas J. (Jeff) Bond III, BMDO SBIR Program Manager

Type of Program

R&D funds (technical and commercial criteria are considered). The program is based on a three-phase process:

1. Phase I—the start-up phase; typically exploration of the technical merit or feasibility of an idea or technology

2. Phase II—the work phase; typically prototype development, evaluation of commercial potential

3. Phase III—the commercialization phase; no SBIR funds available for this purpose (although SBIR program managers can be useful contacts)

Technology Preferences

The BMDO SBIR program sponsors projects that are relevant to ballistic defense systems. Basically, any innovative technology that makes things lighter, faster, stronger, or more reliable, is of interest. A number of specific technical topics are developed for each solicitation, a large share of them within electronics and computer science. Note that the BMDO has a topic area called "Surprises and Opportunities." This area is held open for any new and unique advanced technologies that do not fit into the others topics of the solicitation.

Type of Financing
Contracts

Maximum amounts
$100,000 for Phase I projects (but normally less than $65,000 is awarded for a merit or concept examination, in general lasting six months).

$750,000 for Phase II projects (two years).

Special Considerations
Oriented to small firms (fewer than 500 employees).

Deadlines
The BMDO participates in the first annual Department of Defense solicitation (invitation to compete for funding in certain technological areas). It is released in October, accepting proposals from December, and closing in January. In the period after release but before proposals are accepted, all "topic authors" (scientists and engineers who have come up with scientific and technological focus areas) are available for questioning. After that, potential applicants have the opportunity of using the DOD online interactive topic information system to get (anonymous) answers to technical questions.

Additional Information
Commercial potential is quite important in the BMDO program for Phase II proposals. This means that applicants with private sponsors/confirmations of follow-on funding will have a greater chance of succeeding.

Principal investigators who are also tenured faculty will not be considered primarily employed by the small firm if they receive compensation from the university/college while performing the SBIR contract (waivers from this can be requested).

Name
Small Business Innovation Research Program (SBIR)

Agency/Organization
Defense Advanced Research Projects Agency (DARPA, part of the Department of Defense)

Address
DARPA/OASB/SBIR
3701 North Fairfax Drive
Arlington, VA 22203-1714

Phone   **Fax**
(703) 526-4170   (703) 696-4884

E-mail
SBIR@darpa.mil

Web Page
http://www.darpa.mil/sbir/

Program Officer
Connie Jacobs

Phone
(703) 696-2398

E-mail
CJacobs@arpa.mil

Type of Program
R&D funds (technical and commercial criteria are considered). The program is based on a three-phase process:

1. Phase I—the start-up phase; typically exploration of the technical merit or feasibility of an idea or technology

2. Phase II—the work phase; typically prototype development, evaluation of commercial potential

3. Phase III—the commercialization phase; no SBIR funds available for this purpose (although SBIR program managers can be useful contacts)

Technology Preferences
DARPA's mission is to advance state-of-the-art defense technology. Specific topics change from one solicitation to the next.

Type of Financing
Contracts

Maximum amounts

$100,000 for Phase I projects (in general lasting six months).

$750,000 for Phase II projects (two years). More common in DARPA is to receive $375,000 for the development phase, but that additional funding is available for "optional tasks."

Special Considerations

Oriented to small firms (fewer than 500 employees).

Deadlines

DARPA participates in both annual Department of Defense solicitations (invitation to compete for funding in certain technological areas). This means that DARPA proposal deadlines are in January and August. In the period after release of a solicitation but before proposals are accepted, all "topic authors" (scientists and engineers who have come up with scientific and technological focus areas) are available for questioning. After that, potential applicants have the opportunity of using the DOD online interactive topic information system to get (anonymous) answers to technical questions.

Additional Information

DARPA is one of the most competitive Department of Defense SBIR participants. Only around one out of ten Phase I applicants has received funding in recent years.

A potential for follow-on funding from another source, preferably a private investor, is an advantage when applying for Phase II funding. For DARPA, this signifies that the firm is willing to go all the way through a commercialization phase.

Name
Small Business Innovation Research Program (SBIR)

Agency/Organization
Department of Commerce (DOC)—National Oceanic and Atmospheric Administration (NOAA)

Address
SBIR Program
U.S. Department of Commerce
1315 East-West Highway (SSMC 3 #15342)
Silver Spring, MD 20910

Phone   **Fax**
(301) 713-3565   (301) 713-4100

Web Page
http://www.oar.noaa.gov/orta/

Program Officer
Dr. Joseph Bishop, Program Manager

E-mail
joseph.bishop@noaa.gov

Type of Program
R&D funds (technical and commercial criteria are considered). The program is based on a three-phase process:

1. Phase I—the start-up phase; typically exploration of the technical merit or feasibility of an idea or technology

2. Phase II—the work phase; typically prototype development, evaluation of commercial potential

3. Phase III—the commercialization phase; no SBIR funds available for this purpose (although SBIR program managers can be useful contacts)

Technology Preferences
In fiscal year 1999, the NOAA topic headlines were:

1. Atmospheric sciences

2. Ocean Observation Systems

3. Living Marine Resources

4. Ocean Science

5. Cartography and Photogrammetry

Although these can change, they indicate some of NOAA's general interests.

Type of Financing
Contracts

Maximum amounts
$75,000 for Phase I projects (in general lasting six months). $300,000 for Phase II projects (two years).

Special Considerations
Oriented to small firms (fewer than 500 employees).

Deadlines
DOC releases one solicitation each year. Expected release date for the fiscal year 2000 solicitation is October 1, 1999, with an indicated closing date mid-January 2000.

Additional Information
DOC is a relatively small participant in SBIR, and NOAA is also smaller than the National Institute of Standards and Technology. In fiscal year 1998 DOC made 45 Phase I and 19 Phase II awards.

Phase I applications are reviewed by two NOAA scientists/engineers if the formal requirements of length, format, etc., are met. Phase II applications undergo evaluations by three reviewers, some of which may come from outside DOC.

Name
Small Business Innovation Research Program (SBIR)

Agency/Organization
Department of Commerce (DOC)—National Institute of Standards and Technology (NIST)

Address
NIST
U.S. Department of Commerce
North Campus—Building 820—Room 306
Gaithersburg, MD 20899

Phone   **Fax**
(301) 975-4517   (301) 548-0624

Web Page
http://www.nist.gov/sbir

Program Officer
Norman Taylor, NIST SBIR Program Manager

E-mail
norman.taylor@nist.gov

Type of Program
R&D funds (technical and commercial criteria are considered). The program is based on a three-phase process:

1. Phase I—the start-up phase; typically exploration of the technical merit or feasibility of an idea or technology

2. Phase II—the work phase; typically prototype development, evaluation of commercial potential

3. Phase III—the commercialization phase; no SBIR funds available for this purpose (although SBIR program managers can be useful contacts)

Technology Preferences
The SBIR program has two participants in DOC: NIST and the National Oceanic and Atmospheric Administration (see separate entry in directory). In fiscal year 1999, the NIST topic headlines were:

1. Adaptive Learning Systems

2. Advanced Building Materials and Systems

3. Advanced Detection and Suppression of Fire

4. Combinatorial Discovery of Materials and Chemicals

5. Condition-based Maintenance

6. Intelligent Control

7. Intelligent and Distributed CAD

8. Infrastructures for Distributed Electronic Commerce

9. Measurement and Standards for Catalysis and Biocatalysis

10. Measurement and Standards for Composite Materials

11. Measurement and Standards for Membrane Materials

12. Microelectronics Manufacturing Infrastructure

13. Microfabrication and Micromachining

14. Organic Electronic Materials Technology

15. Photonics Manufacturing

16. Supporting Technologies for Semiconductor Lithography

17. Integration of Manufacturing Applications

Although these can change, they indicate some of NIST's general interests.

Type of Financing
Grants

Maximum amounts
$75,000 for Phase I projects (in general lasting six months).
$300,000 for Phase II projects (two years).

Special Considerations
Oriented at small firms (fewer than 500 employees).

Deadlines
DOC releases one solicitation each year. Expected release date for the fiscal year 2000 solicitation is October 1, 1999, with an indicated closing date mid-January 2000.

Additional Information
DOC is a relatively small participant in SBIR. In fiscal year 1998 DOC made 45 Phase I and 19 Phase II awards.

Phase I applications are reviewed by two NIST scientists/engineers if the formal requirements of length, format, etc., are met. Phase II applications undergo evaluations by three reviewers, some of which may come from outside DOC.

Name
Small Business Innovation Research Program (SBIR)

Agency/Organization
Department of Education (ED)

Address
Small Business Innovation Research Program
U.S. Department of Education
Room 508D, Capitol Place
555 New Jersey Avenue, N.W.
Washington, DC 20208-5644
Phone: 202/219-2004 SBIR Program Office

Phone   **Fax**
(202) 219-2004   (202) 219-1528

Web Page
http://www.ed.gov/offices/OERI/SBIR
[Note: The ED Web server is case-sensitive—write OERI/SBIR in CAPI-TAL LETTERS.]

Program Officer
Lee Eiden, SBIR Program Coordinator

E-mail
Lee_Eiden@ed.gov

Type of Program
R&D funds (technical and commercial criteria are considered). The program is based on a three-phase process:

1. Phase I—the start-up phase; typically exploration of the technical merit or feasibility of an idea or technology

2. Phase II—the work phase; typically prototype development, evaluation of commercial potential

3. Phase III—the commercialization phase; no SBIR funds available for this purpose (although SBIR program managers can be useful contacts)

Technology Preferences
For the 1999 solicitation, 17 different topics were developed. These are likely to be changed in the future, at least to some extent. The names of the offices that develop the topics might give some indications as to what their interests are:

1. Office of Special Education and Rehabilitative Services, which has the most topics, and in general displays interest in technologies with relevance for people with disabilities
2. Office of Vocational and Adult Education
3. Office of Educational Research and Improvement

Type of Financing
Grants

Maximum amounts
$50,000 for Phase I projects (in general lasting six months).
$300,000 for Phase II projects (two years).

Special Considerations
Oriented to small firms (fewer than 500 employees).

Deadlines
The ED solicitation (invitation to compete for funding in certain technological areas) is released once every year in the beginning of February. Proposals are due in early April.

Additional Information
ED is the smallest SBIR participant, having a total SBIR budget of $5.1 million in fiscal year 1998. This resulted in 41 Phase I and 18 Phase II awards.

Success rates are average: 18 percent of the Phase I applications and 37 percent of the Phase II applications got funded in 1998.

Name
Small Business Innovation Research Program (SBIR)

Agency/Organization
Department of Energy (DOE)

Address
SBIR Program Office
SC-32
U.S. Department of Energy,
19901 Germantown Road
Germantown, MD 20874-1290

Phone   **Fax**
(301) 903-1414   (301) 903-6067

E-mail
sbir-sttr@oer.doe.gov

Web Page
http://sbir.er.doe.gov/sbir/

Program Officer
Robert E. Berger, Ph.D., Acting SBIR Program Manager

Type of Program
R&D funds (technical and commercial criteria are considered). The program is based on a three-phase process:

1. Phase I—the start-up phase; typically exploration of the technical merit or feasibility of an idea or technology
2. Phase II—the work phase; typically prototype development, evaluation of commercial potential
3. Phase III—the commercialization phase; no SBIR funds available for this purpose (although SBIR program managers can be useful contacts)

Technology Preferences
About 40 specific topics are developed each year within the following areas:

1. Basic Energy Sciences
2. Biological and Environmental Research
3. High Energy and Nuclear Physics
4. Fusion Energy Sciences

5. Computational and Technology Research

6. Energy Efficiency and Renewable Energy

7. Nuclear Energy

8. Fossil Energy

9. Environmental Management

10. Nonproliferation and National Security.

Type of Financing
Grants

Maximum amounts
$100,000 for Phase I projects (in general lasting six months).
$750,000 for Phase II projects (two years).

Special Considerations
Oriented tosmall firms (fewer than 500 employees).

Deadlines
The DOE solicitation (invitation to compete for funding in certain technological areas) is released once every year in the beginning of December. Proposals are due in the beginning of March.

Additional Information
DOE is the fourth largest participant in SBIR. In fiscal year 1999 DOE expects to fund around 200 Phase I and 75 Phase II projects, based on an expected budget of $75 million.

Success rates are quite low for Phase I :12 percent, but higher for Phase 2; 45 percent.

Name
Small Business Innovation Research Program (SBIR)

Agency/Organization
Department of Transportation (DOT)

Address
DOT/SBIR Program Office, DTS-22
U.S. Department of Transportation
Research and Special Programs Administration
Volpe National Transportation Systems Center
55 Broadway, Kendall Square
Cambridge, MA 02142-1093

Phone   **Fax**
(617) 494-2051   (617) 494-2497

Web Page
http://www.volpe.dot.gov/sbir/

Program Officer
Joseph Henebury, DOT SBIR Program Director

E-mail
henebury@volpe.dot.gov

Type of Program
R&D funds (technical and commercial criteria are considered). The program is based on a three-phase process:

1. Phase I—the start-up phase; typically exploration of the technical merit or feasibility of an idea or technology

2. Phase II—the work phase; typically prototype development, evaluation of commercial potential

3. Phase III—the commercialization phase; no SBIR funds available for this purpose (although SBIR program managers can be useful contacts)

Technology Preferences
Specific topics are likely to change from year to year. The technological focus areas are developed by the following organizations (numbers in parenthesis refer to the maximum number of awards to be made by this organization in fiscal year 1999):

1. Federal Aviation Administration (5)
2. Federal Railroad Administration (3)
3. Federal Transit Administration (2)
4. National Highway Traffic Safety Administration (3)
5. Research and Special Programs Administration (4)
6. United States Coast Guard (3)

Type of Financing
Grants

Maximum amounts
$100,000 for Phase I projects (in general lasting six months). $750,000 for Phase II projects (two years).

Special Considerations
Oriented tosmall firms (fewer than 500 employees).

Deadlines
The DOT solicitation (invitation to compete for funding in certain technological areas) is released once every year in mid-February. Proposals are due in the beginning of May. Note that the DOT SBIR solicitation is only available electronically (in Microsoft Word format for 1999).

Additional Information
DOT is one of the small participants in SBIR; twice the size of the Department of Education and about the same size as the Environmental Protection Agency. Note that although DOT is a small player in SBIR, the award sizes are as large as in the bigger agencies.

Projects with follow-on funding committments have better chances of winning awards. Some follow-on funding can also be available from DOT organizations if the project concerns a technology/product very useful to them.

Name

Small Business Innovation Research Program (SBIR)

Agency/Organization

Environmental Protection Agency (EPA)

Address

Environmental Engineering Research Div. (8722)
Office of Research and Development
U.S. Environmental Protection Agency
401 M St SW
Washington, DC 20460

Phone	**Fax**
1-800-490-9194	(202) 401-1014

Web Page

http://es.epa.gov/ncerqa/sbir/

Program Officer

Donald F. Carey, SBIR Program Director

Phone

(202) 260-7899

Type of Program

R&D funds (technical and commercial criteria are considered). The program is based on a three-phase process:

1. Phase I—the start-up phase; typically exploration of the technical merit or feasibility of an idea or technology

2. Phase II—the work phase; typically prototype development, evaluation of commercial potential

3. Phase III—the commercialization phase; no SBIR funds available for this purpose (although SBIR program managers can be useful contacts)

Technology Preferences

Specific topics are likely to change from year to year. EPA states that some of the topics that will be emphasized over the next few years include Drinking Water Disinfection, Particulate Matter, Human Health Protection, Ecosystem Protection, Endocrine Disruptors, Pollution Prevention and New Technologies, Technologies for prevention and control of air emissions, Waste reduction/pollution prevention techniques, Drinking water treatment technologies, Technologies for municipal and industrial wastewater treatment and pollution control, Treatment, recycling, and disposal of solid wastes, hazardous wastes, and sediments, Technologies for in-situ site remediation of organically contaminated soil, sediments, and groundwater, Technologies for treatment or removal of heavy metals at contaminated sites, Technologies for prevention and control of indoor air pollution, Biosensors and immunoassay for pesticide residue identification and monitoring, Technologies for wet weather flow treatment and pollution control, and Innovative Monitoring Technologies.

Note that many of the other SBIR participants also release topics within environmental fields. Many of the large Department of Defense participants (for example the Air Force and the Navy) fund more SBIR projects oriented at technologies for improving the environment/quality of life than EPA itself. Also the Department of Energy and some of the smaller SBIR participants develop topics in such fields.

Type of Financing
Grants

Maximum amounts
$70,000 for Phase I projects (in general lasting six months).
$295,000 for Phase II projects (two years).

Special Considerations
Oriented tosmall firms (fewer than 500 employees).

Deadlines
The EPA solicitation (invitation to compete for funding in certain technological areas) is released once every year in September. Proposals are due in November. Note that EPA also issues a separate Phase II solicitation (whereas the other agencies accept proposals for Phase II continuously or several times during the year without an explicit invitation).

Additional Information
EPA is one of the small participants in SBIR; about the same size as the Department of Transportation.

The success rate for Phase II is one of the highest in the SBIR; over the past six years 58 percent of the Phase II applicants have received funding.

Name
Small Business Innovation Research Program (SBIR)

Agency/Organization
National Aeronautics and Space Administration (NASA)

Address
Technology Program Management Office
Code 705
National Aeronautics and Space Administration
Goddard Space Flight Center
Greenbelt, MD 20771

Phone   **Fax**
(301) 286-8888   (301) 286-0321

Web Page
http://sbir.nasa.gov/

Program Officer
Paul Mexcur, Program Manager, SBIR/STTR

E-mail
Paul.Mexcur@hq.nasa.gov

Type of Program
R&D funds (technical and commercial criteria are considered). The program is based on a three-phase process:

1. Phase I—the start-up phase; typically exploration of the technical merit or feasibility of an idea or technology
2. Phase II—the work phase; typically prototype development, evaluation of commercial potential
3. Phase III—the commercialization phase; no SBIR funds available for this purpose (although SBIR program managers can be useful contacts)

Technology Preferences
Specific topics are likely to change from year to year. The NASA strategic technical areas are:

1. Space science
2. Mission to planet earth (use of e.g. satellites to expand our understanding of earth)
3. Aeronautics and space transportation technology
4. Human exploration and development of space

5. Crosscutting technologies (that are relevant to many of the above—for instance, related to power, materials, environment issues, data systems and storage, instruments, and communication)

Type of Financing
Grants

Maximum amounts
$70,000 for Phase I projects (in general lasting six months). $600,000 for Phase II projects (two years).

Special Considerations
Oriented to small firms (fewer than 500 employees).

Deadlines
The NASA solicitation (invitation to compete for funding in certain technological areas) is released once every year in April. Proposals are due in July. Note that the solicitation is only available in electronic form, either on the World Wide Web or through other electronic services. If requested, NASA also sends the program information on diskettes.

Additional Information
NASA is one of the large SBIR participants—the third largest after the Department of Defense and the Department of Health and Human Services.

Name
Small Business Innovation Research Program (SBIR)

Agency/Organization
National Science Foundation (NSF)

Address
U.S. National Science Foundation
SBIR Program
4201 Wilson Blvd
Arlington, VA 22230

Phone   **Fax**
(703) 306-1390   (703) 306-0337

E-mail
sbir@nsf.gov

Web Page
http://www.eng.nsf.gov/sbir/

Program Officer
Dr. Kesh S. Narayanan, SBIR Director

E-mail
Knarayan@nsf.gov

Type of Program
R&D funds (technical and commercial criteria are considered). The program is based on a three-phase process:

1. Phase I—the start-up phase; typically exploration of the technical merit or feasibility of an idea or technology

2. Phase II—the work phase; typically prototype development, evaluation of commercial potential

3. Phase III—the commercialization phase; no SBIR funds available for this purpose (although SBIR program managers can be useful contacts)

Technology Preferences
NSF's mission is different from most of the other agencies' (with the possible exception of the National Institutes of Health). Instead of having specific tasks related to e.g. transportation and energy, the main task of NSF is to support the best fundamental research and technology in a large number of fields and specialties. This means that the proposed technology should not (necessarily) display a specific relevance to one practical mis-

sion. NSF is instead likely to fund projects that are "cutting edge" or "state-of-the-art" technology. In addition, program goals are intended to contribute to develop intellectual capital, strengthen the physical infrastructure, integrate research and education, and promote partnerships.

Specific topics are likely to change from year to year, and they are developed by the foundation's subdivisions. In FY 1998, some "critical technology areas of national importance" were emphasized: Applied Molecular Biology, Distributed Computing and Telecommunication, Integrated, Flexible Manufacturing, Materials Synthesis and Processing, Microelectronics and Optoelectronics, Pollution Minimization and Remediation, Software, and Transportation.

Type of Financing
Grants

Maximum amounts
$100,000 for Phase I projects (in general lasting six months). $400,000 for Phase II projects (two years).

Special Considerations
Oriented to small firms (fewer than 500 employees).

Deadlines
The NSF solicitation (invitation to compete for funding in certain technological areas) is released once every year in March or April. Proposals are due in June.

Additional Information
NSF is the fifth largest SBIR participants (and the smallest STTR participant).

The SBIR program was initiated in NSF in the late 1970s as an experiment. On the basis of its success, a law was passed in 1982 mandating SBIR at all agencies conducting more than $100 million of research..Many of the program personnel in NSF have extensive experience in selecting projects and dealing with entrepreneurs.

Name

Small Business Technology Transfer Program (STTR)

Participating Agencies/Organizations (Sorted by Program Size)

Department of Defense (DOD)

Department of Health and Human Service (DHHS) (mainly the National Institutes of Health, NIH)

National Aeronautic and Space Administration (NASA)

Department of Energy (DOE)

National Science Foundation (NSF)

Address

See entries for the SBIR programs in the participating agencies. Most of them use the same Web pages, addresses, personnel, etc. for both the SBIR and the STTR program. See below for more specific information

Program Officers/Contact Information

In DOD, the program officers and general contact addresses (Help Desk, etc.) are the same for the SBIR and STTR programs.

This is also the case of DHHS/NIH.

NASA has its own STTR contact:

Carl G. Ray

E-mail: cray@hq.nasa.gov

In DOE, the general e-mail help address and other contact information is the same for SBIR and STTR. The STTR has its own Web page, though: http://sbir.er.doe.gov/sttr/

NSF has its own STTR Program Manager:

Darryl Gorman

E-mail: dgorman@nsf.gov

Type of Program

R&D funds (technical and commercial criteria are considered). The program is based on a three-phase process:

1. Phase I—the start-up phase; typically exploration of the technical merit or feasibility of an idea or technology

2. Phase II—the work phase; typically prototype development, evaluation of commercial potential

3. Phase III—the commercialization phase; no SBIR funds available for this purpose (although SBIR program managers can be useful contacts)

The major difference compared to the SBIR program, is that STTR requires the applicant (the private firm) to cooperate with a non-profit research institution, which has to meet the following criteria:

1. Located in the U.S.
2. Meet one of three definitions:
   - Nonprofit college or university
   - Domestic nonprofit research organization
   - Federally funded R&D center (FFRDC)

Technology Preferences
The set-aside of the agencies R&D budget to the STTR program is very small; only 0.15 percent (the SBIR program is based on a 2.5 percent set-aside). This means that the participants will rarely develop a broad set of topics for the STTR program, as they do for SBIR.

Often, only a couple of technological areas are targeted through STTR. For example, in fiscal year 1998, the National Science Foundation only accepted proposals in the areas of Nanotechnology and Sensors in Harsh Environments. The STTR solicitations should therefore be watched closely.

Type of Financing
Grants

Maximum amounts
$100,000 for Phase I projects (in general lasting one year).
$500,000 for Phase II projects (two years).

These are the same in all the participating agencies. Note that the project period is twice as long in STTR Phase I compared to SBIR.

Special Considerations
Oriented to small firms (fewer than 500 employees) cooperating with nonprofit research institutions.

Deadlines
DOD: The STTR solicitation (invitation to compete within certain technological areas called "topics") is released every year in January. Proposals are accepted from early March with a final deadline in April.

DHHS: Three STTR solicitations are released annually, with deadlines on the first day of April, August, and December.

NASA: One solicitation is released every year in March, and proposals are due by mid-May.

DOE: The annual solicitation is released in October, with a final proposal deadline in January.

NSF: Final deadline for proposals is in December, and the solicitation is released two to three months before that.

Additional Information
The application forms and the award process are very similar in the STTR and SBIR program. In the STTR, however, a formal agreement between the applying firm and the independent non-profit R&D organization has to be submitted along with the proposal. Model agreements are found at all the STTR Web sites.

Name

The U.S. Small Business Administration (SBA)

Address

409 Third Street, S.W.
Washington, DC 20416

Phone

(800) 8-ASK-SBA (TDD number: (704) 344-6640)

Fax

(202) 205-7064

Web Page

http://www.sba.gov

Type of Programs

Educational, networking, and administrative programs relevant to small business. Advice and help of various kinds is offered—for instance, help with finding funding in the private market and courses in starting a business and writing a business plan. General advice and guidance on starting a business are available online (and in paper versions from local offices)—for instance, through a Small Business Startup Kit.

Technology Preferences

None in particular. Small Business Development Centers are often, but not always, oriented toward certain businesses in their local area. To get help, financial support, etc., the company must have fewer than 500 employees and must not be dominant within its field.

Type of Financing

Loan guarantees.

Maximum Amount

Up to $750,000 guaranteed in loans from participating banks. For loans with fast application review processes and/or low requirements for documentation, the maximum limit is $150,000. There are special programs oriented, for example, at export and cyclical needs for working capital.

Special Considerations

SBA runs a number of loan programs and a number of centers oriented—for instance, toward women, minorities, and war veterans. Loans are also available for defense-dependent firms that have been adversely affected by defense cuts.

Deadlines

Applications for loans are accepted throughout the year. For specific courses and advice, contact your local SBA office.

Additional Information

Most of the SBA loans are not awarded by Small Business Administration itself, but by a private financial institution. SBA issues a guarantee for the loan (up to 75% for large loans and 80% for small loans).

Note that SBA also has many other responsibilities—for instance, disaster assistance and help with the Year 2000 problem (Y2K). Their Web site is a good starting point for finding federal, state and private Internet resources for small firms. SBA is responsible for administering (and reporting to Congress) the SBIR and STTR programs, and annual reports from these, as well as links and other information, can be found on the SBA Web site.

SBA at the Local and Regional Levels

In addition to the central administration office in Washington, DC, there are both regional offices and district offices. The regional offices have mainly administrative responsibilities, plus some educational and networking tasks. The SBA district offices, on the other hand, are the points of delivery for most SBA programs and services.

It is important to bear in mind, however, that many of the SBA programs are offered through distinct organizations. Small Business Development Centers and the Service Corps of Retired Executives have already been mentioned. There are also centers oriented toward businesses owned by women, companies run by native Americans, socially and economically disadvantaged businesses, and more. The closest field office of the SBA should be able to lead you in the right direction.

Almost all the different centers are found locally in states and cities. There are more than 900 Small Business Development Centers. For the firms, the federal level of the SBA will function mainly as a gateway to more locally available information and service. SBA field offices are found in the following cities (please contact SBA headquarters or look at their Internet home page to receive local contact information):

AK	Anchorage		CO	Denver
AL	Birmingham		CT	Hartford
AR	Little Rock		DC	Washington, DC
AZ	Phoenix		DE	Wilmington
CA	Fresno		FL	Coral Gables
	Glendale			Jacksonville
	Sacramento		GA	Atlanta
	San Diego		HI	Honolulu
	San Francisco		IA	Cedar Rapids
	Santa Ana			Des Moines

ID	Boise	OH	Cincinnati
IL	Chicago		Cleveland
	Springfield		Columbus
IN	Indianapolis	OK	Oklahoma City
KS	Wichita	OR	Portland
KY	Louisville	PA	Harrisburg
LA	New Orleans		King of Prussia
MA	Boston		Pittsburgh
	Springfield		Wilkes-Barre
MD	Baltimore	PR	Hato Rey
ME	Augusta	RI	Providence
MI	Detroit	SC	Columbia
	Marquette	SD	Sioux Falls
MN	Minneapolis	TN	Nashville
MO	Kansas City	TX	Corpus Christi
	St. Louis		El Paso
	Springfield		Fort Worth
MS	Gulfport		Harlingen
	Jackson		Houston
MT	Helena		Lubbock
NC	Charlotte		San Antonio
ND	Fargo	UT	Salt Lake City
NE	Omaha	VA	Richmond
NH	Concord	VT	Montpelier
NJ	Newark	WA	Seattle
NM	Albuquerque		Spokane
NV	Las Vegas	WI	Madison
NY	Buffalo		Milwaukee
	Elmira	WV	Charleston
	Melville		Clarksburg
	New York City	WY	Casper
	Rochester		
	Syracuse		

Part V Indexes

Science and Technology Preference Index

Page numbers in this index refer to Part IV—the Quick Reference section with contact information. For more information on a specific program, please consult the Program Index below (and the list of acronyms if necessary).

Note that not all agencies list their general interests under the topics used in this index. There could be alternatives for a specific technology that are not listed below. For instance, electronics materials and computer science are very central parts of many Defense projects under the SBIR and other programs, although they most often will not list their special interests as "Sensors," "Electronics," etc., as we do, but rather as improved weapons systems, improved vehicles, improved communication devices, etc.

For specific topics such as audio compression or encryption, you must use your judgement as to where they fit under the more general technology headings, such as electronics or computer science. Also, you must think creatively to figure out where else they may fit. For example, areas such as Deafness and Other Communication Disorders in NIH/SBIR might be a home for audio compression, while Defense Sciences and Advanced Military Technology in DOD might be a home for encryption. You should view the use of this index as a way to get started and begin a conversation with a possibly relevant program manager.

Program Index

The first page number in the list refers to Part II, where the programs are described in more detail. The second page number refers to Part IV, where information in brief, including points of contacts, web page addresses, etc., are found.

People Index by Name

Page numbers below refer to Part IV—the reference section that you can use to get contact information or find out more about the program in brief.

Name	Program/Agency/Laboratory/Fields	Page
Jones, Ted	SBIR/CDC/National Center for Injury Prevention & Control	240
Kaplan, Jonathan	SBIR/Army/Army Research Institute for Social Sciences	275
Kelty, Miriam F.	SBIR/NIH/National Institute of Aging	211
Kiley, James	SBIR/NIH/Sleep Disorders Research	238
Koehler, Karl	SBIR/NIH/Biomedical Technology	233
Lange, Ruth	SBIR/USDA/Assistant Program Director	206
Larriva, Diane	COSSI/Office of the Secretary of Defense	200
Lemondes, John	ACTII, Army Material Command	195
Levy, Abraham	SBIR/NIH/Biomedical Technology: Electron Microscopy, Spectrometry	233
Lide, Bettijoyce	ATP/Medical Informatics, Biomedical, Healthcare	193
Linder, Barbara	SBIR/NIH/Diabetes, Endocrinology & Metabiological Diseases	223
Linsenmeyer, Ed	SBIR/Navy/NSWCCSS/Naval Warfare Center	303
Lutterman, Kenneth G.	SBIR/NIH/NI of Mental Health/Services and Intervention Research	230
Lynn, Richard	SBIR/NIH/Muscle Biology	214
Lyons, Reba	ACTII, Army TRADOC Battle Lab	195
Marino, Charles	SBIR/Navy/Strategic Systems Program	307
Markwell, Mary Ann	SBIR/NIH/Biomedical Technology: Electron Microscopy Spectrometry	233
Mazumdar, Purabi	ATP/Electronics & Photonics Technology	193
McAuliffe, Mark	SBIR/Army/STRICOM/Simulation, Training & Instrumentation Command	276
McDonald, Tom	COSSI/Navy	200
McGowan, Joan	SBIR/NIH/Cartilage & Connective Tissue	215
Mexcur, Paul	SBIR/National Aeronautics and Space Administration	324
Mihina, Carol	SBIR/Army/Construction Engineering Research Laboratory	277
Millan, Juan	COSSI/Army	200
Mirsky, Rich	COSSI/Office of the Secretary of Defense	200
Mitchell, Mary	ATP/Information Technology & Applications	193
Moshell, Alan	SBIR/NIH/Skin Diseases	214
Munozrovira, Francisco	SBIR/Navy/Strategic Systems Program	307
Musson, Robert	SBIR/NIH/Lung Diseases	227
Narayanan, Kesh	SBIR/NSF	326
Nichols, Susan	SBIR/Army/Topographic Engineering Center	278
Nodgaard, Cathy	Dual Use Science & Technology/Navy	197
Norelli, Janis	SBIR/Air Force/Information Directorate	260
O'Donnell, Pete	SBIR/Navy/Naval Air Warfare Center Aircraft Division	294
Olah, Nick	SBIR/Navy/NFESC/Naval Facilities Engineering Service Center	299
Orthwein, Jayne	ATP/Information Technology & Applications	193
Panagis, James	SBIR/NIH/Orthopedics	215
Pearl, Scott	COSSI/Air Force	200
Petonito, Dan	Dual Use Science & Technology/Office of the Secretary of Defense	197
Podskalny, Judith	SBIR/NIH/Digestive Diseases & Nutrition	223

People Index by Program/Agency

Page numbers below refer to Part IV—the reference section that you can use to get contact information or find out more about the program in brief.

Name	Program/Agency/Laboratory/Fields	Page
Wassink, Bill	SBIR/Air Force/Air Logistics Center	264
Tillman, Madie	SBIR/Air Force/Air Vehicles Directorate	252
Zysk, Kevin	SBIR/Air Force/Arnold Engineering Development Center	261
Hancock, Bob	SBIR/Air Force/Directed Energy Directorate and Space Vehicles Directorate	258, 259
Williams, Belva	SBIR/Air Force/Human Efficiency Directorate	257
Norelli, Janis	SBIR/Air Force/Information Directorate	260
Starr, Sharon	SBIR/Air Force/Materials & Manufacturing Directorate	255
Bixby, Dick	SBIR/Air Force/Munitions Directorate	256
Zobrist, Dottie	SBIR/Air Force/Propulsion Directorate	253
Fannin, Marleen	SBIR/Air Force/Sensors Directorate	254
Bannister, Ken	SBIR/Army	266
Saarman, John	SBIR/Army/Armament Research, Development & Engineering Center	280
Kaplan, Jonathan	SBIR/Army/Army Research Institute for Social Sciences	275
Hudson, Dean	SBIR/Army/Army Research Laboratory	273
Jones, Ken	SBIR/Army/Army Research Office	274
Haglich, Brenda	SBIR/Army/AVRDEC	271
Crisci, Joyce	SBIR/Army/CECOM	270
Weeks, Suzanne	SBIR/Army/CECOM	270
Mihina, Carol	SBIR/Army/Construction Engineering Research Laboratory	277
Salls, Theresa	SBIR/Army/CRREL	281
Willis, Herman	SBIR/Army/Medical Research & Material Command	285
Thomas, Buddy	SBIR/Army/MRDEC	284
Raisanen, Gerald	SBIR/Army/NCOE	279
Hohenstein, Marvin	SBIR/Army/Soldier & Biological Chemical Command	272
Hinkle, Ron	SBIR/Army/Soldier and Biological Chemical Command	272
Bauer, Terry	SBIR/Army/Space & Missile Defense Command	268
McAuliffe, Mark	SBIR/Army/STRICOM/Simulation, Training & Instrumentation Command	276
Sandel, Alex	SBIR/Army/Tank Automotive Research, Development & Engineering Center	282
Schnell, John	SBIR/Army/Test & Evaluation Command	269
Nichols, Susan	SBIR/Army/Topographic Engineering Center	278
Stewart, Phillip	SBIR/Army/Waterways Experiment Station	283
Fulton, Janet	SBIR/CDC/National Center for Chronic Disease Prevention & Health	242
Harry, Alfred	SBIR/CDC/National Center for HIV, STP & TB Prevention	244
Fortune, Ken	SBIR/CDC/National Center for Infectious Diseases	241
Jones, Ted	SBIR/CDC/National Center for Injury Prevention & Control	240
Weniger, Bruce G.	SBIR/CDC/National Immunization Program	243
Fleming, Roy	SBIR/CDC/National Institute for Occupational Safety and Health	239
Cleland, Charles F.	SBIR/Department of Agriculture	206

List of Acronyms and Abbreviations

ACTII	Army Advanced Concepts & Technology II Program
ATP	Advanced Technology Program
COSSI	Commercial Operations and Support Savings Initiative
CRADA	Cooperative Research and Development Agreement
DARPA	Defense Advanced Research Projects Agency
DHHS	Department of Health and Human Services
DOC	Department of Commerce
DOD	Department of Defense
DOE	Department of Energy
DOT	Department of Transportation
DU S&T	Dual Use Science and Technology Program
ED	Department of Education
ManTech	Manufacturing Technology Program
MEP	Manufacturing Extension Partnership
NASA	National Aeronautics and Space Administration
NIH	National Institutes of Health
NIST	National Institute of Standards and Technology
NOAA	National Oceanic and Atmospheric Administration
NSF	National Science Foundation
SBA	Small Business Administration
SBIR	Small Business Innovation Research Program
STTR	Small Business Technology Transfer Program
USDA	U.S. Department of Agriculture

HARCOURT SOFTWARE LICENSE AGREEMENT